Georgia
Real Estate:
Practice & Law

Consulting Editor
GREGORY J. DUNN

Real Estate Education

Prepared in cooperation with the
Georgia Institute of Real Estate,
a service of the Atlanta Board of
REALTORS® Educational Foundation, Inc.

This publication is designed to provide accurate and authoritative information in regard to the subject matter covered. It is sold with the understanding that a publisher is not engaged in rendering legal, accounting, or other professional service. If legal advice or other expert assistance is required, the services of a competent professional person should be sought.

Senior Vice President and General Manager: Roy Lipner
Publisher and Director of Distance Learning: Evan Butterfield
Development Editor: Michael J. Scafuri
Production Manager: Bryan Samolinski
Creative Director: Lucy Jenkins
Typesetting: Ellen Gurak, Janet Schroeder

Published by Dearborn™ Real Estate Education,
a division of Dearborn Financial Publishing, Inc.®
a Kaplan Professional Company
155 North Wacker Drive
Chicago, Illinois 60606-1719
(312) 836-4400
http://www.dearbornRE.com

Printed in the United States of America.

10   9   8   7   6   5   4

Contents

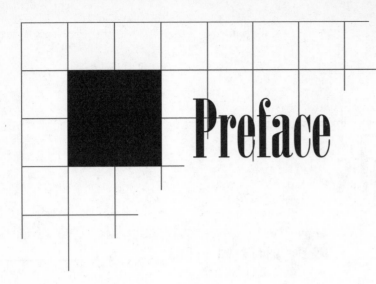

Preface

Welcome to *Georgia Real Estate: Practice & Law.* This text has been prepared by leading Georgia real estate experts in a straightforward, easy-to-read format featuring examples and notes to help explain difficult topics. Further, this text incorporates references to the forms and contracts commonly used in Georgia, providing you with first-hand experience and exposure to the documents you will encounter throughout your real estate career.

Georgia Real Estate: Practice & Law is designed to be used with equal effectiveness with *any* of our real estate principles products; including the following:

- *Modern Real Estate Practice*
- *Real Estate Fundamentals*
- *Mastering Real Estate Principles*
- *National Real Estate Principles Software (SuccessMaster™)*

Georgia Real Estate: Practice & Law also offers current real estate professionals a practical handbook of Georgia's real estate law and rules, along with the most current developments. Every effort has been made to ensure that the information contained in this book is both relevant and current. There are numerous references to Georgia License Law so users can look up the law themselves in most public and university libraries, as well as online.

Readers using *Georgia Real Estate: Practice & Law* to prepare for the state real estate licensing exam should note that this book does not address the national topics that comprise most of the real estate examination. Students are advised to first read the relevant material in one of the main principles products, then turn to *Georgia Real Estate* for a focus on Georgia's laws and practices as they relate to that subject.

ACKNOWLEDGMENTS

The publisher would like to thank Robert Hart, Director of Education, Georgia MLS Training Institute, and Mary S. Shern, Georgia Institute of Real Estate, for their invaluable assistance in preparing this first edition of *Georgia Real Estate: Practice & Law.* The forms in this book have been reprinted with permission from the Georgia Association of REALTORS®.

HOW TO USE THIS BOOK

The conversion table below provides a quick and easy reference for using *Georgia Real Estate: Practice & Law* in conjunction with various real estate principles products. For instance, *Georgia Real Estate's* Chapter 5, "Legal Descriptions," may be read in conjunction with Chapter 9 in *Modern Real Estate Practice*, 15th Edition; Chapter 2 in *Real Estate Fundamentals*, 5th Edition; Chapter 6 in *Mastering Real Estate Principles*, 3rd Edition; and Lesson 6 in *National Real Estate Principles (SuccessMaster™)* software.

Chapter Conversion Table

Georgia Real Estate: Practice & Law	Modern Real Estate Practice	Real Estate Fundamentals	Mastering Real Estate Principles	National Real Estate Principles Software (SuccessMaster™)
1. Georgia Real Estate License Law	–	–	16	16
2. Rules of the Georgia Real Estate Commission			16	16
3. Georgia's Brokerage Relationships in Real Estate Transactions Act (BRRETA)	4/5	9	13	13
4. Antitrust Laws	5	9	13	13
5. Legal Descriptions	9	2	6	6
6. Listing the Seller	6	7	15	15
7. Pricing Property	18	11	19	19
8. Seller's Cost	6, 22	17	12	12
9. Listing the Buyer	6	7, 9	13, 15	13, 15
10. Buyer's Cost	6, 22	17	12	12
11. Writing Real Estate Contracts	11	7	14	14
12. Property Management	17	–	24	24
13. Writing Leases	16	8	8	8
14. Community Association Management	8	5	9	9

1 Georgia Real Estate License Law

PRIMARY PURPOSE

The primary purpose of the Georgia Real Estate License Law is to protect the public from dishonest or incompetent real estate agents. It is also designed to enhance the standards by which licensees perform their duties and to protect them from unfair competition. In essence it provides that one cannot practice as a real estate agent for a fee without first obtaining a license. The license in turn is obtained by proving that one has the necessary degree of knowledge and integrity. There are similar laws in all states. Real estate is one of many vocations and professions for which a license is required.

Based upon the police power of government, the Georgia License Law was first passed by the state legislature in 1925 and has been changed and modified many times since. It sets up the Georgia Real Estate Commission as the authority over all real estate licensees.

Note: Do not confuse the Real Estate Commission with the Board of REALTORS®, a private trade association to which licensees can choose to but are not obligated to join. All licensees are subject to the control of the Real Estate Commission.

 WWWeb.Link
You can find the text of the Georgia License Law at http://www2.state.ga.us/grec/grecforms/grecforms.html, or you can go to www.grec.state.ga.us, click on the button for the Georgia Real Estate Commission, then click on the button for license law. You can find the Georgia Association of Realtors® at http://www.garealtor.com/

THE GEORGIA REAL ESTATE COMMISSION (43–40–2)

The Real Estate Commission has six members, appointed by the governor and confirmed by the state senate. Five of the six members must be licensees, actively licensed for at least five years, and residents of Georgia for at least five years. The sixth member must have an interest in consumer affairs and must *not* have any interest in the real estate industry.

Members serve five-year terms, staggered, so that only one licensee member's term expires each year. The governor fills any vacancy that occurs. Members appoint their own Chairperson each year. Only those who have served at least one year are eligible. Commission meetings are held at least once a month. Four members are a quorum.

The governor can remove a commission member from office for incompetence, dishonesty, and neglect of duties or inability to perform the necessary duties.

Role of the Real Estate Commissioner (43–40–4 & 5)

The commissioner is hired by the commission to act as the department's chief executive officer, administering the policies the commission has adopted. The commissioner is *not* a member of the commission. The commissioner hires and oversees staff necessary for the day-to-day activities. He or she *cannot* hold an active real estate license nor can any other employee of the Real Estate Commission.

Authority of the Real Estate Commission (43–40–2 & 6)

The commission's authority is based upon the statutory law, and can be divided into the following four categories:

1. Issuing Licenses (43–40–7, 8, 9, 10, & 11). The commission can issue licenses to qualified applicants or can refuse to issue a license for cause. Applicants apply first for the right to sit for the required examination, and then having passed the examination, the applicant applies for the license. Misrepresenting information on an application would be a reason for the commission, after a hearing, to refuse to issue a license.

FOR EXAMPLE David states on his application to sit for the examination that he is a high school graduate, when in fact he is not. The commission learns the truth and refuses to issue a license to David.

2. Disciplinary Actions (43–40—14, 15, 16, 17, 25 & 26). For any violation of the license law or of its rules and regulations, the commission can take disciplinary action. Disciplinary actions might include

- a reprimand or *censure* for a minor infraction;
- required attendance at a particular educational program;
- periodic reports from an independent accountant (for a trust account infraction);
- imposition of fines, up to $1,000 for a single infraction and up to $5,000 for multiple infractions;
- suspension of the license (for a temporary period); or
- revocation of the license (permanent removal).

Any combination of disciplinary actions is also possible.

The commission has the authority to issue citations when investigation reveals a relatively minor infraction, bypassing the formal hearing process. A list of maximum fines for typical violations has been adopted. However, a licensee who wishes to contest the citation can still request a hearing.

F OR EXAMPLE Broker Anderson is cited for failing to properly display his license in his office. Because such violations do not seriously affect the public, Anderson is simply censured.

F OR EXAMPLE Julian fails to properly turn over an earnest money deposit to his broker. Investigation disclosed that the broker had not trained Julian in the procedures. Both Julian and the broker were required to attend a course dealing with the handling of earnest money.

Suspension or revocation of the license are reserved for serious violations and are only imposed after a hearing has taken place. Once a license has been revoked, the individual cannot apply for a new license for ten years.

F OR EXAMPLE After signing a contract to buy a home through Broker Jones, Roberta finds that she cannot obtain the necessary loan. She asks Broker Jones to return her earnest money deposit, but he is unable to do so, having used the money for personal debts. Jones's license is revoked.

3. Passing Rules and Regulations (43–40–2). The commission has the authority to pass rules and regulations having to do with the professional conduct of licensees and with the administration of the license law. However, these rules must fall within the scope of the license law. Violation of the rules can result in the same disciplinary actions as are imposed for violations of the law itself.

The rules are passed to clarify sections of the license law that may be misunderstood or misinterpreted. Also, they serve a purpose when the commission observes a situation taking place that is not in the public's best interests and wishes to correct the matter promptly rather than to wait for the next legislative session.

F OR EXAMPLE The license law states that "failing to account for and remit money coming into the licensee's possession which belongs to others" is an unfair practice. To clarify this, the commission passed Rule 520–1–26 having to do with proper trust account procedures.

4. Establishment of Fees. (43–40–3, 12 & 13). In Georgia the Real Estate Commission is a separate budgetary unit of the state government. In order to meet its budget it has the authority to set or adjust any fees by a reasonable amount for original licensure, renewals, change of license, and certain penalty fees. See Rule 520-1-.29.

LICENSING DESIGNATIONS (43–40–1)

The Broker License   A broker (the brokerage firm) is the only licensee authorized to enter into a contract with another person, who has promised to pay the broker a fee or commission. To earn a fee, the broker may list, sell, purchase, lease, rent, exchange, or auction real estate, collect rent, or deal in options to buy. The fee for these services can be anything of value, not necessarily money. Charging an advertising fee to promote property through listings in a publication primarily for such purposes is not considered to be a brokerage service.

Associate Brokers and Salespeople

All of the functions that the broker is authorized to perform can also be performed by associate brokers and salespeople, but with one reservation. They cannot act in their own name but must act as agents of the broker holding their licenses. Only the broker can act independently.

The Community Association Manager

This license is described in detail in Chapter 14.

Real Estate Schools and Pre-license Instructors Also Require a License (43–40–8)

Practicing without a license (43–40–30). When the commission learns of someone practicing real estate without the proper license, they can issue cease and desist orders and can impose a fine of up to $1,000 per day. The commission does not have the power to impose a jail sentence. However, violation of this law is a misdemeanor, and a court might not only impose a fine but also a sentence of up to one year in jail.

License law exemptions (43–40–29). Certain individuals are exempt from the requirements of the license law even though they are performing the same services as a broker. *Note*: The 11 exemptions listed below apply only to unlicensed persons. They do not apply to anyone holding a license even if it is inactive. Once licensed, an agent must always act as a licensee and cannot claim to have acted under one of the exemptions.

1. Owners. Owners of real estate including individuals, corporations, partnerships, general partners of limited partnerships, landlords, or prospective purchasers, or their full-time employees or spouses when buying, selling, or leasing for their own purposes are exempt.

FOR EXAMPLE Kennedy owns a 36-unit apartment complex and is planning to sell it "by owner." Must he have a license to do this? No, he is exempt because he is the owner. (The size of his real estate holdings does not matter.)

2. Attorney-in-fact. Agency law provides that a *principal* may execute a *power of attorney*, authorizing another person (not necessarily an attorney) to act as an agent on his/her behalf.

FOR EXAMPLE Griffin owns an office building that is fully occupied. Since she plans to be out of town on an extended vacation trip, she signs a power of attorney, authorizing her brother to manage the property for a $2,000 fee during her absence. Does her brother need a license to perform this service? No. As the attorney-in-fact of the owner, he has an exemption.

3. Attorney at law. Attorneys enjoy an exemption from license law, but only when performing brokerage services as part of their regular professional legal services rendered to a client.

FOR EXAMPLE The heirs of William Hart have retained the services of attorney Bass to handle the disposition of an estate that includes a 35-acre parcel of land. Bass sells the land for $125,000 and charges the estate a fee of $10,000 for the sale. Did he need a license? No, because selling the property was part of his professional duty. *Note*: An attorney who takes clients only for real estate brokerage or who advertises real estate brokerage services must have a real estate license.

4. Executor, administrator, receiver, trustee in bankruptcy, or guardian. Any person performing brokerage services under the authority of the court is exempt.

FOR EXAMPLE When Gordon died without a will, the court appointed Herman to administer the estate. As part of his duties, Herman must sell 50 acres of Gordon's land to settle a debt. Herman can be paid a fee for the sale and does not need a license because he is acting under the authority of the court.

5. Full-time employees of government agencies, utility companies, lending institutions, and other business concerns. Full-time employees are exempt from license law when authorized by their employers to buy, sell, or lease property on the employer's behalf.

FOR EXAMPLE Freddy is an employee of the FHA, handling the sale of properties acquired through foreclosure. Freddy does not need a license because he is employed by a government agency.

6. General partners of limited partnerships. General partners have an exemption when managing property owned by the limited partnership. They may also employ unlicensed persons to assist.

7. Managers of residential properties under a contract approved by a federal agency.

8. A person who acts as a referral agent. As long as a person making a referral does not perform any brokerage services, does not receive any advance fee, and does not receive a fee from the person being referred, the person is exempt.

FOR EXAMPLE Peggy hears that Margaret Ann is looking for a home in the Westover Community. Peggy also knows that her friend, Joyce, has a home in that area and plans to sell it. She refers Margaret Ann to Joyce and in time a sale results. Joyce paid Peggy $100 for the referral. Does Peggy need a license to accept this money? No. She acted only as a referral agent and was not compensated by the person she referred. *Note:* It is important to remember that it is unlawful for a broker to pay a fee to an unlicensed referral agent.

9. A person employed by a broker managing residential property. A broker who is managing property under a written contract with the owner may employ unlicensed persons who are salaried and under the direct supervision of the broker. However, the activities performed by unlicensed personnel are limited to

- delivering an application or a lease;
- receiving an application, lease, deposit, or payment;
- showing units or executing leases under broker's direct supervision;
- providing authorized information to prospects;

- providing information to tenants regarding payment accounts; and
- performing ministerial acts authorized by the broker in writing.

10. The "innkeeper's exemption." An exemption is accorded to persons who make accommodations available to the public on a daily or weekly basis as in the operation of hotels, motels, and vacation-type rentals. They do not need a real estate license as long as they can meet the following conditions:

- The manager must have a written management agreement with the owner.
- The agreement specifies that the manager may not rent or lease the property and that the guest or occupant is not a tenant.
- Zoning laws do not prohibit short-term occupancy uses.
- Occupancy is for less than 90 days.
- No deposit can exceed the cost charged for a minimum occupancy period.
- The manager pays required state or local business license fees and permits; and the guest pays any required sales or excise taxes.
- The manager can specify which rooms the guests are to occupy.
- No additional charge is made for basic utilities.
- Notice is required for the guest to terminate occupancy.
- The room does not serve as a permanent residence.

The "innkeeper exemption" does not apply if the "innkeeper" engages in other types of brokerage activities. In that case a license is necessary and all "innkeeping" activities must be handled as a licensee would handle rentals. *Note:* A real estate licensee handling some short-term vacation rentals must deposit all funds collected for the owner in a trust account.

11. A person who provides community association management services. As long as the person provides services to only one community association of which that person is a member they are exempt. A person who provides maintenance services to a community association is exempt. A certified public accountant providing accounting services to a community association is exempt. *Note:* The exceptions to the license law are not applicable if a person uses them or tries to use them to evade the need for having a license.

A Proper License Is Required To Collect a Commission (43–40–24)

License law prohibits anyone from going to court to collect a commission for services rendered without first proving that he or she held a valid license at the time the services were performed.

OBTAINING AND RETAINING THE LICENSE (43–40–8)

All applicants for a license must be residents of Georgia unless qualifying as nonresident licensees.

Basic Requirements for the Salesperson's License

An applicant must be at least 18 years old and must be a high school graduate or the holder of a certificate of equivalency. In addition, the applicant must successfully complete 75 hours of instruction by

- attending and passing a 75-hour approved course; or

- completing an approved independent study course; or
- showing by transcript 10 quarter or 6 semester hours of real estate subjects taken at an accredited college, university, or law school;

and applying for and passing the state real estate examination.

An employing broker must sign the application for license, unless the licensee wishes to be on inactive status.

The rules provide that the applicant has three months after completing the examination successfully to apply for the license, or can apply after three months have passed and up to one year for a double fee.

The holder of a new salesperson's license must also complete an additional 25 hours of approved post license study during the first year of licensure.

Basic Requirements for the Broker's License

Applicants for the broker's license must be at least 21 years old and must have been actively licensed for at least three years.

(They can sit for the state broker's examination when licensed for only two years, but then must wait another year before applying for the license.) In addition, a broker applicant must

- successfully complete 60 hours of instruction or the equivalent by
  - attending a 60-hour commission approved course; or
  - completing a commission approved independent study course; or
  - showing by transcript at least 15 quarter hours or 9 semester hours in real estate subjects from an accredited college, university, or law school; or
- applying for and passing a state examination.

The applicant must apply for the license within 12 months of passing the state exam.

Basic Requirements for the Community Association Management License

An applicant for the community association management (CAM) license must be at least 18 years old, a high school graduate or holder of a certificate of equivalence, must pass an approved 25-hour course, and must also pass a state examination.

Post License Educational Requirement

1. Post license. The holder of a new salesperson's license must complete an additional 25 hours of approved post license study during the first year of licensure.

2. Continuing education. All licensees, brokers as well as salespersons, unless licensed before 1980, must complete 6 hours of approved continuing education for each year of licensure or, in other words, 24 hours at each renewal, which takes place every 4 years.

The 25-hour post license course new agents must complete in their first year of licensure counts for 6 hours of continuing education.

License Renewal

When first applying for a license, the applicant pays an application and license fee, valid for four years, expiring on the last day of the applicant's birth month. After that, the licensee renews the license every four years on the last day of the applicant's birth month by showing proof of completion of all continuing education requirements and payment of a renewal fee.

Reinstatement of a Lapsed License

Failure to submit a renewal application in a timely manner and with the required fee causes a license to lapse. The licensee then has two years in which to reinstate the license by paying a reinstatement fee, all renewal fees, and charges that would have been due, and by submitting verification that the continuing education requirement has been met. If the license has lapsed for more than two years and up to ten years, it can be reinstated by paying the fees and by taking the appropriate prelicense course (CAM course for CAM licensees, salespersons course for salespersons, and broker's course for brokers).

After ten years, an applicant for reinstatement must qualify as an original applicant.

Failure to complete the required 25-hour course for new licensees within the first year might necessitate qualifying as an original applicant, unless the applicant registered and paid for the course within the year, in which case they are given six months to complete it.

Inactive Status

The license law provides an inactive status for licensees who might temporarily wish to cease to be actively involved in real estate. An inactive agent may not practice real estate brokerage in any way except for personal transactions. Inactive licensees are not exempt from the 25-hour course requirement for new licensees. Inactive agents pay the same renewal fees as active agents. A license can be on inactive status for an indefinite period of time. Applying to the commission reactivates an inactive license. If the license has been on inactive status for two years or longer, approved courses totaling at least six hours for each year the license was inactive must be completed within one year before activation.

Sole Proprietorship, Corporate, Partnership, and Limited Liability Company Licensure

Before a license is issued to a sole proprietorship, corporation, partnership, or a limited liability company, one person (a human being, not a legal entity) who is the holder of a broker's license, must be designated as the qualifying broker. This individual must

- be able to bind the company to any agreement;
- be able to settle any contested claim before the commission in which the company was named; and
- have signatory power over trust accounts.

Note: Salespersons can participate in company ownership as long as there is at least one broker. Associate brokers and salespersons may personally incorporate themselves as long as the corporate license is assigned to the licensed broker under whom they practice.

In other words, at least two broker's licenses are issued to a sole proprietorship, corporation, partnership, or limited partnership; one to the company and one to the qualifying broker.

Branch offices do not need a separate broker's license. The manager does not have to be a broker.

Nonresident Licensure

Georgia permits residents of other states to hold a Georgia license. The applicant must simply meet the same requirements of age, education, and examination as a resident must and pay the necessary fees. The applicant must designate the commissioner as their agent to receive any legal or judicial notices that might be filed. The applicant must agree to cooperate in any investigation the commission might bring.

Applicants from some states (depending on whether or not reciprocity has been approved) might be required to take the state specific portion of the real estate examination.

A licensee from another state who is moving to Georgia may obtain a license by submitting documents from the Real Estate Commission where they were licensed, showing

- the education and examination requirements that were met;
- whether the license is in good standing; and
- whether there have been any disciplinary actions taken.

Georgia residents who move to another state may choose to put the license on inactive status or keep it active. They must notify the commission of their new address.

WORKING WITH OUT-OF-STATE BROKERS (43–40–9)

Brokers from other states may participate in real estate transactions in Georgia and earn a fee in the following three ways:

1. Participating in referrals of clients and customers. In the referral process, an out-of-state broker refers a prospect to a Georgia licensee but takes no part in the listing, showing, negotiating, or any other brokerage function. A referral fee paid to the broker referring the prospect is permissible. On the same basis, a Georgia broker may refer a prospect to an out-of-state broker but participate in no other way and collect a fee.
2. Participating in nonresident licensure. Nonresident licensure is permitted in Georgia. (The requirements for a nonresident license are explained above.) A nonresident applicant who is not licensed as a broker must be affiliated with a resident or nonresident broker licensed to do business in Georgia.
3. Written agreement with a Georgia broker. Nonresident licensees who wish to do business in Georgia but do not hold nonresident licenses may do so by entering into a written agreement with a Georgia broker. There must be a separate agreement for each transaction, and it must spell out specific procedures to be followed during and after a transaction. The Georgia broker is responsible for the acts of the nonresident and should verify that the person does hold a valid license in his or her state.

BROKER RESPONSIBILITY (43–40–18)

Violations by Affiliates

A broker is responsible if licensees affiliated with the broker's firm violate the license law or the rules and regulations of the commission. This liability might be eliminated or reduced if the broker can show

- that the firm had a training program;
- that the firm had proper procedures for supervising affiliates; and
- that the broker did not participate in the violation.

A broker is required to adhere to the following ten procedures:

1. Review all advertisements.
2. Provide regular updates of law changes for affiliates.
3. Review all offers within 30 days of the writing.
4. Review all trust account journals and other records.
5. Make sure that affiliates maintain active licenses.
6. Make sure that trust fund payments are properly made.
7. Provide for the safekeeping of all records.
8. Provide a written policies and procedures manual for affiliates.
9. See that affiliates have written, signed employment agreements.
10. See that someone with management authority is always available to assist affiliates and the public.

TRUST ACCOUNT PROCEDURES (43–40–20)

Public Protection Provided

License law provides that all licensees must place any funds or valuables to be held on behalf of others in a trust account. The funds in an account specifically designated as a trust or escrow account are protected in that they cannot be seized for the broker's or the firm's debts.

The law also prohibits the broker from using any portion of the funds while they are being held. Trust funds must be kept separate from the broker's own funds or the firm's funds. To mix them in any way (*commingling*) could result in a disciplinary action.

Trust Account

Every broker who accepts funds to be held in trust for a client or customer in a real estate transaction (earnest money, security deposits, rents, etc.) must have a separate, federally insured account for holding such funds. Only brokers who never hold trust funds are exempt from this requirement. A broker may have more than one trust account if good business practice dictates this. The license law also requires the following:

- That the Real Estate Commission be notified of the name of the bank and account number for each account and must be given the right to audit the account at any time.
- That interest-bearing accounts are permitted as long as there is written agreement by all parties, including who is to receive the interest.
- Funds received in trust must be deposited immediately unless there is an agreement in writing by all parties, allowing them to be held for a stated period of time.

- A broker may not remove earnest money from a trust account until the transaction has been consummated or terminated.
- Licensees handling their own property must also place client funds into a trust account, either their broker's account or one they opened themselves. If a licensee uses his or her own account, the Real Estate Commission must be notified and also the broker.

FOR EXAMPLE Broker Barnes sells some land he owns to Gresham on a land contract. Gresham is to pay $10,000 down and $1,200 per month for ten years. He receives possession of the land and will receive the title when the loan is paid off. Barnes still has a mortgage on which he makes payments of $6,000 per year. License law requires Barnes to put Gresham's payments into a trust account each month until his mortgage payment is made. This insures Gresham of the fact that Barnes is paying off his mortgage and a clear title will be available when the ten years have passed.

Nonresident brokers may open a trust account in their state of residence as long as all of the rules regarding notification and management of the account are met. Community association managers, salespersons, and associate brokers must place all client funds in a designated trust account.

Unfair Practices (43–40–25)

The license law lists seven areas where unfair practices constitute violations, as follows:

Discrimination

Any licensee who denies equal service to anyone because of race, color, religion, sex, national origin, familial status, or handicap has not only violated the Federal Fair Housing Law and any similar state or local laws, but has also violated the license law. Such violations cannot only result in civil penalties and in some cases criminal charges, but can also result in loss of license. Licensees should be familiar with Fair Housing law and must constantly evaluate the intent and effect of their actions with respect to these laws so as to avoid even unintentional violations.

Advertising

Advertising rules apply to ads of any sort and in all media ranging from a simple sign to an elaborate TV commercial. No matter what form is used, the subject property must be displayed in a fair way with no misleading or inaccurate statements. License law forbids misrepresenting the property, its value, the terms under which it can be sold, or the services the broker is willing to offer.

FOR EXAMPLE ABC REALTY advertised that they offered a "Free Appraisal" when in fact they were not licensed by the Georgia Real Estate Appraisers Board and were therefore prohibited from using that term. Probably what they intended to offer was a free estimate of market price, and that should have been stated and explained.

It is also an unfair practice for a broker to advertise a property in any way without the written consent of the owner, and the permission granted must have a definite date of expiration.

Inducements

Inducing a prospect to purchase a property by promising that this property will earn a profit when resold is an unfair practice. Violations also include inducing a party to cancel an existing contract in order to substitute a new contract.

FOR EXAMPLE Purchaser Stephenson signed an offer to purchase a certain property through Broker Deal. Broker Conway offers Stephenson $1,000 to forfeit his $500 earnest money deposit and buy another property. Conway would be subject to disciplinary action.

Earnest Money

Licensees are obligated to properly account for and remit any money coming into their hands that belongs to others. This money can never be commingled with business or personal accounts. Because trust funds must be turned over to the broker as soon as possible, the broker should have a policy as to when funds can be received by the broker or someone delegated to receive them on the broker's behalf and to how the receipt of these funds will be acknowledged.

There must also be a procedure for handling cash deposits or other items of personal property. Even when permission to hold an earnest money check for a period of time is given by the parties to a contract, the check must be turned over to the broker. A salesperson or associate broker cannot hold it. Licensees must be carefully trained to follow the procedures for proper handling of trust funds.

FOR EXAMPLE Fran's broker requires that earnest money deposits be turned over to the office bookkeeper during normal business hours from 9:00 A.M. to 5:30 P.M., Monday through Friday. She receives a large earnest money check on Friday night preceding a three-day holiday weekend. When can she turn over the money? Probably not until Tuesday morning. Can she keep it in her own account until then? No, this would be commingling. Is the broker's policy reasonable? Yes.

Broker-Client Relationships

A *client* is a party with whom a broker has entered into a principal/agent relationship. In a listing contract, the seller is the client. In a buyer brokerage contract, the buyer is the client. In a property management agreement, the owner is the client. A prospective tenant might also become a client. The following provisions in the license law arise out of the client relationship:

- A written agency agreement must have a definite ending date. An automatic renewal provision would be a violation.
- All parties signing a contract should be given a copy of the contract.
- A written disclosure as to which party a licensee represented as agent must be made at the time a written offer is made or before that time.
- A dual agency is permissible only if both parties agree in writing.
- A broker may not offer a property for sale, describe terms on which the sale can be made, or place a sign on the property without the written consent of the owner.
- Except for the broker, a licensee cannot conduct a closing unless acting under supervision of the broker or the supervision of an attorney with the broker's knowledge.
- All offers must be presented as soon as possible.

- A broker must keep copies of all sales contracts, listing, closing statements, and any other documents related to real estate transactions for three years.
- A broker may not appraise a property unless the broker has a appraiser classification.
- When a licensee (even an inactive license-holder) is also the seller, buyer, lessor, or lessee in a transaction, the fact that that individual holds a real estate license must be disclosed in any contract. The other party is thereby given notice that he or she is dealing with a person who has special training in real estate.

FOR EXAMPLE Purchaser Salesperson Perkins buys a property listed with Broker Parrish. The seller was told that Perkins was a licensed salesperson with Parrish, and that fact was never disputed; but it was not disclosed *in writing* on the sales contract. This was a violation.

- Another unfair practice is *falsifying contracts* (also referred to as writing *dual contracts*). This often involves writing a second (false) contract to accompany a loan application.

FOR EXAMPLE A buyer wants to purchase a condominium for $55,000, but the maximum loan that is obtainable is for 90 percent of the value, or $49,500. The buyer can only put $2,500 down, and the seller is agreeable to lending the other $3,000 with a second mortgage. But because the lender will not agree to so small a down payment, the broker writes two contracts. One shows the buyer paying $2,500 down and then $49,500 by way of a first mortgage and $3,000 by way of a purchase money second mortgage. The other (the one the lender will see) shows the buyer paying $5,500 down. This could lead to the broker losing his or her license, and all parties to the contract are subject to civil action and/or criminal action and could even go to jail. In fact, falsification in any part of a real estate transaction is prohibited.

FOR EXAMPLE All the following constitute falsifications: concealing from the lender the actual sale price, or the fact that the buyer is getting a second mortgage, or telling the seller that a buyer's credit appears to be okay when the licensee knows otherwise.

- A broker may not accept any undisclosed compensation unless all parties to the transaction agree.
- A broker may not refer a prospect to another broker without the knowledge of the person being referred. The person being referred must be informed of whether or not the referring broker will receive compensation for the referral.

Substantial Misrepresentation

All parties to a transaction must be treated honestly, regardless of whether a party is or is not a "client." Misrepresentation occurs when a licensee misleads (by action, statement, or silence) a party concerning a material fact on which the party relies, to his or her detriment. Stating a fact that is not true, or concealing a defect, can constitute fraud. This is true even when concealment was just a failure to correct an assumption on the purchaser's part, known by the licensee to be incorrect.

FOR EXAMPLE Salesperson Jones asked the seller if there were any defects in the property and was assured there were none. He also inspected and saw no problems.

After the sale it turned out that there was a serious foundation problem. Was Jones guilty? Probably not because he did not intentionally mislead the purchaser.

FOR EXAMPLE Salesperson Jones is showing a vacant residential lot to a customer. Although he knew, he failed to mention to the purchaser that the vacant land next door had been rezoned and purchased for industrial purposes. Was Jones guilty? Yes. His silence about a material fact was misrepresentation.

Working with Other Brokers

It is often the case that brokers cooperate (sometimes called co-brokering) in a transaction, one representing the seller and the other the buyer.

In most residential transactions, the listing broker collects a commission from the seller and shares it with the selling broker in a prearranged agreement. In some cases the buyer-client compensates the selling broker. In any case compensation is only paid to the broker. Salespersons and associate brokers may only receive their share of the compensation from the broker holding their license. They cannot receive compensation from another broker or from the public except when their own broker has full knowledge and has agreed.

When a broker knows that another broker has an exclusive listing on a property, it is a violation to contact the seller or to try to sell the property without the listing broker's permission. Also, any offer must go to the listing broker.

It is a violation to induce any person to alter, modify, or change another licensee's fee or commission without prior written permission.

THE INVESTIGATIVE PROCESS (43–40–27)

The investigative process is necessary because the Real Estate Commission's purpose is to protect the public from unscrupulous licensees. The Georgia Administrative Procedures Act, which outlines permitted disciplinary procedures for all state agencies, controls the commission's investigative powers.

The commission may investigate any licensee upon its own motion or will initiate an investigation whenever anyone files a sworn, written request. This triggers the following four-step procedure:

Step #1: The case is assigned to a commission investigator, who has the power to use subpoenas if necessary to gather evidence. When the investigation is completed, a report is given to the commissioner indicating that there is or is not evidence of a possible violation. If no infraction is found, the matter ends at this point.

Step #2: When evidence is found of a minor infraction, a citation might be issued and a fine imposed. More serious matters are at this point referred to the attorney general and a formal hearing is scheduled. The licensee is notified and can choose to be represented by an attorney if he or she so desires. The hearing is held even if the licensee does not attend.

Step #3: The hearing officer reports the "findings of fact' to the Real Estate Commission. The commission meets to decide what disciplinary action might be appropriate.

Step #4: If a sanction is imposed against the licensee, there is a right to appeal the decision to the Superior Court, and no actions are imposed until appeals are exhausted.

When a license is revoked or is suspended for more than sixty days, the licensee's name must be published on the commission's web site. Also, the commission may share this information with the commissions of other states.

 WWWeb.Link
You will find the names of those sanctioned by the commission at http://www2.state.ga.us/grec/grec/grecsanctions/grecsanctions.html, or you can to to www.grec.state.ga.us, click on the button for the Georgia Real Estate Commission, then click on the button for disciplinary sanctions.

Applications for a license may be denied to anyone who has been convicted of fraud, forgery, embezzlement, obtaining money under false premises, theft, extortion, conspiracy, or other offenses involving moral turpitude. When a licensee is convicted of any of these offenses, the commission must be informed immediately. Sixty days later the license will be automatically revoked unless the licensee has requested a hearing, after which the commission can decide what action is appropriate.

REAL ESTATE EDUCATION, RESEARCH, AND RECOVERY FUND (43–40–22)

Nature and Purpose   The Real Estate Education, Research, and Recovery Fund was established to compensate consumers who suffer damages at the hands of a licensee but who are unable to recover through normal legal procedures.

The fund is maintained by the Real Estate Commission and is funded by charging every applicant a $20 fee for a *new* license. Funds are held separate from other state funds and are invested in legal securities. The income generated can be used by the commission for purposes linked to real estate education and research.

If the fund were to fall below a required minimum total of $1,000,000, all licensees could be assessed up to $30 per year.

Limitations   There are five limitations to compensating consumers from the Recovery Fund:

1. If the fund is to be involved, the aggrieved citizen must bring suit against the licensee in court within two years of when the damage was suffered.
2. Real estate licensees and their families have no claim against the fund.

3. The fund cannot pay more than $15,000 per transaction, regardless of how many persons were cheated and how large the claims.
4. No person shall be paid more than $15,000.
5. The fund is limited to $45,000 per licensee, no matter how many people that licensee may have cheated.

The following three steps are required in order to receive payment from the Recovery Fund:

1. Obtain a judgment. The person claiming to have suffered damages sues the licensee, notifies the Real Estate Commission, and is awarded a judgment.
2. Sell the licensee's property. With a writ of execution from the court, any real or personal nonexempt property belonging to the licensee can be seized to satisfy the judgment.
3. Obtain a court order. When attempts to seize property do not produce enough to satisfy the judgment, the court can now order payment from the Recovery Fund, up to the limits allowed. *Note:* When the commission pays out of the Recovery Fund, the license of the accused licensee is automatically revoked. If all the money is later repaid, the licensee, after ten years, can again apply for a license as an original applicant.

BUSINESS LICENSES (48–13–17)

Local governments may charge a business license to a broker but only in the place where the broker physically maintains an office.

Local governments may charge a gross receipts tax but only for transactions that occurred in their particular town or county.

Questions

1. The maximum period a license may be placed on inactive status is for
   a. one year.
   b. two years.
   c. three years.
   d. no time limit.

2. A broker shall not be entitled to any part of the earnest money or other money paid to him or her in connection with any real estate transaction as part or all of his or her commission until the transaction has been
   a. consummated.
   b. inactivated.
   c. approved.
   d. cemented.

3. The Georgia Real Estate Commission must follow certain procedures when dealing with an alleged violation. Which comes first?
   a. Hearing
   b. Report to the attorney general
   c. Disciplinary action
   d. Investigation

4. A broker may collect a commission from both the seller and the purchaser if
   a. the total commission does not exceed the usury limit.
   b. both the seller and purchaser agree in writing.
   c. the Real Estate Commission is notified.
   d. the seller gives his or her written permission.

5. Which of the following licenses may be placed on inactive status?
   a. Hunting
   b. Fishing
   c. Boating
   d. Associate Broker

6. Salesperson Roberts plans to purchase a piece of property he has listed for sale. Before presenting the offer, he must
   a. disclose to the seller the purpose for which the property is being purchased.
   b. furnish his broker with written notice of his intent to purchase the property so that no commission will be paid.
   c. furnish his broker with written notice of his intent to purchase and state in the contract that he is a licensed real estate salesperson.
   d. provide the commission with a copy of the sales contract so the seller's rights will be protected.

7. Which of the following is exempt from the licensing requirement?
   a. Attorneys who solicit property for sale
   b. Elected officials who deal in real estate in their county of residence
   c. Persons operating under a duly executed power-of-attorney to convey property
   d. Relatives of the owner

8. Licensing fees are set by the
   a. Real Estate Commission.
   b. secretary of state.
   c. state legislature.
   d. governor.

9. Before suspending or revoking a license, the commission shall
   a. provide a hearing for the licensee.
   b. get permission from the attorney general.
   c. refund the licensee's Recovery Fund deposit.
   d. inform the governor.

10. Salesperson Wilson shows a prospective purchaser a home on Wednesday afternoon. That evening Wilson obtains an offer and an earnest money deposit. The offer is to remain effective until Saturday at 6:00 P.M., but it is accepted Friday. When should Wilson turn over the earnest money to the broker?
   a. Probably Thursday
   b. Probably Friday
   c. Probably Saturday
   d. Probably Monday

11. The license law gives the commission the power to
   a. set all commissions.
   b. revoke or suspend licenses.
   c. pass rules and change the license law.
   d. fine licensees up to $1,000 or send them to jail for one year.

12. Which of the following is true about the qualifying broker of a corporation?
   a. The qualifying broker must be an officer of the corporation.
   b. The qualifying broker must own all interest in the company.
   c. The qualifying broker must live in the state of Georgia.
   d. The qualifying broker must have had a broker's license at least five years.

13. What will a broker first be required to prove in court before he or she can recover a commission?
   a. He or she had a contract of employment.
   b. He or she was properly licensed at the time of the cause of the action.
   c. He or she showed the property to the purchaser.
   d. He or she was a resident of Georgia at the time of the cause of the action.

14. The commission may suspend or revoke a license if
   a. a salesperson delivers a signed offer to the seller within a reasonable time.
   b. a broker advertises real estate for sale with the consent of the owner.
   c. a broker deposits earnest money belonging to the principal into a trust account.
   d. a salesperson accepts a commission from anyone except their broker.

15. If a licensee does not renew his or her license within the time period required by law
   a. he or she must reapply as an original applicant.
   b. he or she may renew within one year of the date of its lapsing by paying a reinstatement fee.
   c. he or she may renew within two years of the date of its lapsing by paying a reinstatement fee.
   d. he or she may renew within two years of the date of its lapsing by paying all renewal fees and late charges that would have been due, plus a reinstatement fee.

16. The liability of the Real Estate Education, Research, and Recovery Fund for the acts of one licensee is terminated upon the payment of how much money on behalf of that licensee?
   a. $20,000   c. $45,000
   b. $15,000   d. $10,000

17. A licensee would subject his/her license to sanction by the commission for all of the following EXCEPT
   a. failing to leave a copy of the listing agreement with the seller.
   b. accepting compensation from the employing broker.
   c. placing a For Sale sign on property without the written consent of the owner.
   d. failing to disclose licensure when acting as a principal.

18. When a licensed broker closes a real estate transaction, the broker must retain a copy of the closing statement for
   a. one year.   c. seven years.
   b. three years.   d. forever.

19. Which of the following is considered to be an "unfair practice" of the License Law?
   a. Maintaining more than one trust account
   b. Acting as a real estate broker or salesperson without a license
   c. Offering free gifts to influence prospective buyers
   d. Acting as agent and undisclosed principal in a transaction

20. Which of the following statements concerning a broker's trust account is true?
    a. A broker is never entitled to any portion of an earnest money deposit.
    b. Any bank may be used for a trust account.
    c. Violations of trust account provisions may result in an action by the attorney general to impound such an account.
    d. All trust accounts must pay interest.

21. The Georgia Real Estate Commission has
    a. five members, all licensed.
    b. five members, four licensed.
    c. six members, all licensed.
    d. six members, five licensed.

22. In order to receive a Georgia salesperson's license you must
    a. be at least 21 years of age.
    b. be a graduate of a high school.
    c. take a 75-hour in-class prelicense course.
    d. pass the state exam.

23. A broker in another state who wishes to be paid for selling a piece of property in Georgia must
    a. get a nonresident license.
    b. refer the buyer to a Georgia salesperson.
    c. enter into a verbal agreement to co-op with a Georgia broker.
    d. post a bond at least as large as the commission.

24. A broker is *NOT* required to do which of the following?
    a. Review all advertising
    b. Review all agent tax returns
    c. Review all offers within 30 days
    d. Review all trust account records

25. A licensee who denies equal service to anyone because of race, color, religion, sex, national origin, familial status, or handicap has violated the
    a. Law of Selection.
    b. Georgia Community Housing Law.
    c. Federal Antitrust Law.
    d. Georgia License Law.

2 Rules of the Georgia Real Estate Commission

PURPOSE

The Georgia Real Estate Commission under authority granted in the license law adopts the rules and regulations. They are designed to clarify and further explain sections of the law. Also, if a matter comes to the Commission's attention that is not in the public's best interests, the commission can pass a rule to correct the situation without waiting for the legislature to meet. However, no rule can be passed that is not based on the license law or which in any way conflicts with it.

 WWWeb.Link
You can find the Rules of the Georgia Real Estate Commission at http://ww2.state.ga.us/grec/grec/grecforms/grecforms.html or you can go to www.grec.state.ga.us, click on the button for the Georgia Real Estate Commission, then click on the button for rules.

Violating a rule has the same effect as violating the law itself and can result in the same disciplinary action.

FOR EXAMPLE The term "net listing" does not appear in the law, but the commission felt it was in the best interests of the public to pass a rule that prohibits net listings. A licensee who accepts a net listing is subject to a disciplinary action.

Any citizen can ask for the passage, amendment, or repeal of a rule. The request must be in writing with a notarized signature. Within 30 days of receipt of the request, the commission will either deny it, stating the reasons why, or initiate a rule-making procedure.

Also, upon request, within 90 days, the commission will furnish a *declaratory ruling* to clarify its position and intent with regard to a particular rule. These rulings are *not* intended to (nor will they)

- render legal advice;
- settle disputes between a broker and a salesperson;

- settle disputes between real estate companies; or
- tell a licensee whether or not a contemplated action will be a violation.

To resolve such matters, the licensee should seek legal advice.

LICENSURE OF A BUSINESS (520–1–.10)

Sole Proprietorship   A broker who elects to do business as a sole proprietorship may operate in his own name or in a registered trade name. Two broker licenses will be needed, one for the qualifying broker and one for the sole proprietorship.

Corporation   Brokers who choose to form a corporation will need two broker licenses, one for the qualifying broker and one for the corporation. The application will include a copy of the corporate charter.

Partnership   Like corporations, partnerships will have at least two broker licenses: one for the qualifying broker and one for the partnership.

FOR EXAMPLE Al and Jim both have broker licenses, and they decide to go into business together as a partnership. Al is to be the qualifying broker. Two licenses are necessary, one for the qualifying broker and one for the partnership. Jim will be an associate broker.

Limited Liability Company   Like a corporation or partnership, the limited liability company (LLC) must have two licenses, one for the qualifying broker and one for the company, as registered with the secretary of state.

Note: A broker may operate only in the name in which the commission issues the license.

LICENSURE OF INDIVIDUALS (520–1–.11) AND THE LICENSE EXAMINATION (520–1–.13)

Applicants for a license must apply to take the state examination and pay a nonrefundable fee. A passing grade of 75 percent is required. Honorably discharged veterans with one year or more of service (of which 90 days was during wartime) receive a five-point credit; and veterans discharged due to injury or illness with at least a 10 percent disability receive a ten-point credit.

If licensed in another state, an applicant might be exempt from education and examination requirements, if the real estate commission in each state in which they were licensed can certify that the applicant

- passed an examination similar to the one Georgia requires;
- has met prelicense and continuing education requirements of the other state(s);

- has kept an active license with no more than 90 days of inactive or lapsed time; and
- has had no disciplinary actions imposed.

Note: To determine reciprocity, an applicant should contact the Georgia Real Estate Commission.

APPLYING FOR THE LICENSE (520–1–.25)

Applicants for the *salesperson* license must make application within three months of the examination date and pay a fee, or after three months but before twelve months for a double fee. The signature of an employing broker is needed, or application can be made for an inactive license. A salesperson can begin work when the employing broker receives the wall license. *Note:* A salesperson cannot be licensed under more than one broker at any given time.

Applicants for the broker's license have one year from the examination date to apply for the license. Failure to apply for any license within the time limits nullifies the examination and necessitates a retake.

Any applicant who has been convicted of a serious crime or sanctioned by a licensing board must give the commission a certified copy of the conviction or the final order when applying. *Note:* A person who wants to know, prior to going through the education and examination procedures, whether a conviction or sanction on their record might result in denial of the license can receive an early review of the matter.

TRANSFER OF LICENSE (520–1–.11)

Any licensee always has the right to leave their employing broker and either go to inactive status or join another broker. The present broker cannot refuse to sign a release form.

If going inactive, the license is surrendered to the commission and the broker sends the commission a signed "change" (release) form and the wall license.

If joining a new firm, the licensee can deliver the wall license to the new broker, who then signs the "change" (transfer) application and sends it to the commission. The former broker notifies the commission in writing that the wall license has been moved. All notifications to the commission must be made within 30 days of the move.

REINSTATEMENT OF A LAPSED LICENSE (520–1–.14)

When a license lapses, the broker must forward the license along with the licensee's pocket card to the commission. The licensee can no longer practice until the license is reinstated. A license lapses because of

- nonpayment of fees, and/or
- failure to complete certain educational requirements in time.

A lapsed license may be reinstated with two years, provided necessary continuing education credits are complete, by paying all renewal fees, late charges, plus a reinstatement fee.

After two years and before ten years have passed, reinstatement of a lapsed license not only requires paying all fees, but also re-taking the approved pre-license course that applies, i.e., salesperson course for salespeople, broker course for brokers, etc.

Reinstatement of a license after ten years requires applying again as an original applicant.

A license lapsed due to failure to complete the 25-hour post license course for new salespeople within one year cannot be reinstated. However, if the licensee can prove that he or she enrolled in and paid for an approved course, but for some valid reason was unable to complete it on time, a six-month extension of the time limit is granted. Otherwise the licensee must retake the license exam and complete the post license course before becoming licensed again.

Note: When the license of someone who has a "grandfathered" exemption from continuing education requirements (i.e., was licensed before 1980) lapses, the exemption no longer applies.

Any required courses must be taken within one year of reinstatement.

SURRENDERING A LICENSE TO THE COMMISSION (520–1–.12)

Both wall license and pocket card must be returned to the commission when a license is surrendered. This might be done voluntarily, or it might be done at the commission's request due to a suspension or revocation. This differs from inactive status in that the right to reactivate is not necessarily present.

If a qualifying broker surrenders a license, the affiliated agents do not need to return their licenses as long as a new qualifying broker is named.

RETENTION OF WALL LICENSES (520–1–.32)

A written request to the commission will afford a licensee who is retiring after 20 years of active licensure, or the family of a deceased licensee, the right to keep the wall license and pocket card for nonbrokerage purposes.

THE BROKER-SALESPERSON RELATIONSHIP (520–1–.11)

The Employer-Employee Relationship

A broker who wants to control such things as work schedules, office hours, floor duty time, and general procedures might choose to have employees. The agent is then accountable to the broker, not only for end results, but also for how the work is performed.

In turn, the broker must withhold state and federal income taxes, pay a Social Security contribution, and provide unemployment and worker's compensation insurance.

The Independent Contractor Relationship

Under the independent contractor arrangement, much preferred in most real estate sales offices, the broker has fewer costs and accounting responsibilities because there is nothing to withhold and no contributions to make.

The agents pay their own estimated taxes and manage their own business expenses.

The broker has less control. The agents are accountable to the broker only for the end results of their work but not for the way they perform. (Of course independent contractors *can* be required to attend training sessions on the license law and to abide by the law.)

Note: Regardless of the relationship chosen, salespeople owe the same obligations to the client as does the broker.

The Employment Agreement

A written employment agreement is required when an affiliate joins a firm. Regardless of whatever else it might provide, it must include

- how the licensee will be compensated while working for the broker;
- how the licensee will be compensated for work begun but not completed when the affiliation ends; and
- what accounting is to take place for prospects, listings, records, signs, plats, and keys when the licensee leaves the broker.

The commission will *not* enforce these contracts. Disputes must be resolved elsewhere.

Personal Assistants (520–1–.40)

A sharp increase in the number of busy agents employing assistants has generated some new rules regarding this role; among them are the following three:

1. There must be a three-way agreement among the broker, the licensee, and the support personnel, including duties to be performed and compensation. No one licensed in one firm can be employed to assist an agent in another.
2. An unlicensed assistant can perform "ministerial duties" such as scheduling appointments, closings, or inspections; placing or removing signs, securing public information; and acting as a courier.
3. Prohibited activities for unlicensed assistants include cold calling, holding open houses, preparing advertising without supervision, showing property, answering questions about a listing, explaining a contract, negotiating, giving advice, and holding trust funds.

Broker's Responsibilities To Affiliate Licensees

A broker is responsible for the performance of affiliated licensees and can be held accountable if any one of them breaks the law unless able to prove that adequate training and managerial oversight were available, and that the broker did not know of or participate in the infraction. The broker must also

- provide and distribute written company policies and procedures;
- instruct agents on the law and on any changes in the law that occur;
- be responsible for retaining legal advice when needed; and
- review all contracts within 30 days.

Salesperson's Duties To the Broker

A salesperson should become familiar with and follow the company's policies. The broker should be consulted whenever there is something that the salesperson does not understand or whenever a problem arises.

Brokers must also be informed before a salesperson sells, buys, leases, or rents a property in their own name.

THE REAL ESTATE TRANSACTION

Exclusive Seller Brokerage Engagements— Listings (520–1–.03)

Following are some rules regarding listings:

- All listing agreements must be in writing.
- Net listings are illegal.
- The compensation must be a definite percentage or amount.
- Listings must have a definite ending date.
- People who sign a listing contract must be given a copy of what they signed.
- Brokers must keep copies of listings for three years.
- Salespeople can sign a listing on behalf of their broker if written permission is granted. (It is often contained in the employment agreement.)
- A licensee promising to buy the property as an inducement must put it in writing.

FOR EXAMPLE Agent Jennifer, in an attempt to list the Andersons' house, tells them that if it does not sell in 60 days she will buy it herself. Jennifer must accompany her listing contract with a signed agreement to purchase.

Presenting Offers (520–1–.06)

Licensees have an obligation to see that all offers are clear and unambiguous. License law provides that they must be presented as soon as possible, no matter how unreasonable or unworkable they might seem to be. Complaints often arise about prompt presentation of offers. A delay might be due to the seller being out of town. This represents poor business practice because the listing agent should have instructed the seller to leave information about where he or she could be contacted. Much more serious is a delay due to greed.

FOR EXAMPLE On Tuesday morning, Grady received from a salesperson with another company an offer of $50,000 on his listing. Because Grady has a prospect of his own for this property and would make twice as much commission if she would buy, he holds onto the first offer until he can get in touch with his own prospect. She comes into the office on Wednesday morning and makes a $51,000 offer. Both offers are presented to the seller on Wednesday evening. The $51,000 offer is accepted. The licensee who writes the first offer complains. Is the complaint justified? *Yes,* his offer was not presented as soon as possible. Only the seller could have chosen to wait and see a second offer before acting on the first.

Closing the Transaction (520–1–.17)

The closing is the final step; it occurs when title is transferred and all the necessary papers are signed. An attorney usually conducts the closing. Occasionally it might be the broker, but a broker is not authorized to prepare legal documents. A salesperson may conduct the closing if under the direct supervision of the broker or an attorney approved by the broker. Parties to the closing are usually accompanied by the licensees who represented them. A complete and detailed closing statement must be prepared, and copies given to all parties. The broker is responsible for receiving and maintaining a copy of the statement.

ADVERTISING (520–1–.04)

Some rules regarding real estate advertising *in any of the media* are as follows:

- A broker may not advertise without the owner's permission, given in writing and with a definite expiration date. This applies even to open listings.
- Advertising must not misrepresent the property or the terms of sale.

FOR EXAMPLE A broker lists a home for $75,000 cash. Thinking it might be hard to sell under those terms, his newspaper ad stated "OWNER FINANCING AVAILABLE." This is an obvious violation because it misrepresents the terms.

Each advertisement must contain the broker's (Company's) name as registered with the commission. If this is omitted, it is called a *blind ad.*

Any broker using a trade name or a franchise name in advertising must include the following statement: "Each (franchise or trade name) office is independently owned and operated"; plus the name of the brokerage firm as registered with the commission. This allows the public to know who is the responsible party.

Note: Rules regarding advertising apply to the Internet and Web sites. A listing advertised on the Internet must be removed within ten days after expiration.

LICENSEES AS PRINCIPALS (520–1–.08 & .15)

Once licensed, people can no longer act as unlicensed persons even when dealing with sales, purchases, leases, or rentals of their own property. Active or inactive licensees must disclose on all contracts that they are licensed in real estate, so that the special knowledge they have attained does not put the other party at a disadvantage. The disclosure must also appear on any advertising they do of their own property.

Active agents must realize that their broker has accountability for their actions even in transactions undertaken on their own behalf with no commission involved. The broker must be informed in writing and must approve both the procedure and any advertising that is to be done. This also applies if a licensee wants to use the services of another firm (for example, for property management).

A licensee has the following three choices when planning to sell or lease his or her own property:

1. List it with the broker, and trust deposits can go in the broker's account.
2. List it with another broker (with your own broker's permission), and trust deposits will go in that other broker's account.
3. Handle it yourself, opening a personal trust account set up under the broker's supervision and registered with the commission.

TRUST ACCOUNT PROCEDURES

Handling Earnest Money (520–1–.26, .30, & .34)

The commission requires that the public receive maximum protection when licensees handle funds belonging to others, i.e., earnest money, security deposits, etc. It is the responsibility of the broker to have written policies in place for the handling of money and to train affiliated licensees in those policies.

Earnest money must be deposited in a trust account immediately unless the contract provides otherwise. It is the listing broker who deposits the money unless the contract provides otherwise.

Often a buyer might want the earnest money check held until the offer is accepted. This is permissible if it is clearly stated in the contract, but the salesperson must turn the check over to the broker. Only the broker can hold the check.

Earnest money can be deposited in an interest-bearing account if the contract provides for this and states who is to receive the interest.

Trust Account Records (520–1–.26)

Any broker who handles client funds must have at least one trust account and must notify the commission within 30 days where the account is located and its number. The bookkeeping system used for accounting for deposits and withdrawals from the trust account will depend in part on the size of the company and the transactions they handle. Many software programs are available for handling this on computers.

A Trust Account Journal and Ledgers are kept to log in deposits or withdrawals as they occur, noting the property involved, names of the parties, amount of money, date, and purpose.

After a closing, the deposit less the total of all checks written on the deposit should be zero.

An exception to that rule occurs when the broker retains a portion of the deposit as commission earned. It is so designated in the accounting and transferred within a month by writing a check to the broker.

Property managers must also keep separate ledger accounts for each property managed, noting receipts and disbursals for that account. There must always be enough money in property management accounts to cover security deposits held.

A broker is allowed to place a small amount of money in the trust account if needed to take care of a minimum requirement or of service charges. Otherwise no personal or company funds can be mingled with trust funds.

Only the broker can make disbursements from the account. This can be done under the following circumstances:

- When the offer is rejected and the offeror is entitled to a refund of earnest money because there is no contract.
- When the offer is withdrawn before it is accepted and the offeror is entitled to a refund of the earnest money. There is no contract.
- At the time of closing. The earnest money is refunded or is a credit to the buyer at the closing.

When the sale falls through, both parties must agree in writing as to how the earnest money should be allocated.

If the sale fails and the parties to the contract do not agree, the broker can do the following:

- File an *interpleader* action, asking the court to make a decision. (This is rarely used because of the expense and the time it would consume.)
- Wait for a court order. If the parties have resorted to litigation, the court will make a decision.
- Make a *reasonable interpretation* of the contract, notifying all parties of the decision. (A prudent broker might seek legal counsel before doing this.)

Note: If the customer or client of a salesperson asks for a return of earnest money, the salesperson should refer them to the broker, making no statement as to whether or not that might be possible.

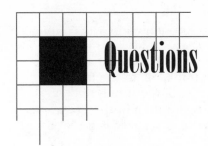

Questions

1. Rules passed by the Real Estate
   Commission
   a. are contained in the license law.
   b. regulate the commission staff.
   c. are based upon some provision in the
      license law.
   d. are effective until the next legislative ses-
      sion.

2. The Real Estate Commission _____ the
   use of net listings in Georgia.
   a. permits   c. prefers
   b. prohibits   d. approves

3. A salesperson may conduct the closing of a
   real estate transaction if
   a. the broker gives the salesperson written
      permission in his or her contract of
      employment.
   b. both the seller and the purchaser
      approve of the action and sign a state-
      ment releasing the salesperson of any
      liability.
   c. the salesperson is under the direct
      supervision of the broker or an attorney
      approved by the broker.
   d. the broker is present or the attorney is
      present with the broker's approval.

4. A salesperson may advertise personal real
   estate for sale or lease, without using the
   broker's name, provided
   a. a minimum brokerage fees is to be paid.
   b. the broker is told.
   c. the ad states that the "owner is a
      licensed real estate agent."
   d. the broker verbally approves of both the
      procedure and the advertisement.

5. A broker may maintain a separate trust
   account for each office location, provided
   a. a separate trust account journal is main-
      tained for each trust account.
   b. the commission is advised of the name of
      the bank and the name of the account
      within 14 days of opening the account.
   c. the broker agrees to have the account
      examined by the Georgia association.
   d. the office manager agrees to be responsi-
      ble for the account.

6. An applicant passing the salesperson's
   licensing examination has three months to
   apply for his or her license (without paying
   double fees) from the date that
   a. the applicant filed an application to sit
      for the examination.
   b. the commission advised the applicant
      that he or she passed the examination.
   c. the applicant took the examination.
   d. the applicant finished the prelicense
      course.

7. Upon notice of revocation of his or her
   license, the broker shall
   a. immediately forward to the commission
      the license and pocket card.
   b. return all wall licenses and pocket cards
      in his or her possession within 30 days
      or as soon as all pending sales close,
      whichever occurs first.
   c. forward to the commission all licenses
      and pocket cards in his or her posses-
      sion within 60 days.
   d. transfer all licenses to another broker.

8. Brokers may have their own funds in the trust account
   a. if the bank requires a minimum balance and the funds are identified in the journal.
   b. if the broker is leasing and managing property.
   c. when she or he is maintaining enough money to cover repairs for owners.
   d. to have money available to pay the broker's bills.

9. When salespersons sell their own property, they
   a. must always deposit the earnest money into their broker's trust account.
   b. may deposit the earnest money into their trust account, as long as it is approved by their broker and properly registered with the commission.
   c. need not deposit earnest money into a trust account, if their license is on inactive status.
   d. need not deposit the money if they notify the commission.

10. Earnest money checks received by a salesperson
    a. should be held by the salesperson, until the offer is accepted.
    b. should be turned over to the broker the next business day.
    c. should be placed in the broker's custody, as soon after receipt as is practicably possible.
    d. may never be shown to the seller while presenting the offer.

11. The commission requires
    a. all exclusive listings must be in writing.
    b. all gross listings must be in writing.
    c. all open listings must be in writing.
    d. all listings must be in writing.

12. If a sale does not close, and the broker wishes to disburse the earnest money, which of the following might be a violation?
    a. Filing an interpleader action with the courts
    b. Obtaining a separate agreement signed by all interested parties
    c. Transferring the funds to the broker's operating account
    d. Waiting on a court order

13. "Blind Ads" are prohibited by the commission, because they
    a. discriminate based on race.
    b. mislead the public as to the true price, terms, or value of the property.
    c. fail to give the location of the property.
    d. fail to state the advertiser is a real estate licensee.

14. When advertising a specific property either for sale in a publication or with signs on the property, the broker is required to
    a. use letters not less than three inches in height.
    b. name the salesperson listing the property.
    c. show the name of the brokerage firm as registered with the commission.
    d. use his or her telephone number and trade name, if any, in the ad.

15. A nonresident licensee who qualified for a nonresident license by meeting the age, education, and examination requirements, and who later becomes a resident of Georgia, may
    a. not be required to meet the education and examination requirements.
    b. apply for a tax exemption.
    c. not be required to have a escrow account.
    d. apply for a continuing education exemption.

16. Which of the following statements about commission rule(s) is (are) correct?
    a. The commission is not authorized to pass any rule it believes to be in the public interest, if the rule is confined to real estate brokerage activities.
    b. Any interested person may not petition the commission for a rule change.
    c. The commission will supply declaratory rulings as to the applicability of the license law, or any of its rules.
    d. The commission shall supply declaratory rulings as to matter under investigation.

17. A license may lapse for nonpayment of fees or failure to complete certain educational requirements within the time allowed by law. Which statement is correct concerning a license that lapsed for nonpayment of fees?
    a. The license may be reinstated within two years simply by paying a reinstatement fee.
    b. The license may be reinstated at any time, by paying a reinstatement fee plus all late charges and renewal fees that would have been due during the lapsed period.
    c. The license may not be reinstated; and the licensee must pass another examination before he or she can be issued another license.
    d. The license may be reinstated within two years by paying a reinstatement fee plus all late charges and renewal fees that would have been due during the lapsed period.

18. All exclusive listing contracts must
    a. end at midnight.
    b. begin the day the listing is signed.
    c. have a definite ending date.
    d. end at noon.

19. A licensed real estate salesperson is selling his or her home without his or her company being involved. All of the following statements are true *EXCEPT*
    a. the licensee's broker must be informed.
    b. the salesperson can deposit earnest money in his or her own personal account.
    c. ads run must disclose that the owner is a licensee.
    d. a sales contract must contain a disclosure that the seller is a licensee.

20. Sally works for ABC Realty Company, but she hires XYZ Realty Company to manage her rental property. Deposits made by tenants are held in
    a. the licensee's trust account.
    b. ABC Realty's trust account.
    c. XYZ Realty's trust account.
    d. the commission's trust account.

3 Georgia's Brokerage Relationships in Real Estate Transactions Act (BRRETA)

The Brokerage Relationships in Real Estate Transactions Act (BRRETA) is a Georgia law, effective in 1994, that governs the agency relationships of brokers with sellers, buyers, landlords, and tenants. A revised version was effective as of July 1, 2000. It is not intended to interfere with any contractual relationships the parties may have agreed upon. *Note:* In reading this law, the word "broker" refers to any person holding a real estate license.

 WWWeb.Link
You can find the text of the Brokerage Relationships in Real Estate Transactions Act at http://www2.state.ga.us/grec/greclegal/revised_brreta.html, or you can go to www.grec.state.ga.us, click on the button for the Georgia Real Estate Commission, click on the button for license law, and then click on the link to BRRETA.

DEFINITIONS

Licensees will find it profitable to know the meanings of the following terms:

- A *brokerage relationship* is defined as any agency or nonagency relationship between a broker and a client or customer.
- A *brokerage engagement* describes the agency relationship between broker and a client. This can only be created by a written contract. (This law, then, eliminates the liability that can be caused by unintentional agency.) Because an agent is not a *fiduciary*, only reasonable standards of performance are required.
- A *customer* is a person for whom the broker can perform ministerial acts; this requires either a verbal or written agreement.
- *Ministerial acts* are acts that do not require the broker to exercise professional judgment or skill.
- Payment of compensation does not create agency (so receiving a commission from a seller does not make a buyer broker a dual agent.)
- Joining an information source such as a multiple-listing service (MLS) does not create an agency relationship.
- *Dual agency* occurs when a broker has a client relationship with both parties to a transaction. It requires that both parties give written, informed consent.

- *Designated agency* occurs when both parties to a transaction are clients of two agents attached to the same firm; and it occurs when each of the agents is assigned by the broker to represent one client and not the other. Neither the broker nor the agents designated to act are considered to be dual agents.
- A *transaction broker* is one who has no client relationships with either party to a transaction.
- *Material facts* are facts a party does not know, could not reasonably discover, and would reasonably want to know.

THE BROKER'S DUTIES

In representing a client who is a seller, buyer, landlord, or tenant, in addition to complying with the terms of their agreement, the broker shall

- seek a sale or lease at the price and on the terms named or, in the case of a buyer or tenant, find a suitable property;
- present all offers in a timely manner;
- disclose to the client all material facts;
- advise the client to seek expert advice for matters beyond the broker's area of expertise;
- properly account for all monies and valuables received;
- exercise reasonable skill and care, obeying all applicable laws; and
- keep information confidential when specifically asked to do so, unless law requires disclosure. (A broker can discuss confidential facts with affiliates.)

A broker must treat all parties to a transaction honestly and must disclose the following to all parties in a transaction:

- All adverse material facts concerning the property and the improvements
- All known adverse factors concerning the neighborhood within one mile of the property

Note: The broker cannot be held accountable for false information if the source of the facts is revealed and if the broker did not know it was false. Also, the buyer or tenant is not relieved of a responsibility to make a reasonably diligent inspection.

If there is a conflict between a request for confidentiality and a need to avoid giving false information, the need to avoid false information must prevail.

It is not a violation of this law if a listing broker shows properties other than the one listed or if a buyer broker shows properties in which the client is interested to others.

A broker cannot be held liable for failure to reveal information that is beyond what is described in this law unless fraud could be proven.

DURATION OF THE AGENCY RELATIONSHIP

An agency agreement begins when the broker is engaged. It usually ends because the task has been performed or the time limit has expired or by mutual agreement. If the task has not been performed and no expiration is otherwise provided, BRRETA provides that it will end in one year. Then the broker has no further obligations to the client except

- to account for funds or property held, and
- to keep information confidential unless the client allows it to be revealed or the law requires that it be revealed.

DISCLOSURES

At the time of entering into brokerage engagements, the prospective client must be informed of the following:

- The types of agency relationships offered by the broker
- Any other relationships the agent has that might be considered a conflict of interest—for example, the case of a listing broker who might already have listed a similar house belonging to a relative
- How the broker will be compensated and how compensation might be shared with cooperating brokers
- The broker's obligation to keep information confidential under this law

A further disclosure is needed whenever the agency role changes.

DUAL AGENCY

Written consent is required of all parties to a dual agency. This written consent must include the following:

- A description of the transaction in which the broker will be acting as dual agent
- A statement that the broker will be serving clients whose interests may be different or even adverse
- A statement that the agent will disclose all material facts to all parties except those kept confidential by request
- A full disclosure of any material relationship the broker might have with either party to the transaction
- A statement that a client does not have to consent to dual agency
- A statement that the client has read this disclosure, understands it, and is consenting voluntarily

Note: The signing of this statement provides proof that informed consent was given.

If a client does not consent to dual agency, the broker may withdraw from the contract with that client without liability. The broker may receive a referral fee for referring the client to another company.

Every broker must adopt a written agency policy, including a statement as to whether dual agency is or is not practiced in that company.

DESIGNATED AGENCY

Under the year 2000 version of BRETTA, designated agency is described in detail with particular emphasis on the obligation to keep information confidential when there is no consent to disclosure, when there has been a request for confidentiality, or when the information could harm the client's position. The designated agents may disclose information to the broker, but the broker cannot disclose information from one agent to the other.

TRANSACTION BROKER

A transaction broker has no agency obligation to either party but may receive compensation for performing ministerial acts such as identifying a property, providing statistics, using and filling out forms, locating subsidiary services, and identifying neighborhood amenities.

The transaction broker must reveal adverse facts about a property or the neighborhood within one mile of the property if the buyer or tenant could not readily discover these facts.

Questions

1. BRRETA will act to end an agency agreement
   a. if the owner declares bankruptcy.
   b. by supervening illegality.
   c. if the home is destroyed by fire.
   d. after one year.

2. According to the BRRETA, an agency relationship exists between the
   a. listing broker and seller.
   b. selling broker and seller.
   c. selling broker and listing broker.
   d. salesperson and buyer.

3. Under BRRETA, a listing agent is required to present to the seller
   a. all written offers.
   b. all qualified offers.
   c. all signed offers.
   d. all offers.

4. Agent Norris is working with a buyer prospect who chooses to be a customer. The prospect wants to see a listing on Pine Street, but the listing company has indicated it will not offer subagency. What can Norris do?
   a. Norris can show the house as a transaction broker.
   b. The house can be shown only by buyer brokers.
   c. The listing company had no right to refuse subagency.
   d. A dual agency will result if Norris's buyer decides to make an offer on the Pine Street house.

5. A broker engaged by a seller who performs such acts as locating lenders, inspectors, attorneys, surveyors, and schools for the purchaser would be performing
   a. buyer agent duties.
   b. transactional broker responsibilities.
   c. ministerial acts.
   d. contractual obligations on behalf of the seller.

6. Prior to entering into brokerage engagement relationships, a broker must do all of the following EXCEPT:
   a. advise the prospective client of the types of brokerage relationships available through the broker.
   b. advise the prospective client of any other brokerage relationships held by the broker that would conflict with any interests of the prospective client actually known to the broker.
   c. advise the prospective client as to the broker's compensation and whether the broker will share such compensation with other brokers who may represent their parties to the transaction.
   d. advise the prospective client as to the manner in which the broker will allocate the commission between agents.

7. The buyer brokerage agreement is a contract between
   a. buyer and multiple-listing system.
   b. buyer and selling salesperson.
   c. buyer and broker.
   d. broker and selling salesperson.

8. When a prospective purchaser comes to an "open house" being held by the listing salesperson, the prospect should be treated as
   a. a customer.   c. an agent.
   b. a client.   d. a subagent.

4 Antitrust Laws

THE FEDERAL ANTITRUST ACT: SHERMAN ANTITRUST ACT

The prices that the public pays for goods and services are fair when there is competition in the marketplace or, in other words, a free exercise of supply and demand. Any limit on competition or restraint of free trading leads to monopolistic practices, where one entity or group controls a product or service and can charge exorbitant prices for it. Antitrust laws are designed to restrict monopolistic practices.

The Sherman Antitrust Act is a federal law on the books since 1890 relating to interstate commerce. The act applies to real estate brokerage for the following reasons:

- Brokerage is viewed as a *trade* because it is commercial and for profit; it is not a profession like law or medicine that are not covered by this act.
- Brokerage is classified as *interstate commerce* because state lines are crossed by people moving, by interstate transfer of funds for financing and insurance, interstate advertising by large companies with offices in several states, and by national franchises.

Although salespeople in real estate are probably more likely to be sued for fraud than for antitrust violations, brokers are aware that enforcement of this act has been vigorous in recent years.

Violations of the Sherman Antitrust Act include

- any two or more brokers going into collusion to set commission rates;
- any brokers going into collusion to set prices on properties;
- any agreement by brokers not to compete in certain areas and/or for certain types of properties;
- refusal by real estate boards to admit qualified members; and
- multiple-listing services restricting the availability of their services, prohibiting membership in more than one service, and refusing to take nonexclusive listings.

For violations, individuals can be fined up to $100,000 and get up to three years in prison. Corporations can be fined up to $1,000,000. Private antitrust suits can result in triple damages plus attorney fees and costs.

Note: The Real Estate Commission also has the power to sanction a licensee who violates a federal law. Moreover, the errors and omissions insurance that many brokers and licensees carry does not, as a rule, cover violations of federal laws.

THE GEORGIA FAIR BUSINESS PRACTICES ACT

In protecting the public, the focus of the Georgia Fair Business Practices Act (FBPA) is primarily on deceptive advertising. The highlights are as follows:

- It deals primarily with fraudulent or misleading advertisements.
- The advertising must have an impact on the public as a whole.
- An actual transaction must occur in order to prosecute.
- The term "advertising" applies to any media.
- The law prohibits any type of misleading advertising.
- The law is administered by the governor through the Office of Consumer Affairs.

THE GEORGIA UNIFORM DECEPTIVE TRADE PRACTICES ACT

The Georgia Uniform Deceptive Trade Practices Act (UDTPA) deals primarily with price-fixing and any other practices that would restrict competition. The highlights are as follows:

- The law is similar to FBPA but covers a wider area of deceptive practices.
- No actual consumer transaction must take place.
- The state of Georgia, another broker, or an individual can sue.
- Prosecution can result in injunctions, fines, and/or triple damages.

COMPLIANCE WITH ANTITRUST LAWS

Not only are brokers, agents, and companies liable under antitrust laws, but the laws also apply to real estate boards, associations, and multiple-listing services. Violations include not only price-fixing and allocation of customers or markets but also certain types of boycotts and "tie-in" arrangements. *Note:* A tie-in occurs when one contract is made dependent on another.

FOR EXAMPLE: A developer agrees to sell a choice property to a client only if the client will also agree to buy a not-so-choice property. This "tie-in" is an antitrust violation.

TRAINING LICENSEES FOR COMPLIANCE

Licensees must clearly understand that the critical terms of a contract are never "standard' or "nonnegotiable." In a listing presentation, phrases to avoid include the following:

"I have to charge a 7 percent commission. That's what all the brokers charge."

"The Board of REALTORS® requires that I charge 7 percent."

"I am not allowed to list your house for less than 120 days."

"The standard listing period in this town is 90 days."

"Don't list with ABC Realty. Most of the agents in the area refuse to work with them."

The one acceptable phrase that can be used to defend the rate or term a licensee is proposing is the following:

"This is my company's policy."

WHEN LICENSEES MEET WITH OTHER LICENSEES

Licensees should avoid using the following phrases when they talk to other licensees:

"We never cooperate with anyone who charges a flat fee."

"If that broker decides to list for a 5 percent commission, we won't work with him any more."

"We should all agree not to accept listings for less than 120 days."

"This is our territory. They should stay in their own county."

In fact, when any discussion arises among licensees that relates to prices, commissions, or territories, a wise licensee turns his back and runs away as fast as possible.

CONTRACT PROVISIONS TO AVOID

Printed forms used in contracts should not include

- preprinted commission rates;
- a predetermined "listing duration" printed in the contract; and
- a predetermined "protection period" printed in the contract. (A protection period is a time period following the expiration of the contract during which the agent's commission is protected.)

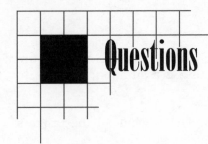

Questions

1. A provision in a contract of sale that obligates the purchaser to list the property with a specific broker when the property is resold is
   a. in violation of antitrust laws.
   b. good business practice and perfectly legal.
   c. called a shoe tie.
   d. okay if the broker is related to the seller.

2. The Sherman Antitrust Act was created to regulate the formation of
   a. intrastate competitive practices.
   b. monopolistic practices.
   c. competition among very large corporations.
   d. illegal lending practices.

3. All of the following actions could represent violations of antitrust laws *EXCEPT*
   a. an owner listing property at a rate that he or she has been told is "the going rate."
   b. a multiple-listing system that refuses to accept nonexclusive listings.
   c. a real estate company that instructs its agents to take no listings for less than 7 percent commission.
   d. a real estate company that is refused membership in the local Board of REALTORS®.

4. Under federal antitrust law, an individual found guilty of a violation can be fined up to
   a. $1,000.   c. $100,000.
   b. $10,000.   d. $1,000,000.

5. Georgia's Uniform Deceptive Trade Practices Act
   a. requires a transaction take place before a violation is charged.
   b. has a narrower application than the Georgia Fair Business Practices Act.
   c. is a vehicle for regulating interstate antitrust violations.
   d. has a broader application than the Georgia Fair Business Practices Act.

5 Legal Descriptions

DESCRIPTIONS OF REAL PROPERTY

Legal Description   No two parcels of land are exactly alike. Each parcel occupies a unique location. A street address is not enough to legally describe a parcel of land because it only tells us where to find it, not what it consists of. Over the years, street names and street numbers change. A legal description is one that is precise and unambiguous; it is what the courts require in contracts such as real estate sale contracts, mortgages, deeds, and leases.

A legal description will identify the property in such a way that it can be found at any later date in spite of changes which might have taken place and that it cannot be mistaken for any other parcel. The street address is usually included in the legal description if available just to be sure both parties to a contract are thinking of the same property.

The more formal ways of describing property require the technical skills of a surveyor. The survey a buyer receives at closing is called a *spot survey*. See Figure 5.1. Real estate professionals are not expected to have this expertise,

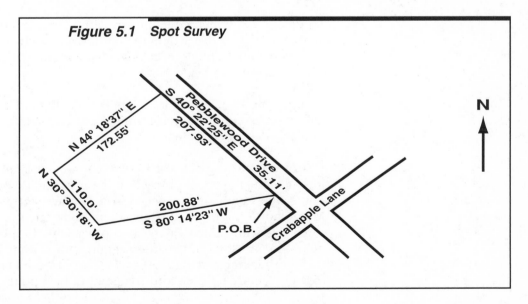

Figure 5.1   *Spot Survey*

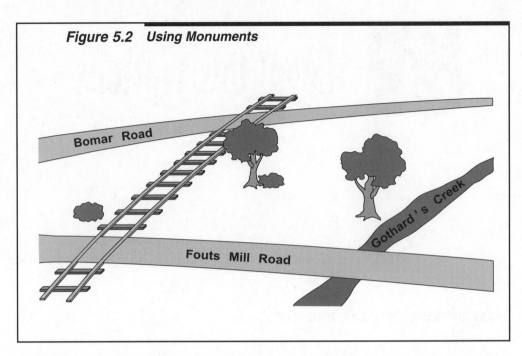

Figure 5.2 **Using Monuments**

but they must be able to read and understand information on a plat of survey the surveyor has prepared in order to advise clients.

Two different forms of legal description are used in Georgia: metes and bounds and recorded plat.

Metes-and-Bounds (Long-Form) Description

The *metes-and-bounds* method of legal description identifies the parcel by describing its boundaries. It can be compared to a walk around the border of the property. It is the most authoritative method, but it is also usually the longest and most difficult to prepare and to interpret. Metes are distances and directions. Bounds are landmarks or monuments that serve as markers each time the distance and direction must change. Objects like trees and rocks are natural monuments, while human-made markers such as stakes, metal pins, concrete markers; roads, walls, or fences are artificial monuments.

Before modern surveying technology came along, monuments served as the primary method for describing the land. Even today, land of little value or in remote areas might be described solely by monuments. (See Figure 5.2 and the legal description below.)

All that tract or parcel of land lying and being in Land Lot 217 of the First District, Second Section of Simple County, Georgia, and being more particularly described as follows:

BEGINNING at the old oak tree on the west side of Gothard's Creek, following along the creek proceed to the intersection of Gothard's Creek and Fouts Mill Road; then proceed in a northwesterly direction along Fouts Mill Road to the railroad track; then follow the railroad track to where it intersects with Bomar Road, then proceeding in a northeasterly direction along Bomar Road to the intersection with Gothard's Creek; then following southwesterly along Gothard's Creek to the old oak tree on the west side of Gothard's Creek and the point of beginning.

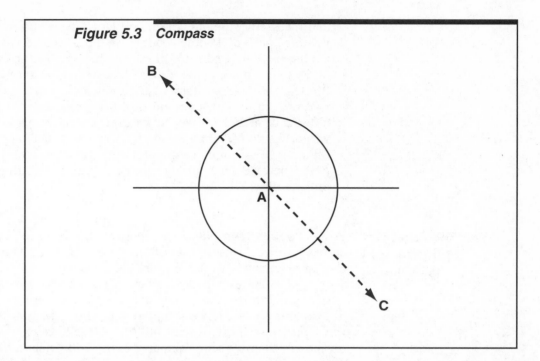

Figure 5.3   Compass

Metes-and-Bounds Description Using Compass Points

More typical today are metes-and-bounds descriptions that use bearings that are compass directions that take us from one monument to another. See Figure 5.3.

The north-south line through the middle of the compass is a meridian. Bearings are shown in degrees (°), minutes (′) and seconds (″). There are 360 degrees in the circle. Each degree is divided into 60 minutes, and each minute into 60 seconds. On the illustration in Figure 5.3, the line from A to B runs 30 degrees, 10 minutes and 45 seconds west of due north. The line from A to C runs 30 degrees, 10 minutes and 45 seconds east of due south.

A metes-and-bounds description must have a definite point of beginning (POB) which is the place in the property where the survey begins. Any uncertainty about this could make it vague and might void a contract or deed. Because this is so important, whenever possible the point of beginning is identified in relation to some permanent point of reference such as a standard *benchmark*. Benchmarks are fixed points, set in place by the U.S. Geological Survey. They are referenced to each other by distance and direction; and they are considered to be the most reliable references because of their permanence and accuracy. If a monument is destroyed or removed, it could be reestablished by relying on the benchmark.

Once the point of beginning is established the description continues with the compass direction and distance for each boundary line. (This is known as a *call*). Finally it must return to the point of beginning for closure. If closure is not possible, the description is incomplete. See the legal description below.

All that tract or parcel of land lying and being in Land Lot 44 of the 7th District, Second Section of Simple County, Georgia, and being more particularly described as follows:

BEGINNING at an iron pin on the southwesterly side of Pebblewood Drive, said iron pin being 35.11 feet northwesterly, as measured along the southwesterly side of Pebblewood Drive, from that point where the southwesterly side of Pebblewood Drive intersects the northwesterly side of Crabapple Lane; running thence south 80 degrees, 14 minutes, 23 seconds west a distance of 200.88 feet to an iron pin; running thence north 30 degrees, 30 minutes, 18 seconds west a distance of 110.0 feet to an iron pin; running thence north 44 degrees, 18 minutes, 37 seconds east a distance of 172.55 feet to an iron pin on the right-of-way of the southwesterly side of Pebblewood Drive; running thence south 40 degrees, 22 minutes, 15 seconds east along the right-of-way of the southwesterly side of Pebblewood Drive a distance of 207.93 feet to the iron pin at the point of beginning.

The Recorded Plat (Short-Form) Description

When a subdivision has been recorded, the recorded plat provides the most convenient legal description of all. When a tract of land is subdivided, most local governments would require that a licensed surveyor or engineer prepare a plat showing how the land would be divided into blocks and lots. Letters and numbers are assigned to each block and lot, with exact sizes and dimensions shown. Once the plan is finally approved, the plat is recorded at the county courthouse. Then all future legal descriptions of lots in that subdivision need only recite the name of the subdivision, the lot and block number, the plat book number and page number, Land Lot, District, Section (if applicable), and name of the county and state.

FOR EXAMPLE "All that tract or parcel of land lying and being in Land Lot 22, of the 17th District of Simple County, Georgia, being known as Lot 17, Block A of the Pineview Subdivision, according to a plat of survey recorded in Plat Book 15, page 42, Simple County, Georgia records."

GUIDELINES FOR USE OF LEGAL DESCRIPTION IN GEORGIA

In Georgia we use only the metes-and-bounds method or the short-form description. For a checklist of basic legal description requirements, see Table 5-1.

A sale contract or lease without a sufficient legal description is not enforceable. The street address is not enough. Obtain the legal description before writing the contract.

A salesperson should be able to compose a short-form description from a recorded subdivision plat. Only surveyors, attorneys, or qualified persons should attempt to compose a metes-and-bounds description.

A listing salesperson should get the legal description of the listed property as soon as possible. It can be found

- in the seller's deed or in the security deed;
- on the seller's plat of survey if one is available;
- on the subdivision plat if it is in a recorded subdivision; and
- as a last resort in the public records of the county where the property lies.

Table 5.1   Checklist for Legal Descriptions Used in Georgia

Eight Basic Requirements For a Metes-And-Bounds or Long-Form Description

1. Land Lot
2. District
3. Section or Militia District, where applicable
4. County
5. State
6. Definite point of beginning
7. Compass direction and distance, from one point to the next, returning to the point of beginning **(closure)**
8. Address of property, if available

Eight Basic Requirements For a Recorded Plat or Short-Form Description

1. Land Lot
2. District
3. Section or Militia District, where applicable
4. County
5. State
6. Subdivision—lot, block, and unit
7. Recorded reference—book and page number
8. Address of property, if available

There are three circumstances where one cannot use an existing legal description:

1. When the seller is not selling the entire tract. *A new survey is needed.*
2. When the seller has previously sold part of the land. *A new survey is needed.*
3. When a recent survey is in conflict with the description on the deed.

These circumstances indicate a possible title problem. *Consult your broker.*

Questions

1. When used in a deed or other real estate document, a legal description describes only the land because
   a. a bill of sale is used to convey title to the buildings and other improvements.
   b. artificial attachments, such as buildings, cannot be adequately surveyed.
   c. buildings and other improvements are considered to be part of the real estate.
   d. a street address must be used to identify the buildings and improvements.

2. The method of land description that identifies a parcel by specifying its boundary lines along with the terminal points and the bearing of each side is known as
   a. lot, block, and tract.
   b. recorded plat.
   c. government survey.
   d. metes and bounds.

3. Which of the following is *NOT* an acceptable method of legally describing a parcel of real estate?
   a. Street addresses, county, and state
   b. Metes and bounds
   c. Rectangular survey
   d. Recorded plat

4. Which of the following would be considered an artificial monument when used in a metes-and-bounds legal description?
   a. A tree   c. A river
   b. A fence corner d. A large rock

5. An adequate metes-and-bounds description will have all of the following *EXCEPT*
   a. a definite point of beginning.
   b. four sides.
   c. closure.
   d. linear measurements and compass directions.

6. A metes-and-bounds description must have all of the following *EXCEPT:*
   a. a definite point of beginning.
   b. the name of the county and state.
   c. the approximate square footage or acreage.
   d. compass directions and distances from one point to the next.

7. Which of the following would be acceptable on a sales contract?
   a. Legal description to be attached
   b. Legal description attached and made a part hereof by reference
   c. The legal description and survey to be provided at closing
   d. Purchaser to be provided with legal description within ten days

8. When it is necessary to prepare a new metes-and-bounds description it should be done by
   a. the seller.
   b. an attorney or surveyor.
   c. the listing salesperson.
   d. the selling salesperson.

9. You have a prospective purchaser for a home, and the listing agent has not been able to provide you with a legal description. Which statement describes your best course of action?
   a. Complain to the Real Estate Commission
   b. Write an offer without a legal description
   c. Find the legal description yourself at the courthouse
   d. Contact the seller yourself

10. If the only land description you have provided on your offer is the street address
    a. this could be sufficient provided there is no other street by the same name.
    b. this contract is probably unenforceable.
    c. this amounts to a contingency that must be resolved.
    d. the contract may be legal but is unprofessional.

6 Listing the Seller

THE LISTING DEFINED

A *listing* is the broker's contract of employment with an owner. It authorizes the broker to find a buyer or tenant who is "ready, willing, and able" to meet the owner's terms. In general, this means that the broker has earned the commission if a buyer can be found who will offer the price asked, who is willing to pay, and who can afford to pay the price on the exact terms specified.

The commission has been earned even if the seller refuses the offer, changes the terms, or is unwilling or unable to close. Not infrequently an offer is obtained that is at less than listed price or provides other than specified terms. In this case the broker has earned the commission only if the seller chooses to accept the offer.

Note: The typical listing contract does *not* authorize the broker to enter into a contract to sell or lease the property, nor does it obligate the seller to sell.

FOR EXAMPLE Broker Josh has listed the Gordons's house for $170,000 and brings them a full-price, cash offer. However, at this point, the Gordons have changed their minds and refuse to accept the offer. Are they within their rights? *Yes.* But do they owe Josh the commission specified in the listing? *Yes.*

TYPES OF LISTINGS

Open Listing

In an open listing an owner promises to pay a commission to a broker who produces a ready, willing, and able buyer at the named price. The contract must be in writing to be enforceable. The owner can give open listings to as many brokers as he or she chooses or even sell the property by owner with no obligation to pay anyone a commission. In return, the broker makes no promise to actively seek a buyer; and few brokers will devote much time and money to an open listing arrangement. When the property is sold, all other open listings on that property end.

Note: An open listing is an express, unilateral, executory contract.

Exclusive-Agency Listing

In an exclusive-agency listing only one broker is authorized to market the property, but the owner reserves the right to sell it himself or herself without any obligation to pay a commission. The broker in turn promises to actively seek a buyer. This contract must be in writing to be enforceable. Few brokers choose to accept exclusive-agency contracts because of the risk that their time and money will be wasted if the owner sells the property. There is also a concern that the seller may quote a lower price than the one the broker is quoting.

Note: The exclusive-agency listing is an express, bilateral, executory contract.

Exclusive-Right-To-Sell Listing

The most widely used type of listing is the exclusive-right-to-sell listing because it affords the broker the maximum of protection. The broker's right to market is exclusive and there's assurance of compensation if the property sells during the listing, no matter by whom. The contract must be in writing and must have a definite date of termination. Owners as well as brokers benefit from this arrangement in that it provides the broker with more incentive.

Note: The exclusive-right-to-sell listing is an express, bilateral, executory contract.

Net Listing

A net listing results when a seller has a certain sum in mind that he or she wants to realize from the sale and authorizes the broker to market the property for any price desired and to pocket the difference. This causes ethical questions to arise. Does not the broker have an obligation to obtain for the seller the highest possible price? Is the broker obligated to give the seller an estimate of market value? For these reasons, net listings are illegal in Georgia.

MULTIPLE-LISTING SERVICE

A multiple-listing service (MLS) is an organization made up of brokers who wish to exchange listing information and solicit the cooperation of other MLS members in marketing the properties.

The rules of a particular system specify what types of listings can be entered and the fees that the service will charge. Most of the listings submitted are exclusive-rights-to-sell listings. The listing broker retains the primary agency responsibility to the seller. The cooperating agents who choose to show the property might be acting as subagents of the seller, if offered that role, or as agents of the buyer, or they could possibly be neither.

In any case, there is an expressed or implied agreement to share any commission earned.

TERMINATION OF THE LISTING

Because the listing is an agency contract, it can terminate in any of the following ways under the law of agency: performance, expiration of the term, revocation, renunciation, abandonment, agreement, death of either party, incapacity, extinction, or a supervening illegality.

THE LISTING PRESENTATION

A licensee seeking to list a property should follow these eight steps:

1. Research data on comparable properties that have sold and be prepared to make a recommendation about a realistic price.
2. Explain the broker's agency policy, the policy for sharing commissions, and reveal any possible conflict of interest (i.e., a similar property that has been listed and might belong, for example, to a relative).
3. Present a marketing plan and, if the company permits the offering of subagency to cooperating agents, find out if the seller wishes subagency to be offered. (See Chapter 9 for a definition of subagency.) Discuss showing arrangements and how to make the property show at its best.
4. Obtain, if possible, a copy of the deed whereby the seller obtains the title. It is important that any party having an ownership interest, however small, sign the listing contract. The seller's deed also provides a formal legal description. One must also look for unusual conditions or terms in the deed.
5. Explain the necessity for disclosing any property defects to a prospective purchaser. A Seller's Disclosure Form can be used and should be filled out by the seller when possible.
6. Have the seller sign a form authorizing the licensee to obtain information about the existing loan on the property from the lender.
7. If the property data is to be entered into an MLS computer, obtain the necessary data for filling out the Profile Form.
8. Discuss the need for an inspection for termites and other pests.

THE RIGHT TO A COMMISSION

When a seller refuses to pay a commission that the broker feels has been earned, and the broker goes to court for a resolution, the broker must prove three things:

1. That she or he holds a valid real estate license
2. That there was a written listing agreement
3. That the broker was a "procuring cause" of the sale

A licensee who obtains an offer and deposit, and who follows through to the closing, is usually but not always considered to be the sole procuring cause. The claim is supported if the licensee can prove having

1. physically shown the property;
2. followed through and communicated; or

> 3. provided a service, creating events that, without a break in continuity, contributed to the sale.

THE LISTING CONTRACT

Note: There are a number of forms used for listing contracts. The one selected for this exercise is a form approved by the Georgia Association of REALTORS® for an exclusive-right-to-sell listing contract.

The sentence in bold print at the top of the form reminds us that the new BRRETA law requires that any contract establishing an agency relationship be in writing.

Narrative. *On November 2nd, Angela Adams of Adams & Son, Realty, is listing a house owned by Emily and John Johnson. The listing is to begin on November 4th and will extend for 120 days. The price will be $179,000, and the commission will be 6 percent. The legal description of the Johnson house is Land Lot 32 of the 6th District, 2nd Section of Carson County, Georgia, being Lot 122 of Block A in Hidden Hills Subdivision, as recorded on Page 331 of Plat Book 67. The street address is 456 Hilltop Drive, Carson, Georgia, zip code 33333.*

The Johnsons remind Angela that For Sale signs are not permitted in Hidden Hills Subdivision, and they also tell her that they do not want a lockbox on the house. Showings are to be by appointment only. Window treatments and laundry equipment are to be included in the sale. A 60-day safety clause is agreed upon. Adams & Son, Realty, does not offer subagency.

EXCLUSIVE SELLER LISTING AGREEMENT
(ALSO REFERRED TO AS EXCLUSIVE SELLER BROKERAGE AGREEMENT)

Georgia
Association of
REALTORS®

2002 Printing

State law prohibits Broker from representing Seller as a client without first entering into a written agreement with Seller under O.C.G.A. § 10-6A-1 et. seq.

For and in consideration of the mutual promises contained herein and other good and valuable consideration, _____ **Emily and John Johnson** _____ as seller (hereinafter referred to as "Seller"), and _____ **Adams & Son, Realty** _____ as broker and its licensees (hereinafter collectively referred to as "Broker") do hereby enter into this Agreement, this **2nd** day of _____ **November** _____, 20 **02** _____.

1. **Exclusive Listing Agreement**. Seller hereby grants to Broker the exclusive right and privilege as the Agent of the Seller to show and offer for sale the following described property as the real estate broker for Seller: All that tract of land lying and being in Land Lot **32** of the **6th** District, **2nd** Section of _____ **Carson** _____ County, Georgia, and being known as Address _____ **456 Hilltop Drive** _____, _____ **Carson** _____ City, Georgia Zip Code _____ **33333** _____, according to the present system of numbering in and around this area, being more particularly described as Lot **122**, Block __**A**__, Unit **N/A**, Phase/Section __**N/A**__ of _____ **Hidden Hills** _____ subdivision, as recorded in Plat Book __**67**__ Page __**331**__, _____ **Carson** _____ County, Georgia records together with all fixtures, landscaping, improvements, and appurtenances, all being hereinafter collectively referred to as the "Property." The full legal description of the Property is the same as is recorded with the Clerk of the Superior Court of the county in which the Property is located and is made a part of this Agreement by reference. The term of this Agreement shall begin on _____ **November 4** _____, 20 __**02**__ and shall continue through _____ **March 3** _____, 20 __**03**__ (hereinafter referred to as "Listing Period").

Opening Paragraph   The first blank names the seller(s) and the second blank the broker. The third blank is for the date that the contract is being prepared.

1. Exclusive Listing Agreement   Paragraph #1 of the form provides the property's legal description, followed by the listing's beginning and ending dates.

The narrative states that the listing is to begin on November 4th and run for 120 days.

In November it will run for (30 minus 3) days or 27 days.
Now, adding 31 days of December, we have 58 days.
Now, adding 31 days of January, we have 89 days.
Now, adding 28 days of February, we have 117 days.
So, if we add 3 days of March, we have 120 days.

The ending date, then, will be March 3rd.

---

2. **Broker's Duties To Seller.** Broker's sole duties to Seller shall be to: (a) use Broker's best efforts to procure a buyer ready, willing, and able to purchase the Property at a sales price of at least $_____**179,000**_____ (including commission) or any other price acceptable to Seller; (b) assist to the extent requested by Seller, in negotiating the terms of and filling out a pre-printed real estate purchase and sale agreement; and (c) comply with all applicable laws in performing its duties hereunder including the Brokerage Relationships in Real Estate Transaction Act, O.C.G.A. § 10-6A-1 et. seq.

3. **Seller's Duties.** Seller represents that Seller: (a) presently has title to the Property or has full authority to enter into this Agreement; (b) will cooperate with Broker to sell the Property to prospective buyers and will refer all inquiries concerning the sale of the Property to the Broker during the terms of this agreement; (c) will make the Property available for showing at reasonable times as requested by Broker; and (d) will provide Broker with accurate information regarding the Property (including information concerning all adverse material facts pertaining to the physical condition of the Property).

4. **Marketing.**
   A. **Advertisements:** Broker may advertise the Property for sale in all media and may photograph and/or videotape and use the photographs and/or videotapes in connection with Broker's marketing efforts. Seller agrees not to place any advertisements on the property or to advertise the property for sale in any media except with the prior written consent of Broker. ~~Broker is also hereby authorized to place Broker's "For Sale" sign on the Property. Broker is authorized to procure buyers to purchase the Property in cooperation with other real estate brokers and their affiliated licensees. Broker may distribute listing and sales information (including the sales price) to them and other members of the multiple listing service(s), and said cooperating brokers and their licensees may republish such information on their Internet web sites.~~ Broker and other real estate brokers and their affiliated licensees may show the Property without first notifying the Seller.
   B. **Lockboxes:** ~~A lockbox may be used in connection with the marketing of the Property.~~ There have been isolated instances of reported burglaries of homes on which lockboxes have been placed and for which the lockbox has been alleged to have been used to access the home. In order to minimize the risk of misuse of the lockbox, Broker recommends against the use of lockboxes on door handles that can be unscrewed from the outside or on other parts of the home from which the lockbox can be easily removed. Since others will have access to the Property, Seller agrees to either remove all valuables or put them in a secure place.
   C. **Multiple Listing Service(s):** Seller acknowledges that Broker is a member of the following multiple listing service(s): _____ ("Service(s)").
   Broker agrees that Broker will file this listing with said Service(s) within forty eight hours after Seller signs the same (excepting weekends, federal holidays and postal holidays).

   Seller acknowledges that the Service(s) is/are not a party to this Agreement and is/are not responsible for errors or omissions on the part of Seller or of Broker. Seller agrees to indemnify the Service(s) from and against any and all claims, liabilities, damages or losses arising out of or related to the listing and sale of the Property.

---

2. Broker's Duties To Seller   Next, in paragraph #2, we fill in the price selected. The broker is obligated to make an effort to find a ready, willing, and able buyer.

3. Seller's Duties   In paragraph #3 the seller states that he or she has title to the property and will cooperate in the marketing process and will provide the broker with accurate information.

4. Marketing   The marketing program is the subject of paragraph #4. It includes the following:

- The broker's right to advertise, and the seller's promise not to advertise without the broker's consent. The right to place signs on the property and to cooperate with other brokers. (Note that this must be crossed out and the deletion initialed according to our Narrative.)
- The right to use a lockbox. (Another deletion for our client.)
- The broker's obligation to submit the property to the MLS within 48 hours.

---

5.   <u>Commission</u>. Seller agrees to pay Broker no later than at closing a real estate commission of _____**six**_____ percent (__**6**__%) of the purchase price of the Property or $____**N/A**____ in the event that during the term of this Agreement, (1) Broker procures a buyer ready, willing, and able to purchase the Property at the price described above; or (2) Seller enters into an enforceable contract for the sale or exchange of the Property with any buyer, whether through the efforts of Broker or any other person, including Seller. Broker shall share this commission with a cooperating broker, if any, who procures the buyer of the Property by paying such cooperating broker ____**50**____% of Broker's commission or $_____**N/A**_____. Cooperating brokers are expressly intended to be third-party beneficiaries under this Agreement. In the event that Seller sells or contracts to sell the Property to any buyer introduced to the Property by Broker within _____**60**_____ days after the expiration of the Listing Period, then Seller shall pay the commission referenced above to Broker at the closing of the sale or exchange of the Property. Notwithstanding the above, in the event that the Property is sold to the prospective buyer by or through another licensed broker with whom Seller has signed an exclusive right to sell listing agreement, then no commission shall be owed to Broker by virtue of this Agreement. The commission obligations set forth herein shall survive the termination of this Agreement.

6.   <u>Limits on Broker's Authority and Responsibility</u>. Seller acknowledges and agrees that Broker: (a) may show other properties to prospective buyers who are interested in Seller's Property; (b) is not an expert with regard to matters that could be revealed through a survey, title search, or inspection; the condition of property; the necessity or cost of repairs; hazardous or toxic materials; the availability and cost of utilities or community amenities; conditions existing off the property that may affect the property; uses and zoning of the property; the appraised or future value of the property; termites and wood-destroying organisms; building products and construction techniques; the tax or legal consequences of a contemplated transaction; or matters relating to financing (and if these matters are of concern to Seller, Seller is hereby advised to seek independent expert advice on any of these matters of concern to Seller); (c) shall owe no duties to Seller nor have any authority to act on behalf of Seller other than what is set forth in this Agreement; (d) may make all disclosures required by law; (e) may disclose all information about the Property to others; and (f) shall, under no circumstances, have any liability greater than the amount of the real estate commission paid hereunder to Broker (excluding any commission amount paid to a cooperating real estate broker, if any).

Seller agrees to hold Broker harmless from any and all claims, causes of action, or damages arising out of or relating to: (a) Seller providing Broker incomplete and/or inaccurate information; (b) the handling of earnest money by anyone other than Broker; or (c) any injury to persons on the Property and/or loss of or damage to the Property or anything contained therein.

---

5. Commission   In paragraph #5 the commission is stated as either a percentage or dollar amount. (Remember to place a N/A in the blank not used.) The commission is earned if

- the broker procures a buyer on the terms named, or
- if the seller accepts any offer from any source.

There are also blanks to fill in noting how the commission is to be shared with a cooperating broker.

The 60-day *safety clause* protects the broker's right to a commission, if a prospect shown the property during the listing buys within that time period after the listing has expired; unless that sale occurs after the property has been exclusively listed with another broker.

6. Limits on Broker's Authority and Responsibility

Paragraph #6 states that the broker can show prospects, who might be interested in the subject property, other properties. It disclaims broker responsibility to matters requiring outside expertise, and it also limits broker liability for any problem to the amount of the total commission.

The broker is to be held harmless for damages related to incomplete or inaccurate information received from the seller, the handling of earnest money, or any injury on the property or loss or damage to the property.

---

7.   **Extension**. If during the term of this Agreement, Seller and a prospective buyer enter into a real estate sales contract which is not consummated for any reason whatsoever, then the original expiration date of this Agreement shall be extended for the number of days that the Property was under contract.

8.   **Seller's Property Disclosure Statement and Official Georgia Wood Infestation Report**. Within ____ days of the date of this Agreement , Seller agrees to provide Broker with a current, fully executed Seller's Property Disclosure Statement. Additionally, within _____ days of the date of this Agreement, Seller agrees to provide Broker with an Official Georgia Wood Infestation Report dated not more than one hundred eighty days prior to the date of this Agreement. Broker is hereby authorized to distribute the same to prospective buyers interested in the Property.

---

7. Extension

The printed language in the paragraph #7 provides that, if a listed property is off the market for a period of time because a contract was signed, but then comes back on the market when the sale fails to close, the listing broker may add the time that the property was off the market to the listed period.

FOR EXAMPLE Broker James listed the house on May 1st, and the listing was to run until August 31st. A contract was signed on May 20th, and it fell through on June 10th. The property was off the market for 22 days. The listing will now extend to September 22nd.

8. Seller's Property Disclosure Statement and Official Georgia Wood Infestation Report

In paragraph #8 the seller agrees to supply the buyer with a Seller's Property Disclosure form within _____ days; and also to provide an official Georgia Wood Infestation Report that is no more than 180 days old.

9. Required State Law Disclosures, and 10. Broker's Policy on Agency

Paragraphs #9 and #10 contain the following disclosures required by the BRRETA law:

- The broker's agreement to keep information confidential when asked to do so
- The fact that the broker cannot knowingly give the buyer false information
- The fact that the obligation to avoid giving false information, when in conflict with a request for confidentiality, prevails

Paragraph #10 is a statement of the company's agency policy, with a blank to fill in, if there is an agency relationship that is *not* offered.

There follows the disclosures needed for written informed consent when a dual agency arises. The last paragraph states that this is the entire agreement, and it cannot be modified without all parties consenting.

Above the signatures, we will have to note that there are some Special Stipulations that must be included.

All parties then sign the contract.

It is important that all parties who have any interest in the title to the property being listed sign the listing agreement, because their signatures will be required for acceptance of any offer. Our listing agent signs on behalf of her company.

If a corporation had owned the property, the officers so authorized would sign the contract, and a copy of the corporate resolution authorizing them to sign would be attached. In a general partnership, all general partners must sign, except in the case of a partnership in the building business, wherein any general partner can sign.

---

9. **Required State Law Disclosures**. (a) Broker agrees to keep all information which Seller asks to be kept confidential by express request or instruction unless the Seller permits such disclosure by subsequent word or conduct or such disclosure is required by law. (b) Broker may not knowingly give customers false information. (c) In the event of a conflict between Broker's duty not to give customers false information and the duty to keep the confidences of Seller, the duty not to give customers false information shall prevail. (d) Unless specified below, Broker has no other known agency relationships with other parties which would conflict with any interests of Seller (except that Broker may represent other buyers, sellers, landlords, and tenants in buying, selling or leasing property).

10. **Broker's Policy on Agency**. Unless Broker indicates below that Broker is not offering a specific agency relationship, the types of agency relationships offered by Broker are: seller agency, buyer agency, designated agency, dual agency, landlord agency, and tenant agency.

The agency relationship(s), if any, **NOT** offered by Broker is/are the following:_____

Dual Agency Disclosure: *[Applicable only if Broker's agency policy is to practice dual agency]* Seller does hereby consent to Broker acting in a dual agency capacity in transactions in which Broker is representing as clients both the Buyer and Seller and Broker is not acting in a designated agency capacity. By entering this Agreement, Seller acknowledges that Seller understands that Seller does not have to consent to dual agency, is doing so voluntarily, and that this brokerage engagement has been read and understood. In serving as a dual agent, Broker is representing two parties as clients whose interests are or at times could be different or even adverse. As a dual agent, Broker will disclose to both parties all adverse material facts relevant to the transaction actually known to the dual agent except for information made confidential by request or instructions from client and which is not required to be disclosed by law. Seller hereby directs Broker, while acting as a dual agent to keep confidential and not reveal to the Buyer any information which would materially and adversely affect the Seller's negotiating position. Broker or Broker's affiliated licensees will timely disclose to each client the nature of any material relationship the broker and the broker's affiliated licensees have with the other client or clients, other than that incidental to the transaction. A material relationship shall mean any actually known personal, familial, or business relationship between Broker and a client which would impair the ability of Broker to exercise fair and independent judgment relative to another client. The other party whom Broker may represent in the event of dual agency may or may not be identified at the time Seller enters into this Agreement. If any party is identified after the Agreement and has a material relationship with Broker, then Broker shall timely provide to Seller a disclosure of the nature of such relationship.

11. **Entire Agreement**. This Agreement constitutes the sole and entire agreement between the parties hereto, and no modification of this Agreement shall be binding unless signed by all parties. No representation, promise, or inducement not included in this Agreement shall be binding upon any party hereto.

12. **Governing Law**. This Agreement shall be governed by and interpreted pursuant to the laws of the State of Georgia.

SPECIAL STIPULATIONS: The following Special Stipulations, if conflicting with any preceding paragraph, shall control.

    1. Showings to be by appointment only.
    2. Laundry equipment and window treatments to be included in the sale.
    3. No sign to be used and no lockbox.
    4. Subagency is not offered.

Special Stipulations

The special stipulations include the following:

1. Showings to be by appointment only
2. Laundry equipment and window treatments to be included in the sale
3. No sign to be used and no lockbox
4. Subagency is not offered

To see a full copy of the Exclusive Seller Listing Agreement, please see Appendix A.

☐ **(Mark box if additional pages are attached.)**

BY SIGNING THIS AGREEMENT, SELLER ACKNOWLEDGES THAT: (1) SELLER HAS READ ALL PROVISIONS AND DISCLOSURES MADE HEREIN; (2) SELLER UNDERSTANDS ALL SUCH PROVISIONS AND DISCLOSURES AND HAS ENTERED INTO THIS AGREEMENT VOLUNTARILY; AND (3) SELLER IS NOT SUBJECT TO A CURRENT LISTING AGREEMENT WITH ANY OTHER BROKER.

RECEIPT OF A COPY OF THIS AGREEMENT IS HEREBY ACKNOWLEDGED BY SELLER.

The above proposition is hereby accepted, _____ o'clock _____ M., on the _____ day of _____, 20_____.

Adams & Son, Realty	**John Johnson**
Company	Seller SS/FEI#
By: **Angela Adams**	**Emily Johnson**
Broker or Broker's Affiliated Licensee	Seller SS/FEI#
Print/Type Name: _____	Print/Type Name(s): _____
Phone #: _____	Phone #: _____
Fax #: _____	Fax #: _____
	Address: _____

F1, Exclusive Seller Listing Agreement, Page 3 of 3 01/01/02

Questions

1. The primary purpose of a listing agreement is to
   a. serve as a contract of employment between the owner and the broker.
   b. list all improvements and amenities of the property.
   c. serve as a guide for a sales contract.
   d. do none of the above.

2. In some cases a broker's commission can be earned if the broker can prove she or he set in motion a series of events that resulted in the sale. To do so means the broker
   a. had an exclusive-right-to-sell listing.
   b. secured the buyer's signature on the sales contract.
   c. was the procuring cause of sale.
   d. showed the property to the buyer.

3. The provision in a listing agreement that extends the period of the agency on those prospects to whom the broker introduced the property prior to expiration is called
   a. an automatic renewal clause.
   b. an estoppel clause.
   c. an equal dignities clause.
   d. a safety clause.

4. The amount of a broker's commission is
   a. based upon standard rates established in the area.
   b. established by agreement between the broker and the seller.
   c. established by the real estate commission.
   d. 6 percent or 7 percent for single-family residences, depending on the area.

5. Buyer Murphy does not know about the leaking basement and proceeds to make an offer. Should the broker have told Murphy about the defect?
   a. No. Caveat emptor would apply in this case.
   b. Any defects known to the broker should have been disclosed to buyer Murphy.
   c. Because the broker is the agent for the seller, the broker should not mention the basement unless asked about it.
   d. No, because all basements leak, the property is not defective.

6. Which of the following statements about the appointment of subagents is true?
   a. The listing broker may appoint salespersons within the company to act as subagents.
   b. The listing broker must appoint a subagent if the subagent requests it.
   c. The seller may prohibit the listing broker from appointing a subagent.
   d. A subagent is appointed to take over the listing broker's duties to the seller.

7. A listing that allows the owner to sell the property without being liable for a commission but appoints only one broker to act as sole agent is an
   a. exclusive-agency listing.
   b. open listing.
   c. exclusive-right-to-sell listing.
   d. sole listing.

8. Exclusive listings should *NOT* include
   a. a safety clause.
   b. permission for the listing broker to use the multiple-listing service.
   c. a definite date of expiration.
   d. the right of the broker to sign deeds for the seller.

9. If a listing agreement does not specifically
    authorize a broker to accept and hold an
    earnest money deposit on behalf of the sell-
    er, then the
    a. deposit must be turned over to the seller
       immediately.
    b. purchaser cannot be required to pay a
       deposit.
    c. broker has implied authority to accept
       such deposits.
    d. broker must obtain power of attorney
       from a prospective purchaser to hold the
       deposit.

10. Which of the following is characteristic of
    an exclusive-right-to-sell listing?
    a. It may allow more than one broker to
       share a commission paid by the seller.
    b. The seller may sell the property without
       being obligated to pay a broker's com-
       mission.
    c. The seller must sell to a ready, willing,
       and able buyer found by the broker.
    d. The broker may sign a contract of sale
       on behalf of the seller.

7 Pricing Property

SALES COMPARISON OR MARKET DATA PRICING APPROACH

The sales comparison or market data pricing approach estimates value by comparing the property being appraised (the *subject property*) with similar properties (*comparables*) that have sold recently under normal market conditions.

This is based on the *principle of substitution,* which provides that the value of a property tends to be set by the cost of buying an equally desirable substitute. This approach is the one most commonly used by real estate licensees for residential property.

In this approach, the appraiser must gather and analyze sales data from similar properties, compare the features of these properties with those of the subject property, and make adjustments for differences in

- rights,
- conditions of the sale,
- financing,
- market conditions,
- location,
- physical factors, and
- income characteristics.

DATA SOURCES FOR MARKET ANALYSIS

Sales data for comparable properties may be drawn from multiple-listing services (MLSs), professional reporting services, lending institutions, brokers, attorneys, public records, appraisers, and from the agent's own files. When available, the MLS data is usually the best and most complete source for real estate agents. MLS data includes not only listings but also sales. (The listings are only helpful to the extent that they tend to set an upper limit on price because few properties sell for more than the listed price.) In some cases, the market for the type of property being priced is not active enough to provide sufficient comparable data. In this case, the agent will emphasize one of the other approaches to value.

SELECTING COMPARABLES

Because no two properties are exactly alike, the agent is looking for those that are as nearly alike as possible. Those selected as representing comparable sales should be

- *Recent.* If prices are relatively stable the time period might be extended to one year, but when prices are changing even a sale six months ago is out of date.
- *Similar.* They should be near the subject property and in a similar social and economic environment. There should be a high degree of similarity in physical characteristics and amenities.
- *Sold under similar market conditions.* The comparables selected should represent sales that occurred in free and competitive trading. For example, a sale between relatives, or one due to an impending foreclosure, would not be appropriate.

Three to five good comparables, those requiring few adjustments, are generally needed. Once these are in hand, the next step is to adjust for any differences from the subject property.

MAKING ADJUSTMENTS

The purpose of adjustments is to make the comparables as similar to the subject property as possible. *Note:* Never make any adjustments to the subject property.

If the comparable is inferior to the subject property, add. (As a memory aid, think "CIA" for Comparable Inferior? Add.)

FOR EXAMPLE A comparable home sold for $165,000. The subject property has a masonry fireplace worth $4,500, and the comparable has none. Which is more valuable? The subject property, of course, because it has the extra feature. In order to make the two properties as similar as possible, the sale price of the comparable is increased by $4,500.

$165,000 Sales price of the comparable property
+ 4,500 Adjustment for lack of a fireplace
$169,500 Indicated value

If the comparable is better than the subject property, subtract. (As a memory aid, think "CBS" for Comparable Better? Subtract.)

FOR EXAMPLE A comparable home sold for $118,000. It has a full, finished basement estimated to be worth $9,000. The subject property has none. Which is more valuable? The comparable, of course, because it has a basement. In order to make the two properties as similar as possible, the price of the comparable is reduced by $9,000.

$118,000 Sales price of the comparable property
– 9,000 Adjustment for the basement
$109,000 Indicated value

One other adjustment may be necessary. If the seller of one of the comparable properties paid closing costs or points, these amounts should be deducted from the sale price since they represent money that was not actually received. How does the agent know what amount to add or subtract when making adjustments? To some extent reliance is placed on experience and on current knowledge of construction costs. In addition, there are cost manuals and computer programs available for just this purpose and also experts with whom one can consult.

RECONCILIATION

This reconciliation is not simply an averaging. More weight or emphasis is placed on the indicated values of the most similar properties. For example, in the Market Analysis Adjustment Worksheet shown, you will see that Comparable #2 requires four adjustments, #3 has five, and #1 has six. On that basis, #2 was given 50 percent weight, #3 had 30 percent, and #1 had 20 percent. The final step, as shown at the bottom of the worksheet, is the correlation or reconciliation, resulting in an "estimated value by market data approach." See Figure 7.1.

EXERCISE #1—PRICING PROPERTY

Fill out a market analysis adjustment worksheet based on the following information. There is no "right" answer; however, there is a range within which your estimated sales price should fall. Use Figure 7.2.

Subject property is located in Falling Pines subdivision at 1000 Longfellow Court. It is an 8-room, 2-story frame house on an average size lot. It needs repainting on the outside. There are 4 bedrooms, 2½ baths, a separate dining room, a family room with fireplace, a full basement, and pull-down stairs to attic storage. It has central air conditioning; central forced air gas heat, a double garage, and is on sewer. It has a loan balance of $80,200 at 9 percent with 27 years remaining. The owners are Will and Wilma Wilson.

You find the following four properties in the subdivision that have sold within the last six months and are comparable to the subject property:

1. **1005 Longleaf Court:** 8-room, 2-story brick and frame, average lot. Although the lot is average in size and shape, it has a ravine across the back of the lot, making it less desirable than other lots. The house is in good condition. It has the same floor plan and features as the subject property and had a loan balance of $78,900 at 9 percent with 27 years remaining. It was listed for $92,000 and sold on loan assumption after 38 days on the market.
2. **2121 Short Needle Drive:** 7-room, 2-story brick and frame, average lot. The house is in good condition and contains 3 bedrooms, 2½ baths, living room, dining room, family room with fireplace, full basement, and pull-down stairs to attic storage. It has central air conditioning, central forced air gas heat, a double garage and, like all homes in the subdivision, is on sewer. It had a loan balance of $73,600 at 9½ percent with 28 years remaining. It was listed for $89,900 and sold for $86,000 on a new 80 percent conventional loan with the purchaser paying all costs after 76 days on the market.
3. **1449 Resin Circle:** 8-room, 2-story brick, and average lot. House is in good condition with the same features as the subject property, except it has no basement. With a loan balance of $73,900 at 9 percent and

Figure 7.1   *Market Analysis Adjustment Worksheet*

MARKET ANALYSIS ADJUSTMENT WORKSHEET **FORM 10-2**				
ITEM	SUBJECT PROPERTY	COMPARABLE-1	COMPARABLE-2	COMPARABLE-3
Address	618 Pine Drive	358 Hightower Trail	1215 Willowood Wy.	1029 Hillendale Pl.
Sale Price		$81,800	$79,500	$78,900
Date of Sale & Time Adjustment		Current	9 months ago +2,000	Current
Terms and Conditions of Sale		Similar	Similar	Similar
Location	Good	Similar	Similar	Similar
Sq. Ft. of Living Area	2,000 sq. ft.	50 sq. ft. larger –2,000	Similar	60 sq. ft. smaller +2,400
Age	5 years	Similar	Similar	Similar
Type/Quality Construction	Brick/Good	Similar	Similar	Similar
Design and Appeal	Good	Similar	Superior –2,500	Similar
Condition	Good	Similar	Similar	Superior –2,000
No. of Rooms	7	7	7	7
No. of Bedrooms	3	3	3	3
No. of Baths	2	2½ –750	2	2½ –750
Functional Utility	Good	Similar	Similar	Similar
Air Conditioning	Central	Inferior +1,000	Similar	Similar
Garage/Carport	2 Car Garage	Similar	Similar	Similar
Porches, Patio, Pool	Deck	Inferior +500	Inferior +500	Similar
Basement	Full – Part Finished	Similar	Similar	Full All Finished –2,000
Fireplace	Masonry	Similar	Similar	Similar
Special Energy Efficiency Items	Storm Windows	Inferior +500	Similar	Similar
Landscaping	Good	Similar	Superior –750	Similar
Other Amenities	Privacy Fence	Inferior +1,500	Similar	Inferior +1,500
Total NET Adjustments		+750	–750	–850
Sale Price		$81,800	$79,500	$78,900
Less Adjustments		+750	–750	–850
Adjusted Sale Price		$82,550	$78,750	$78,050

Correlation:

	Indicated Value	% Weight	
Comparable-1	$82,550	x .20	= $ 16,510
Comparable-2	$78,750	x .50	= $ 39,375
Comparable-3	$78,050	x .30	= $ 23,415

ESTIMATED VALUE BY MARKET DATA APPROACH $ 79,300

28 years remaining, it listed for $85,000 and sold on a loan assumption for $84,000 after 14 days on the market.

4. **1234 Loblolly Lane:** 7-room, 2-story brick and frame on average lot. House is in good condition with 3 bedrooms, 2½ baths, living room, dining room, family room, fireplace, full basement, and attic storage over the double garage. It has central air conditioning and central gas heat. With a loan balance of $58,350 at 8½ percent with 25 years remaining, the house was listed for $92,000 with the seller offering to pay 4 points discount and 3 points closing costs. After 45 days on the market, it sold for its listed price on a VA contract.

Figure 7.2   Market Analysis Adjustment Worksheet

ITEM	SUBJECT PROPERTY	COMPARABLE-	COMPARABLE-	COMPARABLE-	COMPARABLE-
Address					
Sale Price					
Date of Sale & Time Adjustment					
Terms and Conditions of Sale					
Total NET Adjustments					
Sale Price					
Less Adjustments					
Adjusted Sale Price					

(Title: MARKET ANALYSIS ADJUSTMENT WORKSHEET, FORM 10-2)

Correlation:

	Indicated Value	% Weight		
Comparable-		x	= $
Comparable-		x	= $
Comparable-		x	= $
Comparable-		x	= $

REDUCED (ESTIMATED VALUE BY MARKET DATA APPROACH) $ _____

ROUNDED TO: $ _____

After thoroughly checking, you find there are no homes now for sale in Falling Pines subdivision. You did find an expired listing at 1889 Resin Circle with features similar to 1449 Resin Circle, which had been listed for $94,000 with no terms offered and expired after 90 days on the market. Concerning the subject property, your broker gave you the name of a reputable painting contractor familiar with the neighborhood. After talking with the contractor, you receive an estimate of $1,800 to paint the Wilsons' home. Your broker also suggested an adjustment figure of $4,000 for the lack of a 4th bedroom for 2121 Short Needle Drive and 1234 Loblolly Lane, and $6,000 for the lack of a full basement at 1449 Resin Circle. Your broker suggested adjusting for the bad lot on 1005 Longleaf Court by the original difference of $3,000 in lot prices when the lot was sold. All brick homes in

Falling Pines subdivision sold for $2,000 more than similar homes of frame construction. No adjustment was made for brick and frame versus frame only.

Assign the following:
- 30 percent of value to comparable #1
- 25 percent of value to comparables #2 and #3
- 20 percent of value to comparable #4

For an example of how the Market Analysis Adjustment Worksheet could be filled out for this exercise, see Figure 7.3.

Figure 7.3   Market Analysis Adjustment Worksheet—Exercise 1

MARKET ANALYSIS ADJUSTMENT WORKSHEET
FORM 10-2

ITEM	SUBJECT PROPERTY	COMPARABLE-1	COMPARABLE-2	COMPARABLE-3	COMPARABLE-4
Address	1000 Longfellow	Longleaf	Short	Resin	Loblolly
Sale Price		$92,000	$86,000	$84,000	$92,000
Date of Sale & Time Adjustment					
Terms and Conditions of Sale					
Construction	Frame	Brick/Frame	Brick/Frame	Brick −2,000	Brick/Frame
# Rooms	8	8	7	8	7
Bedrooms	4	4	3 +4,000	4	3 +4,000
Basement	Full	Full	Full	None +6,000	Full
Financing	–	–	–	–	–6,440
Lot	Average	Ravine +3,000	–	–	–
Condition	Needs Paint	Good –1,800	Good –1,800	Good –1,800	Good –1,800
Total NET Adjustments		+1,200	+2,200	+2,200	–4,240
Sale Price		$92,000	$86,000	$84,000	$92,000
Less Adjustments		+1,200	+2,200	+2,200	–4,240
Adjusted Sale Price		$93,200	$88,200	$86,200	$87,760

		Indicated Value	% Weight	
Correlation:	Comparable- 1	$93,200	x	.30	= $ 27,960
	Comparable- 2	$88,200	x	.25	= $ 22,050
	Comparable- 3	$86,200	x	.25	= $ 21,550
	Comparable- 4	$87,760	x	.20	= $ 17,552

REDUCED (ESTIMATED VALUE BY MARKET DATA APPROACH) $ 89,112
ROUNDED TO: $ 89,100

1. When using the market approach to pricing a property, the agent would utilize data derived from
   a. acquisition cost to present owner.
   b. a foreclosure sale.
   c. cubic foot method.
   d. multiple-listing service information.

2. When selecting comparable properties for the market pricing approach, the agent should
   a. utilize as many comparables as can be found.
   b. choose those that require the fewest adjustments.
   c. choose any comparable, if it is in close proximity to the subject property that sold during the previous six months.
   d. choose all comparables that sold in the last two years.

3. Which of the following approaches to value estimation is based upon the calculation of construction costs at current prices of a property that serves the same purpose or function as an original property?
   a. Market   c. Income
   b. Cost   d. Gross Rent

4. In the market approach, the value of a feature present in the subject property but *NOT* in the comparable would be
   a. added to the selling price of comparable property.
   b. subtracted from the comparable property's sales price.
   c. omitted from the final estimate of value.
   d. not be considered since it is not important.

5. Which of the following would *NOT* be important in a market data approach to value?
   a. Difference in sales dates
   b. Difference in age
   c. Different original costs
   d. Difference in location

6. The market price as related to the market value of a property is
   a. never the same.
   b. always the same.
   c. possibly the same.
   d. seldom the same.

7. The ground floor of a home measures 38 feet by 48 feet, the second floor has the same measurements, the basement is half that size. If the ground floor improvements are valued at $62 a square foot, the second floor improvements are valued at $48 a square foot, and the basement area is valued at $21 a square foot, what is the value of the improvements?
   a. $239,654   c. $209,987
   b. $219,792   d. $199,123

8 Seller's Cost

PURPOSE AND USE OF THE ESTIMATE NET TO SELLER FORM

The Estimate Net to Seller form is a summary of calculations, showing deductions from the sale price and also credits that will affect the seller's "bottom line." It represents the seller's half of the final closing statement, prepared by the closing attorney, and shows how much cash the seller will net at that closing. This number might be of more critical importance to a seller than the sale price itself.

When To Use the Form

The Estimate Net to Seller form may be used in three instances during the course of the transaction:

1. *At the time of listing.* Sometimes when listing a property, the seller, in establishing a market price, needs some information about how much cash he or she might net at that price. This estimate depends on projecting a sales price, a closing date, and a division of closing costs. So it is at best an estimate that may or may not prove to be accurate. The seller must understand this is basically guesswork.
2. *At the time of receiving an offer.* Once an offer to purchase is in hand, the net-to-seller calculations can become much more accurate, although they are still only an *estimate*. The form will be helpful to the seller in deciding whether or not to accept the offer, and the agent should be prepared to amend the estimate in case a counteroffer is under consideration.
3. *Prior to closing.* Once the contract has become a binding agreement and contingencies have been removed, a final version of this form should come very close to what will appear on the closing statement. It can still fall short of perfection because some cost may crop up of which the agent was unaware, but it does give the seller a pretty good idea of what to expect at the closing. Avoiding surprises at the closing table is the key to successful closings.

How To Use the Form

Because the numbers on this form are of great importance to a client, the agent must, of course, prepare them with great care. Whenever possible the numbers should be researched, so that there is as little guesswork as possi-

65

ble. For example, do not just take the seller's opinion of how much is owed on an existing loan. Find out. The form is "user friendly" and does not require a mastery of advanced mathematics. Some basic formulas and concepts are the key. When in doubt, ask for help. Always be sure that the seller understands that it is an *estimate*.

MATHEMATICAL STEPS TO FOLLOW WHEN CALCULATING NET-TO-SELLER COSTS

Some General Guidelines

Be aware of the following when figuring out net-to-seller costs:

- It is important to know which party, buyer or seller, is responsible for the day of closing. It is the seller who is charged with all costs of ownership such as property taxes and hazard insurance. The seller is also credited with income (rent) for the day of closing. The buyer is charged with the cost of the day of closing for prepaid items, interest adjustment, mortgage insurance, and impounds.
- Because calculations must be accurate to the day, one must know how many days there are in each month. (The 29th day in February in leap years can be safely ignored.)
- It is a good practice to carry out calculations to four decimal places and then to round the final answer to two places because it is dollars and cents.

Prorations

Prorations are the bookkeeping entries we make to adjust for costs or items of income that do not come out evenly. For example, in a closing to take place on September 10th we see that the seller has paid the dues to a homeowners association for the entire year; but it is the buyer who should be responsible for those dues starting on September 11th. To be fair, on the seller's statement we will place a credit for the cost of the dues from September 11th through December 31st; and that same number will appear as a debit when we get to the Estimate of Cost to Buyer (see Chapter 10).

It is not necessary to compute the number of days from January 1st through September 10th because the seller owed for those days and has already paid for them.

Prorating the property tax. Local jurisdictions differ as to when taxes are due, but for study purposes we will assume that the tax must be paid July 1st and that it covers the calendar year from January 1st through December 31st. This means that

- if the closing date is *before July 1st*, the buyer will receive the next tax bill and must be compensated by the seller for *the time period from January 1st through the day of closing.* Credit the buyer and debit the seller.
- if the closing date is *after July 1st*, the seller has prepaid the tax and must be compensated by the buyer for *the time period from the day after the day of closing through December 31st.* Credit the seller and debit the buyer. The formula is as follows:

Annual Tax ÷ 365 = Daily Rate × Number of Days

Prorating insurance. Hazard insurance is paid for in advance, usually for a year, and therefore it is likely that the coverage the seller has paid for will extend beyond the closing date. *The time period begins with the day after the day of closing and extends through the last day of insurance coverage* (the day before the next premium is due). Credit the seller and debit the buyer.

The formula is as follows:

Annual Premium ÷ 365 = Daily Rate × Number of Days

Note: In most closings, except for those where a loan is being assumed, the buyer pays for a new insurance policy rather than assuming the balance of coverage in the seller's policy. The value of the unused portion of the seller's policy as calculated by this formula will show on the buyer's cost estimate only if the buyer is assuming the coverage. However, the calculation will still show as a credit to the seller because, if the buyer does not assume the coverage, the insurance company will refund the value of the unused portion after closing.

Prorating accrued interest. The interest on a mortgage loan is paid in arrears rather than in advance. For example, if a seller who made his or her last loan payment on March 1st is closing with a buyer on March 15th, the March 1st payment covered the interest for February, but the seller still owes for the period from March 1st through March 15th. If the seller's payment was due on the 20th of the month instead of the 1st, then his or her last payment was on February 20th covering the time through February 19th. When the closing takes place on March 15th he or she owes interest from February 20th through March 15th. The seller does owe for the day of closing.

The formula is as follows:

Loan Amount × Rate of Interest = Annual Interest ÷ 360 =
Daily Interest × Number of Days Owed

Note: Use the actual number of days in the month to calculate how many days are owed. Use a 360-day year to calculate the daily interest. (This is not necessarily the practice in all lending institutions, but it is the method used in this textbook.)

When the buyer is assuming the seller's loan, the accrued interest will show on the seller's statement as a debit and on the buyer's statement as a credit. It is the buyer who will have to make the next payment, including some interest the seller owed. If the buyer is getting a new loan, the figure will only appear as a debit to the seller.

Prorating rent. Most rental agreements provide that rent must be paid in advance. The seller is entitled to receive the rent up to and *including* the day of closing, but any rent already paid that covers a period beyond the closing day should be turned over to the new owner.

Following is the formula:

One Month's Rent ÷ Number of Days in the Month it Was Received =
Daily Rent × Number of Days Owed

Note: If the seller is holding a security deposit that must be returned to the tenant at the end of the lease, this must also be turned over to the buyer by a debit to the seller and a credit to the buyer.

Calculating the Transfer Tax

The transfer tax is a state tax usually charged to the seller when title is transferred. The tax is paid to the Clerk of the Superior Court in the county where the property is located when the deed is recorded.

The tax is charged at the rate of ten cents per hundred dollars of the sale price or portion thereof, the amount of an *assumed loan* is deducted. A new loan is *not* deducted. The sales price is divided by 100 and then, if that does not result in a whole number, rounded *up* to the next whole number. Then multiply by ten cents.

The formula is as follows:

Sales Price (Minus loan assumed if any) ÷ 100 and, if necessary, rounded up to the nearest whole number × 10 Cents.

Calculating the Intangibles Tax

The intangibles tax is assessed against any new loan of more than $1,500 that will require more than three years to repay. The tax is paid to the county in which the property is located, and the question of whether it is to be paid by buyer or seller is negotiable. The lender will make sure it is paid because failure to pay this tax will make the loan unable to be foreclosed.

The rate is $1.50 per $500 or portion thereof. *Note:* Do not use the rate of $3 per $1,000. This seemingly simple shortcut will result in miscalculations.

If dividing the loan amount by 500 results in a fraction, *round up* to a whole number. For example, a loan of $96,200 divided by 500 = 192.4. This becomes 193 before we multiply by $1.50.

If the purchaser is obtaining more than one loan, the tax should be computed on each loan separately.

There is no intangible tax on an assumption. The formula is as follows:

New Loan Amount ÷ 500, rounded up to the next whole number = Taxable Amount × $1.50

Calculating Private Mortgage Insurance

Lenders usually, but not always, require private mortgage insurance (PMI) on conventional loans that exceed an 80 percent loan-to-value ratio. This insures the lender against loss when making a loan with a minimum down payment. Ordinarily the cost of the insurance is charged to the buyer but, like most closing costs, is negotiable. The seller may have agreed, contractually, to pay it.

The cost of PMI varies widely from time to time and from offeror to offeror. Often two rates are quoted, one for loans between 80 percent and 90 percent loan-to-value, and a higher rate for loans from 90 percent to 95 percent loan-to-value.

FILLING OUT THE FORM

Opening Paragraph   The first blank lines at the head of this form ask for information only (no calculations). We insert the name of the seller for whom we are preparing this form, the address of the subject property, the date of our estimate, and the projected closing date. The county the property is in and the month the taxes are paid are also noted.

Sales Price   At the top of the form we insert the sales price.

Present Loan Pay-Off Expenses:

1st mortgage principal balance after last payment	$_____
Failure to notify bank penalty	+ $_____
Pre-payment penalty	+ $_____
Accrued Interest (Principal Balance $_____ x Rate____% ÷ 365 x # of days to closing _____)	+ $_____
2nd mortgage/home equity loan principal balance after last payment	+ $_____
Accrued Interest (Principal Balance $_____ x Rate____% ÷ 365 x # of days to closing _____)	+ $_____
Subtotal Present Loan Pay-Off Expenses	-$_____

Present Loan Pay-Off Expenses   The balance owed on the seller's existing loan is either going to be paid off or assumed. In either case it represents an amount that must be deducted from the sale price because it is money the seller will *not* receive at closing. The balance then is entered on line #1 of the Present Loan Pay-Off Expenses section of the form.

Line #2 and line #3 are for a failure to notify bank penalty or prepayment penalty, which might be charged, if any.

The seller will also owe accrued interest starting from the day of the last payment through the day of closing. Calculate the annual interest, divide by 365, and multiply by the number of days. Enter this number on line #4.

If there is a second mortgage loan outstanding, the balance owed on that loan will be inserted on line #5.

The accrued interest for the 2nd mortgage loan goes on line #6.

On line #7 all of these expenses are added together.

Costs of Sale:

Real Estate Brokerage Fee	$ _____
Termite Letter	+ $ _____
Unpaid Property Taxes (Annual taxes $_____ ÷ 365 x # of days from January 1 to closing _____)	+ $ _____
Special Assessments (i.e., Association Fees)	+ $ _____
Repairs/Clean-Up	+ $ _____
Survey	+ $ _____
State of Georgia Property Transfer Tax	+ $ _____
Seller's Contribution to Closing Costs	+ $ _____
Other_____	+ $ _____
Other_____	+ $ _____
Subtotal Costs of Sale	- $ _____

Costs of Sale   In the Costs of Sales section of the form, a brokerage commission to be paid goes on line #1.

If a termite letter cost is involved it goes on line #2.

Line #3 is for the unpaid property tax proration, to be used only when the taxes for the current year are not yet due as of the closing date, so the seller owes the buyer money. Divide the annual tax by 365 to get a daily rate and then multiply by the number of days from the first of the year through the closing date.

Line #4 is used when the seller is required to pay for an assessment or lien that must be removed.

If a cost of repairs or of cleanup is involved, it goes on line #5.

Line #6 is for any survey cost paid by seller.

The transfer tax is entered on line #7. Divide the sales price (minus an assumption if any) by 100 and round *up* if necessary. Then multiply by $0.10.

Line #8 is for the seller's contribution to the buyer's closing cost.

Line #9 and line #10 are available for any other expense in the Costs of Sale area.

The expenses on line #1 through line #10 are then totaled on line #11, subtotal Costs of Sales.

Credits:

Pre-Paid Property Taxes (Annual taxes $_____
     ÷ 365 x # of days from closing to December 31_____)   + $_____

Escrow Refund of Taxes & Insurance (Usually received
     30 days after closing)   + $_____

Other_____   + $_____

Subtotal Credits   + $_____

TOTAL ESTIMATE OF NET TO SELLER $_____

The above information is based on data available as of this date. Additional monthly payments and accrued interest may reduce the loan payoff. Fees such as warehouse fees, tax service, lender inspection, photos, document preparation, handling fees, courier fees, etc. may also appear on the closing statement. No representation is made as to the accuracy or completeness of this form. This is an estimate only.

Credits   So far, we have been dealing with the seller's costs but, before a final esti-mate can be made, we need to take into account any credits that may be forthcoming.

In the Credits section of the form, line #1 is a companion to line #3 in the Cost of Sale section. We used line #3 there to show how much a seller owes the buyer when the taxes have not been paid up to and through the day of closing. Line #1 in the Credits section is used when the seller has paid the taxes *beyond* the closing date. The seller will be repaid for the days starting with the day after the closing through the end of the year. Divide the annu-al tax by 365 to get a daily rate and then multiply by the number of days.

If the seller had a budget mortgage loan, there is probably a balance in the escrow account held by the lender and it will be returned (probably not at the closing, but shortly thereafter). The amount goes on line #2.

Line #3 can be used for any other credit.

All credits (lines #1 through line #3) are totaled on line #4, Subtotal Credits.

Total Estimate of Net to Seller   This line will show the Sales Price less Loan Pay-Off Expenses and Cost of Sale plus Credits.

Note: There is a disclaimer at the bottom of this form to make sure that the seller understood that it was just an estimate and not necessarily 100 per-cent accurate.

To see a full Estimate of Net to Seller form, go to Appendix A.

Questions

1. If the seller renewed the hazard insurance for one year starting May 15th, and the closing is to be on November 5th, the seller will be
   a. credited 190 days.
   b. debited 174 days.
   c. debited 190 days.
   d. credited 174 days.

2. If the hazard insurance premium for a two-year period is $397, the approximate daily rate will be
   a. $1.08.   c. $ .54.
   b. $ .50.   d. $16.50.

3. When a closing is to take place on September 10th, the borrower's first monthly payment will probably be due on
   a. October 1st.
   b. November 1st.
   c. October 10th.
   d. September 10th.

4. If the seller's existing loan is for $95,000 at 10 percent, and the payment due date is on the first of the month, at a closing to take place on the 25th, the seller will owe interest of approximately
   a. $659.72.   c. $26.25.
   b. $79.00.   d. $9,500.00.

5. A borrower is obtaining a 90 percent loan with a sales price of $125,000 and is closing on February 25th. If the seller is paying 2 percent PMI in cash at closing, the approximate amount will be
   a. $2,258.   c. $2,500.
   b. $2,259.   d. $2,250.

6. A closing is to take place on May 15th. The property is rented, and the tenant pays $600 on the first of each month. At closing
   a. buyer will owe the seller for 15 days rent.
   b. seller will owe the buyer for 16 days rent.
   c. tenant will receive a refund for half a month's rent.
   d. neither seller's nor buyer's closing costs will be affected.

7. If the sales price on a transaction is $112,000 and the purchaser is acquiring a new loan, the transfer tax will be paid
   a. on the sales price.
   b. on the loan amount.
   c. on the price minus the loan.
   d. on the commission.

8. If the sales price is $112,000 and the purchaser is assuming an existing loan in the amount of $80,000 and also obtaining a purchase money mortgage (PMM) for $7,000, the transfer tax will be paid on
   a. the sales price.
   b. the sales price minus the PMM.
   c. the sales price minus the assumption.
   d. the sales price minus the PMM and the assumption.

9. Which of the following is not likely to appear as a debit on the seller's closing statement?
   a. Pay-off of the existing loan
   b. Removal of an existing mechanic's lien
   c. Transfer of a loan escrow account
   d. Proration for unpaid taxes

10. Which of the following is true of a closing taking place on March 10th, where the tax bill for the calendar year will be due on July 1st and has not yet been paid?
    a. Seller owes for 69 days.
    b. Seller owes for 68 days.
    c. Buyer owes for period January 1st to March 10th.
    d. Neither party is charged because the bill has not come due yet.

11. Which of the following statements is true regarding a prepayment penalty on an existing loan?
    a. It will appear as a debit to the seller and a credit to buyer.
    b. It appears as a debit to the seller.
    c. It will often be waived if the loan is assumed.
    d. It is usually too small an amount to be of concern.

12. For the purposes of estimating seller's costs, you can assume the day of closing
    a. belongs to the seller.
    b. belongs to the buyer.
    c. is split between buyer and seller.
    d. does not count for either buyer or seller.

13. The premium for PMI paid at a closing can be charged
    a. only to the seller.
    b. only to the buyer.
    c. to either buyer or seller.
    d. only to the lender.

14. The intangible tax is calculated
    a. on the sales price.
    b. on the sales price minus an assumption.
    c. on the new loan amount.
    d. on the seller's equity.

15. PMI is most likely to be charged when the buyer is getting
    a. an FHA graduated payment plan loan.
    b. a VA loan.
    c. an 80 percent loan-to-value conventional loan.
    d. a 90 percent loan-to-value conventional loan.

16. Which of the following statements regarding a seller's net estimate is true?
    a. You cannot prepare it until you have a contract.
    b. It is only an approximation and, therefore, not very useful.
    c. It can be and often is an important part of a listing presentation.
    d. It should not be used when presenting an offer since it might confuse the issue.

17. Which of the following statements is true?
    a. Hazard insurance is usually paid in advance.
    b. Mortgage loan interest is usually paid in advance.
    c. Rent is usually paid in arrears.
    d. PMI is usually paid in arrears.

18. If a purchaser is buying a home for cash, which of the following closing costs would *NOT* be reduced?
    a. The intangible tax
    b. The transfer tax
    c. The closing attorney's fee
    d. The discount points

19. The transfer tax is paid at the rate of
    a. $1.00 per $1,000.   c. $ .50 per $500.
    b. $1.00 per $500.   d. $ .10 per $100.

20. The intangible tax is paid at the rate of
    a. $ .10 per $100.
    b. $1.00 per $500.
    c. $1.50 per $500.
    d. $3.00 per $1,000.

21. The brokerage fee is usually a percentage of the
    a. buyer's loan amount.
    b. gross equity.
    c. seller's loan amount.
    d. sales price.

9 Listing the Buyer

BUYER REPRESENTATION

In discussing buyer representation it is important to keep in mind the terms *client* and *customer*. When a licensee has entered into an agency relationship with the buyer and is obligated to work in the buyer's best interests with absolute loyalty, that buyer is a *client*. When the licensee showing property to the buyer is not in a principal/agent relationship, the buyer is being treated as a *customer*. A client can be advised and counseled, a customer cannot.

If company policy permits, a licensee has the following five choices in working with a buyer or tenant:

1. Representing the seller as agent or *subagent*. The seller is the client; the buyer is a customer.
2. Representing the buyer as a *buyer's agent*. The buyer is the client; the seller is a customer.
3. Representing both buyer and seller as a *dual agent*. Both are clients.
4. Representing the buyer as a *designated agent* with another agent in the company representing the seller.
5. Representing neither buyer nor seller, as a *transaction agent*. Both are customers.

In other words, a licensee represents the seller, the buyer, both, or neither.

Note: No matter which role is chosen, there is always an obligation to treat all parties to a transaction honestly and to disclose to all parties pertinent facts.

Subagency

When a licensee obtains a listing, the listing contract is between the seller and the broker with whom that licensee is affiliated. It is clear that every agent associated with that company has an agency obligation to the seller. It was also for some time the policy of most, not all, realty companies that salespeople showing a buyer other companies' listings would act as subagents of the listing broker. In other words, everyone represented the seller. Recently, subagency has been declining as more and more sellers and real state companies refuse to offer this option to cooperating brokers for the following four reasons:

1. In subagency, the seller as principal is liable for the acts of not only the listing company's agents but of all subagents who show the property. For example, the subagent misrepresents the utilities available to the property. The seller would be liable for damages or suit.
2. Buyers tend to think that the agent assisting them is acting on their behalf, although in subagency this was not the fact. There was a danger of an implied agency creating an undisclosed dual agency.
3. Buyers are becoming more aware of the agency roles and are asking for representation.
4. It is becoming increasingly clear that a refusal by the listing company or by the seller to offer subagency does little to discourage cooperation from other companies as long as there is an offer to share the commission.

Buyer Agency

A *buyer brokerage agreement* is a contract of employment, similar to a listing contract except that in this case the buyer is the client. Georgia law requires this agreement to be in writing to be enforceable. It obligates the broker to assist the buyer or tenant in finding a suitable property, and it often provides that compensation be paid by the prospect only if it is not forthcoming from the listing agent. Whether it is an open or an exclusive agreement is negotiable. In selecting property and in negotiating an offer, the buyer broker must be absolutely loyal to the buyer's best interests. The following factors should be considered in entering into this agreement:

- The buyer broker must be careful and diligent in researching things like zoning, school locations, availability of utilities, road widening plans, etc. The buyer broker cannot rely on the seller's or the listing agent's information because their accountability for any problem the buyer might later raise is limited once the buyer has his or her own "expert."
- If a buyer client happens to choose a property that is listed with the buyer broker's own company, a dual agency or designated agency will result.

Dual Agency

Dual agency is not illegal as long as both parties have given informed consent in writing. They must be aware of the fact that both are being represented by the same broker despite the fact that their interest may be adverse. As a result, the broker's ability to advise will have important limitations.

Dual agency is a role to be avoided whenever possible because of the difficulty that arises when any helpful advice given to one party could represent disloyalty to the other. The agent becomes a mere conduit for information, unable to give effective counsel to either party. The following factors must be considered:

- The dual agent is aware of the needs of both parties to a transaction so he or she does have some advantage in an effort to produce a "win-win" result. There is also the fact that compensation need not be shared.

- The disadvantage with dual agency lies in the risk of violating the agency accountability to one party. This is sufficiently serious that some companies do not include dual agency in their services offered.
- Whenever working with a buyer who might choose one's own or one's company's listing, it is best to treat that buyer as a customer, so as to avoid dual agency unless the company policy allows designated agency.

Designated Agency

Designated agency occurs when both parties to a transaction are clients of agents attached to the same firm and when each of the agents is assigned by the broker to represent one client and not the other. Neither the broker nor the agents designated to act are considered to be dual agents.

The Transaction Broker

Bearing in mind that an agency agreement requires the consent of both parties, imagine a situation where the seller and/or listing company does not offer subagency and where the buyer the salesperson is working with does not choose to have a buyer broker. In this case the salesperson represents neither buyer nor seller. Like the dual agent, the transaction broker does not offer advice and counsel. Unlike the dual agent, liability is very limited because there are no agency obligations. However, because buyers and sellers usually seek the help of a licensee because they do need professional advice, and will pay for that, the role of the transaction broker is difficult to play, and there is a possibility that playing a lesser role and accepting less liability could lead to less compensation.

Selecting the Agency Role

In deciding how best to represent a prospective client or customer, a licensee must first be aware of the company policy. The next step is to decide what role one wants to play and, finally, to convince the client or customer that the selected arrangement is best.

If a licensee is buying real estate for himself or herself or is representing a buyer who is a relative, buyer brokerage is an obvious choice. When the buyer is a close friend, former client, or perhaps a transferee in need of a great deal of assistance, buyer brokerage is probably indicated. If the buyer chooses to be anonymous, the licensee must choose buyer brokerage. In some cases buyer brokerage should be avoided.

FOR EXAMPLE Agatha is holding an open house at her listing. A prospect that is not represented by an agent shows an interest in the house. Agatha will probably choose to treat the prospect as a customer so as to avoid dual agency.

It is always possible that a customer can later choose to become a client. However, once a person is a client, they cannot be reduced to customer status because confidential matters may have already been shared.

Working with a Customer

A licensee can do many things for a prospective seller or buyer even when not in an agency relationship. A salesperson licensee can perform *ministerial acts* without creating an agency. These are acts that do not require judgment and do not amount to advising or counseling. For example, a licensee can

- show properties that might fit a customer's needs;
- make factual representations about a property's condition;

- provide information about comparable sales;
- point out neighborhood amenities;
- provide information about schools, utilities, taxes, etc.;
- locate lenders, surveyors, attorneys, etc., if needed; and
- prepare and present offers.

Disclosure

Georgia license law requires agency disclosures. The disclosure must be prior to but no later than time of the offer. It is good professional practice for a salesperson to make disclosures at the earliest convenient moment so that the roles being played and any limitations that those rules might entail are clearly understood and no possibility of an unintentional agency relationship can arise. It is also prudent to have written verification of such disclosures.

Dual agency is legal only if both parties to a transaction consent in writing. An undisclosed dual agency, even if entered into unintentionally, is illegal and subjects the agent to a possibility of a civil suit, loss of commission, and also of an action against the license held.

Agency Law Risk Reduction

Licensees can minimize their risks of violating agency law by

- being familiar with company policy and seeking a broker's advice when in doubt;
- choosing one's agency role wisely;
- making full disclosures at the earliest possible time;
- providing written confirmation that disclosures were made;
- making certain that actions are consistent with the role chosen; and
- treating third parties fairly, revealing all pertinent facts.

THE EXCLUSIVE BUYER BROKERAGE ENGAGEMENT

For this exercise we are using the form approved for use by the Georgia Association of REALTORS®. On the very first line in bold print, it reminds us that state law prohibits making a buyer a client without a written agreement.

Narrative *John Johnson has asked Al Blake, a salesperson with Royal Realty, Inc., to assist him in finding a residence. The agreement is signed on March 10th and is to run through April 20th. Johnson agrees to pay a commission of 3 percent of the sales price if the seller's agent does not agree to compensate Royal Realty, Inc. If the buyer leases property or enters into a lease/purchase agreement, the compensation is to be 8 percent of the rent paid. He will allow a safety clause of 60 days.*

EXCLUSIVE BUYER BROKERAGE AGREEMENT

Georgia
Association of
REALTORS®

2002 Printing

**State law prohibits Broker from representing Buyer as a client without first entering into a written agreement
with Buyer under O.C.G.A. § 10-6A-1 et. seq.**

For and in consideration of the mutual promises contained herein and other good and valuable consideration, ____**John Johnson**____
_____ as buyer (hereinafter referred to as "Buyer"), and _____**Royal Realty, Inc.**_____
_____ as broker and its licensees (hereinafter collectively referred to as "Broker") do hereby enter into this
Agreement, this **10th** day of _____**March**_____ , 20__**02**____ .

1. **Exclusive Brokerage Agreement.** Buyer hereby hires Broker to act as Buyer's exclusive real estate broker and agent to assist Buyer
in locating and negotiating the purchase or exchange of real property. Buyer has not entered into a buyer brokerage agreement with
any other real estate broker or any previous buyer brokerage agreement has been terminated. The term of this Agreement shall begin
on _____**March 10**_____ , 20__**02**____ and shall continue through _____**April 20**_____ , 20__**02**____ .

2. **Broker's Duties To Buyer.** Broker's sole duties to Buyer shall be to: (a) attempt to locate property suitable to Buyer for purchase; (b)
assist to the extent requested by Buyer in negotiating the terms of and filling out a pre-printed real estate purchase and sale agreement;
and (c) comply with all applicable laws in performing its duties hereunder including the Brokerage Relationships in Real Estate
Transactions Act, O.C.G.A. § 10-6A-1 et. seq.

3. **Buyer's Duties.** Buyer agrees to: (a) work with only Broker (and not with any other real estate broker or licensee) in identifying,
previewing, and seeing property for purchase by Buyer; (b) be available to meet with Broker to see property; (c) provide Broker with
accurate information as requested by Broker (including financial information about Buyer's financial ability to complete the transaction
and written authorization to obtain verification of funds); and (d) inspect and otherwise become familiar with any potentially adverse
conditions relating to the physical condition of any property in which Buyer becomes interested, any improvements located on such
property and the neighborhood surrounding such property.

4. **Limits on Broker's Authority and Responsibility.** Buyer acknowledges and agrees that Broker: (a) may show property in which Buyer
is interested to other prospective buyers; (b) is not an expert with regard to matters which could have been revealed through a survey,
title search or inspection of the property; the condition of property, any portion thereof, or any item therein; building products and
construction techniques; the necessity or cost of any repairs to property; hazardous or toxic materials; termites and other wood destroying
organisms; the tax and legal consequences of any real estate transaction; the availability and cost of utilities and community amenities;
the appraised or future value of the property; conditions existing off the property that may affect the property; and the uses and zoning
of property and matters relating to financing (and if these matters are of concern to Buyer, Buyer is hereby advised to seek independent
expert advice relative thereto); (c) shall owe no duties to Buyer nor have any authority on behalf of Buyer other than what is set forth in
this Agreement; (d) may make all disclosures required by law; and (e) shall, under no circumstances, have any liability greater than the
amount of the real estate commission paid hereunder to Broker (excluding any commission amount retained by the listing broker, if any).

Opening Paragraph	In the first sentence, it is stated that the buyer, John Johnson, is engaging the broker, Royal Realty, Inc., to find him a suitable property. The agreement is entered into on March 10th.
1. Exclusive Brokerage Agreement	Paragraph #1 sets forth the fact that the contract will begin on March 10th and end on April 20th.
2. Broker's Duties To Buyer	The next two paragraphs outline the broker's duty, which is to find the buyer a suitable property; and the buyer's duty to cooperate in this process. Note that it states that the buyer has a duty to inspect the property and the surroundings for adverse conditions.
4. Limits on Broker's Authority and Responsibility	Paragraph #4 notes that the broker may show properties this buyer is considering to other prospects. It also contains the blanket disclaimers of broker responsibility for matters outside of the broker's expertise and provides a limit in liability.

---

5. **Early Termination**. Broker or Buyer shall have the right to terminate this Brokerage Agreement at any time by giving the other party written notice; however this shall not limit Broker's remedies under the commission paragraph.

6. **Commission**. Broker shall seek to be paid a commission from the listing broker under a cooperative brokerage arrangement or from the seller if there is no listing broker. In the event the seller or listing broker does not pay Broker a commission, then Buyer shall pay Broker at time of closing, a commission of $_____ or ___3___% of the purchase price of all real property in Georgia which Buyer purchases during the term of this Agreement whether or not the property has been identified to Buyer by Broker. In addition, if Buyer leases property or enters into a lease/purchase contract during this Agreement, and the landlord does not agree to pay Broker a leasing commission, Buyer shall also pay Broker for the duration of the lease and any renewal or extension thereof a commission of ___8___% of each rental payment paid by Buyer to Landlord thereunder. Furthermore, in the event that during the __60__ day period following termination of this Brokerage Agreement, Buyer purchases, contracts to purchase, leases or lease purchases any property identified to Buyer by Broker during the term of this Brokerage Agreement, then Buyer shall pay Broker at closing or the commencement of any lease, if applicable, the commission or commissions set forth above. The commission obligations set forth above shall survive the termination of this Agreement.

7. **Extension**. If during the term of this Brokerage Agreement, Buyer and a seller enter into a real estate sales contract which is not consummated for any reason whatsoever, then the original expiration date of this Agreement shall be extended for the number of days that the property was under contract.

8. **Entire Agreement**. This Brokerage Agreement constitutes the sole and entire agreement between the parties hereto, and no modification of this Brokerage Agreement shall be binding unless signed by all parties. No representation, promise, or inducement not included in this Brokerage Agreement shall be binding upon any party hereto.

9. **Required State Law Disclosures**. (a) Broker agrees to keep all information which Buyer asks to be kept confidential by express request or instruction unless the Buyer permits such disclosure by subsequent word or conduct or such disclosure is required by law; (b) Broker may not knowingly give customers false information; (c) In the event of a conflict between Broker's duty not to give customers false information and the duty to keep the confidences of Buyer, the duty not to give customers false information shall prevail; (d) Unless specified below, Broker has no other known agency relationships with other parties which would conflict with any interests of Buyer (with the exception that Broker may represent other buyers, sellers, tenants and landlords in buying, selling or leasing property).

5. Early Termination

In paragraph #5 the right to terminate the agreement on written notice is given to both buyer and broker. The broker, however, can still claim compensation for properties already shown before the contract was terminated.

6. Commission

The commission paragraph, #6, states that the broker is obliged to seek compensation by an agreement to share with the listing broker but, if that fails, the buyer will owe the broker 3 percent of the sale price. A 60-day safety clause protects the broker's right to claim a commission if, after this agreement ends, the buyer buys a property shown during the time this agreement was in effect.

7. Extension

The one sentence in paragraph #7 gives the broker the right to extend the time period of this contract by however many days were lost because a sales contract that had been agreed upon later failed to close.

8. Entire Agreement

Paragraph #8 states that this form contains the entire agreement and that it is binding on both parties. (This is fairly standard contract language.)

In paragraphs #9, #10, and #11 are found the required BRRETA disclosures.

9. Required State Law Disclosures

The basic disclosures in paragraph #9 are four:

1. The buyer's right to request confidentiality
2. The company's agency policy
3. Whether or not there is a conflict of interest
4. How compensation will be shared

10. **Broker's Policy on Agency.** Unless Broker indicates below that Broker is not offering a specific agency relationship, the types of agency relationships offered by Broker are seller agency, buyer agency, designated agency, dual agency, landlord agency, and tenant agency.

The agency relationship(s), if any, **NOT** offered by Broker is/are the following:_____.

11. **Dual Agency Disclosure.** [*Applicable only if Broker's agency policy is to practice dual agency*] Buyer does hereby consent to Broker acting in a dual agency capacity in transactions in which the Broker is representing as clients both the Buyer and a seller of real property in which Buyer is interested in purchasing and the Broker is not acting in a designated agency capacity. By entering into this Agreement, Buyer acknowledges that Buyer does not have to consent to dual agency, is doing so voluntarily, and that this brokerage engagement has been read and understood. In serving as a dual agent, Broker is representing two parties as clients whose interests are or at times could be different or even adverse. As a dual agent, Brokers will disclose to both parties all adverse material facts relevant to the transaction actually known to the dual agent except for information made confidential by request or instructions from either client and which is not required to be disclosed by law. Buyer hereby directs Broker, while acting as a dual agent to keep confidential and not reveal to the seller any information which would materially and adversely affect the Buyer's negotiating position. Broker or Broker's affiliated licensees will timely disclose to each client the nature of any material relationship the Broker and the Broker's affiliated licensees have with the other client or clients, other than that incidental to the transaction. A material relationship shall mean any actually known personal, familial, or business relationship between Broker and a client which would impair the ability of Broker to exercise fair and independent judgment relative to another client. The other party whom Broker may represent in the event of dual agency may or may not be identified at the time Buyer enters into this Agreement. If any party is identified after the Agreement and has a material relationship with Broker, then Broker shall timely provide to Buyer a disclosure of the nature of such relationship.

12. **Governing Law.** This Agreement shall be governed by and interpreted pursuant to the laws of the State of Georgia.

SPECIAL STIPULATIONS: The following Special Stipulations, if conflicting with any exhibit, addendum, or preceding paragraph, shall control.

☐ **(Mark box if additional pages are attached.)**

BY SIGNING THIS AGREEMENT, BUYER ACKNOWLEDGES THAT: (1) BUYER HAS READ ALL PROVISIONS AND DISCLOSURES MADE HEREIN; (2) BUYER UNDERSTANDS ALL SUCH PROVISIONS AND DISCLOSURES AND HAS ENTERED INTO THIS AGREEMENT VOLUNTARILY; AND (3) BUYER IS NOT SUBJECT TO A CURRENT BUYER BROKERAGE ENGAGEMENT WITH ANY OTHER BROKER.

RECEIPT OF A COPY OF THIS AGREEMENT IS HEREBY ACKNOWLEDGED BY BUYER.

The above proposition is hereby accepted, _____ o'clock _____ M., on the _____ day of _____, 20_____.

Company _____

By: _____
    Broker or Broker's Affiliated Licensee

Print/Type Name: _____

Phone #: _____

Fax #: _____

Buyer _____ SS/FEI# _____

Buyer _____ SS/FEI# _____

Print/Type Name(s): _____

Phone #: _____

Fax #: _____

Address: _____
_____

10. Broker's Policy on Agency

Paragraph #10 lists any agency relationships that the company does not practice.

11. Dual Agency Disclosure

Paragraph #11 lists the required disclosures that provide for informed consent to dual agency.

There follows some space for needed special stipulations, and (in the box) the time when it became a binding agreement, followed by the necessary signatures of the buyer and the broker. To see a full Exclusive Buyer Brokerage Agreement, go to Appendix A.

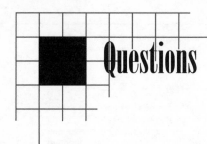

Questions

1. The buyers broker and salesperson owe all but which of the following to the customer?
   a. Negotiation of the highest possible price
   b. Honesty
   c. Integrity
   d. Disclosure of defects

2. Which of the following is *NOT* true regarding a subagency relationship?
   a. The listing broker is the principal of the selling broker.
   b. A subagent has an implied authority to act as a dual agent.
   c. A subagent can only perform the activities delegated and cannot be involved in making decisions which would directly affect the welfare of the seller.
   d. The selling company should contact the listing company before showing property to a prospect.

3. Acting as a dual agent without the consent of all parties is a breach of a broker's duty of
   a. loyalty.
   b. personal performance.
   c. due care.
   d. accountability.

4. A cooperating broker (buyers agent) finds a buyer for a home listed with ABC Realty Company, Inc. The selling broker represents
   a. the seller.
   b. the buyer.
   c. both the buyer and the seller.
   d. neither the buyer nor the seller.

5. ABC Realty has a listing on Aaron Street. The listing information indicates that *no* subagency is being offered. Agent Clark is working with a buyer prospect that chooses to be a customer. The prospect wants to see the listing on Aaron Street.
   a. Clark can show the house as a "transaction broker."
   b. The house can be shown only by buyer brokers.
   c. The listing company had no right to refuse subagency.
   d. A dual agency will result if Clark's buyer decides to offer on the Aaron Street house.

6. A broker engaged by a buyer who performs such acts as locating lenders, inspectors, attorneys, surveyors, and schools for the seller would be performing
   a. buyer agent duties.
   b. transactional broker responsibilities.
   c. ministerial acts.
   d. contractual obligations on behalf of the seller.

7. You have agreed with your broker to split commissions 60 percent to you, 40 percent to the broker. Your listing was just sold by another company for $139,000. Your broker has agreed to pay the selling broker 50 percent of any commission. If the commission on this sale was 6 percent, what was your share?
   a. $8,340.00   c. $1,668.00
   b. $2,502.00   d. $4,170.00

10 Buyer's Cost

PURPOSE AND USE OF THE ESTIMATE OF COST TO BUYER FORM

The Estimate of Cost to Buyer form is designed to show a buyer how much cash will be needed at the closing table for the down payment plus closing costs. In comparison to the Estimate Net to Seller form that was reviewed in Chapter 8, it might be called the other half of the final closing statement. But, like the Estimate Net to Seller form, it is only an *estimate.* For a buyer with minimal cash resources, the numbers on this form can be extremely important. It is not unusual for closing costs to far exceed what an uninformed buyer might expect.

There are two separate calculations on this form: (1) an estimate of cash needed for closing and (2) an estimated monthly payment.

When To Use the Form

The Estimate of Cost to Buyer form may be used in these instances during the course of the transaction:

1. *Prior to the offer.* Before showing property it is necessary to establish the buyers' affordable price range. This in turn is a function of how large a mortgage loan they can qualify for on their income; and how much cash they plan to invest. The Estimate of Cost to Buyer form is useful to show that some of the available cash must be reserved for closing costs –even though filling out the form at this stage involves a lot of suppositions that may or may not prove to be valid.
2. *At the time of an offer.* In making an offer to purchase, the buyer should understand the extent of this commitment, both in terms of cash needed and of monthly payment to be undertaken. At this point an estimate of closing costs can become considerably more accurate, but it is still an estimate because some costs might still be unknown. If the offer is countered, the form must be revised accordingly so that there is a clear picture every step of the way.
3. *Prior to closing.* Once the offer has become a binding agreement, contingencies have been resolved, the buyer has made application for a loan, and has received a Good Faith Estimate of loan costs from the lender, the Estimate of Cost to Buyer form should come very close to what will appear on the closing statement.

The agent should obtain the final closing statement prior to closing, and if there is any significant difference, determine why that is so. The goal is to have no surprises at the closing. The buyer must be advised to bring the needed cash to the closing in the form of a cashier's check.

How to Prepare the Form

As was true of the Estimate Net to Seller form, the numbers on this form can be of great importance. The client or customer has a right to expect that it will be prepared as carefully as possible, never using guesswork or assumptions when the actual numbers can be researched. It is prudent to have someone review the numbers before presenting it. Keep reminding them, though, that it is only an *estimate*.

MATHEMATICAL STEPS TO FOLLOW WHEN ESTIMATING BUYER'S COSTS

Determining the Date of the Buyer's First Monthly Loan Payment

Assuming that loan payments are made monthly on the 1st of each month, the following apply:

- If the closing is on the 1st of the month, the next payment will be due on the 1st of the following month; but,
- If the closing is on *any other day,* the first payment will not be due on the 1st of the following month, but will skip a month. See Table 10.1.

Calculating the Interest Adjustment (Prepaid Interest)

The purpose of the interest adjustment is to allow the buyer's monthly payment to come due on the first day of the month. Interest is paid *in arrears.* In other words, the loan payment made on the 1st of July covers the interest that was due for June. Therefore, when the closing occurs on May 17th, for example, the first payment on the buyer's loan will not be due until July 1st, and this will cover the interest for June; but we still have to provide for the payment of interest starting with May 17th and accruing through the end of May.

Note: This is an exception to our rule that the closing day belongs to the seller. The seller does pay interest on the old loan through the day of closing, but the buyer *also* pays interest for the day of closing on the new loan.

For test purposes, use the actual number of days in each month for calculating how many days are owed but divide the annual interest by 360 to calculate the daily rate of interest.

Table 10.1   First Payment Due Dates

Closing Date	Due Date
September 1st	October 1st
September 5th	November 1st
January 17th	March 1st
December 30th	February 1st

Loan amount × Rate of Interest = Annual Interest
Annual interest ÷ 360 = Daily Rate
Daily Rate × Number of Days Owed (closing date through end of month)

Calculating the Cost of Mortgage Insurance (PMI for Conventional Loans, MIP for FHA Loans)

Note: Percentages used in these exercises are for study purposes only. Rates in the market vary from time to time and between insurance companies.

If the buyer is obtaining a conventional loan for no more than 80 percent loan-to-value (LTV), there will be no cost of private mortgage insurance (PMI).

If the PMI due is to be paid in full at closing, the following apply:

- For a loan between 80 percent and 90 percent LTV, assume the cost to be 2 percent of the loan amount.
- For a loan between 90 percent and 95 percent LTV, assume the cost to be 2.5 percent of the loan amount.

The borrower has another option—to pay part of the PMI cost at closing and the balance as a sum added to monthly payments. In that case, assume the following:

- For the 80 percent to 90 percent LTV, assume the closing cost to be .5 percent of the loan amount.
- For the 90 percent to 95 percent LTV, assume the closing cost to be 1 percent of the loan amount.

The increment to be added to the monthly payment might be calculated by multiplying the loan amount by .0025 for an annual figure and then dividing by 12.

For the mortgage insurance premium (MIP) required in the FHA program there are no payment options. The borrower pays

- 1.5 percent of the loan amount at closing, plus
- a monthly increment calculated by multiplying the loan amount by .5 percent and dividing by 12.

Calculating Escrow Items

If the loan a buyer is arranging is a budget mortgage, then the escrow account for that purpose must be set up at the closing. In a budget mortgage the lender will collect as a monthly payment not only principal and interest but also increments toward the payment of property taxes, hazard insurance, and mortgage insurance, if needed, so that the lender can pay these costs when due.

The Real Estate Settlement Procedures Act (RESPA) regulates the amount that the lender can collect in advance to establish the escrow account.

Property tax. The annual tax bill is divided by 12 to get a monthly figure. This figure in turn is multiplied by the number of months' worth of tax payments the lender can collect. It cannot exceed the number of monthly increments necessary to pay the next tax bill when it comes due, plus two extra months. When the next tax bill comes due, the lender must have 14 months in the escrow account (12 months plus 2 extra).

If, for example, the closing is to be in January, the first monthly payment on the loan will come in March. Before the July 1st tax bill date the lender will only have collected 4 monthly payments (March, April, May, and June). At closing, the lender is entitled to collect 8 months plus 2 extra months, making the total collected at closing 10 months. The lender then would have 14 months available on July 1st (4 monthly payments plus 10 months).

The Tax Escrow Chart will be helpful in making this calculation if one can remember that the months (as represented by the letters on the bottom line) *do not stand for the closing date but for the month the first payment is made.* For example, if the closing is to be in September, the first payment will be made in November. Above the "N" for November we see the number 6, so that is the number we use for the tax escrow.

Note: Exception to the chart: If the closing occurs on July 1st, only 3 months of reserve is required.

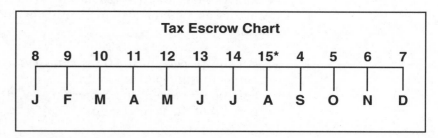

Insurance. The escrow contributions for hazard insurance, and for PMI or MIP if needed, cannot exceed 2 months. The annual cost can be divided by 6 to get this figure.

FILLING OUT THE FORM

Opening Paragraph   At the top of the form there are blank lines for the name of the purchaser, the address of the subject property, the date that the estimate is being prepared, and the estimated closing date. Then the purchase price, loan amount, loan type, interest rate, and term in years are filled in.

Loan Amount   The amount of the mortgage loan the buyer is acquiring may be determined by the type of loan.

If it is to be a conventional loan, multiply the sale price by the LTV percentage and remember to round *down* if necessary.

The maximum VA loan is 100 percent of the LTV.

The maximum FHA loan is 97.75 percent of the sale price above $50,000 (98.75 percent below $50,000); closing costs can be included in the amount borrowed. FHA requires a minimum 3 percent cash investment by the buyer, and the 3 percent may include some closing costs.

If a loan is to be assumed, the exact balance is shown.

Financing Costs:

Down Payment $_____

Closing Costs   + $_____

Loan Discount (Points)   + $_____

Financing Costs

In the Financing Costs section, line #1 shows the cash down payment; it is simply the sales price minus any new or assumed loan amounts.

Because the question of which party pays which items of closing costs is negotiable, one must read a contract or a narrative carefully. This form is for noting only those costs that the buyer will pay.

Line #2 is for closing costs the buyer has agreed to pay. This is usually calculated as a percentage of the amount of the new loan.

Line #3 is for discount "points" the buyer might be charged. This again is a percentage of the amount of the new loan. A "point" is 1 percent of the loan amount.

Escrow Establishment Charges:

Taxes (_____ months @ $_____/month)   + $_____

Homeowner's Insurance (2 Months)   + $_____

Mortgage Insurance (2 Months)   + $_____

Prepaid Interest (____ days @ $_____/day) $_____

Escrow Establishment Charges

Line #1 of the Escrow Establishment Charges section is for the property tax escrow. The annual tax is divided by 12 to get a monthly figure, and this is then multiplied by the number of months the lender is allowed to collect.

Line #2 is for the hazard insurance escrow. The annual premium is divided by 6 to get a figure representing two months.

Line #3 is used only if PMI is required (i.e., for a conventional loan over 80 percent LTV) and only if the cost was not paid in full at closing. The loan amount is multiplied by .0025, and this is divided by 6 to get a figure for 2 months.

If the loan is an FHA, the loan amount is multiplied by .5 to get an annual cost, and this is then divided by 6 to get a figure for 2 months.

If there is any mortgage insurance premium to be paid at closing, show it under Other.

There is no mortgage insurance for VA loans or for conventional loans under 80 percent LTV.

For an FHA loan, the MIP to be paid at closing is 1.5 percent of the loan amount.

For conventional loans where the PMI is to be paid in full at closing, calculate 2 percent of the loan amount for loans from 80 percent to 90 percent LTV, and 2.5 percent of the loan amount for loans from 90 percent to 95 percent LTV.

For conventional loans where the PMI is to paid only in part at closing, calculate .5 percent of the loan amount for loans from 80 percent to 90 percent LTV, and 1 percent of the loan amount for loans from 90 percent to 95 percent LTV.

Line #4 is for the interest adjustment on the new loan. The new loan is multiplied by the interest rate to get the annual interest. This is then divided by 360 to get a daily interest rate. The daily rate is then multiplied by the number of days, starting with the day of closing and through the end of the month.

Miscellaneous Charges:

Homeowner's Insurance (First Year's Premium)	+ $_____
Loan Transfer Fee	+ $_____
Purchase of Seller's Escrow Account	+ $_____
Proration of Property Taxes (County and City)	+ $_____
Other: _____	+ $_____

Miscellaneous Charges

Line #1 in the Miscellaneous Charges section is for a one-year hazard insurance premium or for an insurance proration if the buyer is assuming the seller's coverage. Hazard insurance is paid for in advance, usually for one year.

In most cases the buyer acquires a new policy and the one-year premium for that policy is the number that appears on this line. (The seller will later be refunded the remaining value on the old policy, if any.)

Sometimes—in an assumption, for example—the buyer will assume the seller's policy and will pay the seller for the unused portion.

The three math steps to follow for this calculation are as follows:

1. Divide the annual premium by 365 to get a daily rate.
2. Calculate the number of days starting with the day after the closing.
3. Ending with the day before the anniversary or premium date, multiply the daily rate by the number of unused days.

Line #2 is used only if a loan is being assumed, and it is for whatever transfer fee the buyer is being charged for the assumption.

Line #3 is used only if the buyer is assuming the seller's loan and purchasing the existing escrow account for a dollar amount, which represents the balance in that account as of the closing.

Line #4 is used only if the seller has prepaid the property tax and is therefore entitled to a refund from the buyer.

FOR EXAMPLE The seller paid the tax on July 1st for the calendar year. The closing is to take place on November 3rd, so the seller is entitled to be refunded the tax for the period from November 4th through December 31st. (If the closing had taken place before July 1st, the tax would not have been prepaid so nothing would appear on Line #4.)

To calculate the tax refund, divide the annual tax by 365 to get a daily rate and multiply by the number of days starting with the day after the closing and running through the end of the year.

Line #5 can be used for any other expense items.

Credits:

Proration of Property Taxes (County and City)	- $_____
Earnest Money Deposit	- $_____
Other: _____	- $_____
TOTAL ESTIMATE OF COST TO BUYER	$_____

Credits   We will not have the final figure that shows how much cash the buyer will need at the closing until we enter any credits the buyer might have.

Line #1 in the Credits section is for a credit that the buyer will have if there is some unpaid property tax to be prorated. For example, if the tax is paid on July 1st for the calendar year and the closing is to take place on March 20th, then the seller will be charged the unpaid tax for the period starting with January 1st through and including the day of closing.

(Using our assumption that the tax is due on July 1st for the calendar year, the prepaid tax will show above as a debit under miscellaneous charges, if the closing is after July 1st; and the unpaid tax will show on Line #1, if the closing is before July 1st.)

To calculate, divide the annual tax by 365 to get a daily figure. Then count the days from January 1st through the day of closing. Multiply the daily tax by the number of days.

Line #2 shows a credit for however much earnest money the buyer may have deposited with the contract of sale.

Any other credits can be entered on Line #3.

Total Estimate of Cost To Buyer   The down payment plus all charges less credits represents our estimate of how much cash the buyer will have to bring to the closing. It appears on the Total Estimate of Cost to Buyer line.

Estimated Monthly Payment:

Principal and Interest	+ $_____
Homeowner's Insurance	+ $_____
Mortgage Insurance	+ $_____
Property Taxes	+ $_____
Other: _____	+ $_____
Other: _____	+ $_____
Total	$_____

Projected Due Date of First Payment:

_____, 20_____

The above information is based on data available as of this date. Additional monthly payments and accrued interest may reduce the loan payoff. Fees such as warehouse fees, tax service, lender inspection, photos, document preparation, handling fees, courier fees, etc. may also appear on the closing statement. No representation is made as to the accuracy or completeness of this form. This is an estimate only.

Estimated Monthly Payment

The other calculation on this form is the estimate of how much the buyer's monthly payment will be. It can include the following:

Line #1 in the Estimated Monthly Payment section is for principal and interest. Agents might use a programmed calculator or a computer program to find this number; if those are not available, agents can use a factor table.

On Line #2 enter the monthly hazard insurance payment. (Divide the annual premium by 12.)

Note: Condominium owners do not pay hazard insurance separately, but it is part of their monthly maintenance fee.

Line #3 is for a monthly contribution to PMI or MIP if needed. There would be no entry on this line if there was no need for PMI or MIP, or if it was paid in full at closing.

On Line #4 the monthly tax payment is entered. (Divide annual tax by 12.)

Other monthly payment items could be entered on line #5 and line #6.

Line #7 is for the total of Line #1 through Line #6, and represents the estimated total monthly payment.

To see a full Estimate of Cost to Buyer form, go to Appendix A.

Questions

1. At a closing to take place on June 16th, the purchaser's charge for prepaid interest on a new loan will be for
   a. 15 days.   c. 31 days.
   b. 46 days.   d. 14 days.

2. In estimating prepaid taxes for a purchaser with a new loan who has signed a contract, it is safe to assume an amount equal to
   a. one year.
   b. three months.
   c. six months.
   d. a period based on estimated date of first monthly payment.

3. If a purchaser buys a home for $110,000 and pays $13,200 down, the lender would consider this to be a(n)
   a. 88 percent loan.
   b. 80 percent loan.
   c. 90 percent loan.
   d. 85 percent loan.

4. At a closing, the purchaser's cost for hazard insurance would include
   a. a one-year prepaid policy only.
   b. only two months' cost paid to escrow.
   c. a one-year policy plus at least two months in escrow.
   d. the cost of a one-year policy minus two months.

5. When estimating a purchaser's monthly payment on the desired home, a salesperson should calculate
   a. the payments to principal and interest.
   b. the monthly payment to property taxes.
   c. the monthly cost of hazard insurance.
   d. all of the above.

6. If it costs $9.52 per $1,000 to borrow for 30 years at an amortized rate of 11 percent, what would the monthly payment to principal and interest be on a $96,000 loan?
   a. $923.45.   c. $913.92.
   b. $924.37.   d. $956.17.

7. When a purchaser assumes the seller's loan due the first of each month and the closing is to take place March 10th,
   a. seller gives buyer a credit for 10 days of interest.
   b. buyer gives seller a credit for 10 days of interest.
   c. seller gives buyer a credit for 21 days of interest.
   d. buyer gives seller a credit for 21 days of interest.

8. If a loan is in the amount of $87,000 and the interest rate is 9.5 percent, the daily rate for computing interest proration is
   a. $22.96.   c. $21.45.
   b. $22.64.   d. $21.75.

9. If the purchaser will obtain a purchase money loan from the seller, it will appear on the estimated purchaser cost sheet as
   a. a credit to the buyer.
   b. a debit to the buyer.
   c. a credit to the seller.
   d. as a portion of the purchase price.

10. The earnest money deposited with the contract will appear on the estimated purchaser cost sheet as
    a. a credit to the buyer.
    b. a debit to the buyer.
    c. a credit to buyer and debit to seller.
    d. a debit to buyer and credit to seller.

11. In a contract providing for a conventional loan, the loan discount fee will be
    a. charged to the purchaser.
    b. charged to the seller.
    c. divided between purchaser and seller.
    d. paid according to the provisions in the contract.

12. In a conventional loan contract where the purchaser is obtaining a 90 percent loan, the premium for mortgage insurance can be
    a. paid at closing by either the buyer or the seller.
    b. financed over the period of the loan by the buyer.
    c. paid monthly.
    d. any of the above.

13. The Estimate of Cost to Buyer form is designed to show the buyer both how much cash will be required and
    a. the cost of repairs.
    b. the total finance cost.
    c. the monthly payment.
    d. the seller's net.

14. The agent should complete an Estimate of Cost to Buyer form
    a. prior to the offer.
    b. at the time of the offer.
    c. prior to closing.
    d. at all times mentioned above.

15. A purchaser who closes her new loan on May 1st will have her first payment due on
    a. June 1st.   c. June 10th.
    b. July 1st.   d. July 10th.

16. In calculating the tax escrow, the lender estimates the number of monthly increments necessary to pay the next tax bill then adds how many months?
    a. One   c. Three
    b. Two   d. Four

17. One discount point is what percentage of the loan amount?
    a. 1/8 percent   c. 1/2 percent
    b. 1/4 percent   d. 1 percent

18. The maximum FHA loan, if the sales price is above $50,000, is
    a. 95 percent.   c. 97.75 percent.
    b. 97 percent.   d. 98.75 percent.

19. The purchaser who closes her new loan on October 2nd will have her first payment due on
    a. November 1st.   c. December 1st.
    b. November 10th.   d. December 10th.

20. The purchaser will pay a Mortgage Insurance Premium on what type of loan?
    a. 80 percent Conventional
    b. 90 percent Conventional
    c. FHA
    d. VA

21. A transfer fee is paid to the
    a. county.   c. lender.
    b. state.   d. seller.

22. Escrow establishment charges may include all of the following EXCEPT
    a. repairs.
    b. property tax.
    c. hazard insurance.
    d. interest adjustment.

23. Which item is NOT included in the monthly payment for a condominium loan?
    a. Hazard insurance
    b. Principal
    c. Interest
    d. Property taxes

24. Unpaid property tax would show on the Estimate of Cost to Buyer form as a
    a. debit to the buyer.
    b. credit to the buyer.
    c. debit to the seller.
    d. credit to the seller.

11 Writing Real Estate Contracts

SOME BASIC PRINCIPLES

Before beginning to write a real estate contract, keep in mind the following important general rules:

- The form can be filled in with a computer, a typewriter, or a pen. A pencil would be inappropriate, because pencil marks can be easily erased and changed.
- It is always wise to have a broker or someone else review a contract before it is signed to be sure that the meaning is crystal clear.
- You can cross out the printed language when it is not appropriate, always having all parties to the contract initial the change, adding time and date, so as to make sure they did observe it and to identify the sequence of events.
- When blank space is not adequate you can write "See attached __" and add as many pages or exhibits as needed, making them a part of your contract by reference, and making sure all parties to the contract initial the extra pages.
- If you have no data to put into a blank space, write N/A (not applicable) to show that you did not just overlook it.
- When a sales contract is *contingent* upon loan approval, an inspection, or anything else, the buyer has reserved the right to walk away if the contingency cannot be met. In other words, it is not a firm contract until all contingencies are removed. Therefore, it is a good idea to have time limits for removing contingencies. Note that the clock starts ticking for the time limits included in the contract when it "becomes a binding agreement."
- In the process of negotiating a contract, be careful to avoid giving what might be considered legal advice. When a client asks a legal question about something, such as: (a) how to take title, or (b) what the tax consequences of the transaction might be, or (c) how to get out of the contract once it has become a binding agreement; you answer by suggesting that they *consult an attorney.*

In order to provide a practical application of contract writing, we are using the Purchase and Sale Agreement form, approved for general use by the Georgia Association of REALTORS®.

The following narrative will be used to illustrate how the form is to be filled in.

Narrative *Seller: Peter and Patsy Palmer have listed their home for sale at $175,000 with Franc's Fisher of Southland Realty, Inc. The home is at 1445 Grove Road, Atlanta, Georgia, zip code 30001. The legal description is Land Lot 116 of the 2nd District of Peachtree County, Georgia; Lot 5 in Block 2 of the Fairway Subdivision to be found in Plat Book 477, on Page 21 in the Peachtree County records. The listing is for 90 days at 6 percent commission and is signed on April 5th.*

Purchaser: On May 12th an offer of $170,000 is received from Arthur Altman, an independent broker, buying on his own behalf. He wants to have an 80 percent conventional, fixed-rate mortgage loan and will agree to pay half the closing costs and any loan discount points. He wants to close by June 15th and to have occupancy at closing. He specifies that the refrigerator and laundry equipment be included in the sale at a value of $300, wants the inspection contingency included in the contract, and will provide a $3,000 check as an earnest money deposit.

Conditions: Purchaser expects to receive 50 percent of the commission and wants the sellers to provide a current survey at their expense. He has received and reviewed the sellers' Disclosure Form.

PURCHASE AND SALE AGREEMENT

Date:_____ **May 12** _____, 20 **02** ___

2002
Printing

1. **Purchase and Sale.** The undersigned buyer ("Buyer") agrees to buy and the undersigned seller ("Seller") agrees to sell all that tract or parcel of land, with such improvements as are located thereon, described as follows: All that tract of land lying and being in Land Lot ___**118**___ of the __**2nd**__ District, __**N/A**__ Section of _____**Peachtree**_____ County, Georgia, and being known as Address _____**1445 Grove Road**_____, City_____**Atlanta**_____, Georgia Zip Code __ ____**30001**____, according to the present system of numbering in and around this area, being more particularly described as Lot ___**5**___, Block ____**2**____, Unit ____**N/A**__, Phase/Section ____**N/A**____ of _____**Fairway**_____ Subdivision, as recorded in Plat Book ___**447**___, Page ___**21**___, _____**Peachtree**_____ County, Georgia records together with all fixtures, landscaping, improvements, and appurtenances, all being hereinafter collectively referred to as the "Property." The full legal description of the Property is the same as is recorded with the Clerk of the Superior Court of the county in which the Property is located and is made a part of this Agreement by reference.

The date at the top of page 1 of the Purchase and Sale Agreement is the date the offer is being prepared. In the narrative, the date is May 12th.

1. Purchase and Sale   Paragraph #1 says the buyer will buy and the seller will sell. Then follows the legal description of the property. We filled in the data given in the narrative, using the N/A (for "not applicable") wherever no information was given.

The legal description is essential. It would be improper to use language such as "legal description to be provided within ten days," or "legal description to be produced prior to closing."

If the licensee preparing the offer has not acquired the legal description from the seller or listing agent or cannot find it on the computer, a trip to the county courthouse might be in order, unless it can be pulled up on the computer.

A lengthy metes-and-bounds description will not fit in the blanks in this form. If that were what we had, we would have written "See Attached" and added the description as an *exhibit.*

---

2. **Purchase Price and Method of Payment.** Buyer warrants that Buyer will have sufficient cash at closing, which when combined with the loan(s), if any, referenced herein, will allow Buyer to complete the purchase of the Property. Buyer does not need to sell or lease other real property in order to complete the purchase of the Property. The purchase price of the Property to be paid by Buyer at closing is: _____ **One hundred seventy thousand and 00/100** _____ U.S. Dollars, $____**170,000.00**____ subject to the following: *[Select sections A, B, C, and/or D below. The sections not marked are not a part of this Agreement.]*

☐ A. **All Cash At Closing:** Buyer shall pay the purchase price to Seller in cash, or its equivalent. Buyer's obligation to close shall not be subject to any financial contingency. Buyer shall pay all closing costs.

☐ B. **Loan To Be Assumed**: See Exhibit "_____."

☒ C. **New Loan To Be Obtained:** This Agreement is made conditioned upon Buyer's ability to obtain a loan (except if the loan is denied because Buyer lacks sufficient cash to close excluding the amount of the loan and/or because Buyer has not sold or leased other real property) in the principal amount of ___**80**___ % of the purchase price listed above, with an interest rate at par of not more than ___**7**___% per annum on the unpaid balance, to be secured by a first lien security deed on the Property; the loan to be paid in consecutive monthly installments of principal and interest over a term of not less than ___**30**___ years. "Ability to obtain" as used herein means that Buyer is qualified to receive the loan described herein based upon lender's customary and standard underwriting criteria. The loan shall be of the type selected below: *[The sections not marked are not a part of this Agreement.]*

    (1) Loan Type: ☒ **Conventional**; ☐ **FHA** (see attached exhibit); ☐ **VA** (see attached exhibit) ; ☐ **Other** (see attached exhibit)

    (2) Rate Type: ☒ **Fixed Rate Mortgage Loan;** ☐ **Adjustable Rate Mortgage ("ARM") Loan;**

    (3) Closing Costs and Discount Points: Seller shall, at the time of closing, contribute a sum not to exceed $____**N/A**____ to be used by Buyer to pay for: (a) preparation of the warranty deed and owner's affidavit by the closing attorney; (b) at Buyer's discretion, closing costs, loan discount points, survey costs, and insurance premiums (including flood insurance, if applicable) relating to the Property and/or loan; and (c) at Buyer's discretion, other costs to close including escrow establishment charges and prepaid items, if allowed by lender. Buyer shall pay all other costs, fees, and amounts for the above referenced items and to fulfill lender requirements to otherwise close this transaction.

    (4) Closing Attorney: This transaction shall be closed by the law firm of_____**N/A**_____ _____, provided the firm is approved to close loans for Buyer's lender.

    (5) Loan Obligations: Buyer agrees to: (a) make application for the loan within __**five (5)**__ days from the Binding Agreement Date; (b) immediately notify Seller of having applied for the loan and the name of the lender; and (c) pursue qualification for and approval of the loan diligently and in good faith. Should Buyer not timely apply for the loan, Seller may terminate the Agreement if Buyer does not, within five days after receiving written notice thereof, cure the default by providing Seller with written evidence of loan application. Buyer agrees that a loan with terms consistent with those described herein shall satisfy this loan contingency. Buyer may also apply for a loan with different terms and conditions and close the transaction provided all other terms and conditions of this Agreement are fulfilled, and the new loan does not increase the costs charged to the Seller. Buyer shall be obligated to close this transaction if Buyer has the ability to obtain a loan with terms as described herein and/or any other loan for which Buyer has applied and been approved. From the Binding Agreement Date until closing, Buyer shall not intentionally make any material changes in Buyer's financial condition which would adversely affect Buyer's ability to obtain a loan. In the event any application of Buyer for a loan is denied, Buyer shall promptly provide Seller with a letter from the lender denying the loan stating the basis for the loan denial.

☐ D. **Second Loan to be Obtained,** see Exhibit "_____."

---

2. Purchase Price and Method of Payment

Sentence #1 of paragraph #2 guarantees that the buyer will come to the closing with enough cash to close, and that the offer is *not* contingent upon the sale or lease of another property.

If the buyer *did* have to dispose of another property in order to close, you would have had to cross out that word *"not"* and would have had to add "See attached."

There is another form (not shown here) that can be used as an exhibit to provide the details of an offer that is to be contingent upon the sale or lease of another property. If this form did not happen to be available, the information might be included in a special stipulation.

Now, we write out the offered price in letters and numbers, just as it's done on a bank check. The price must be stated as a definite amount, or in such a way that a definite amount can be determined.

In this narrative, it is specific, but it might have read as follows:

- "The purchase price to be determined by an appraisal of the property" —adding when the appraisal is to be made, by whom, and who is to pay for it; or
- "The purchase price to be $1,200 per acre, with acreage to be determined by a survey made"—adding when the survey is to be made, by whom, and who is to pay for it.

It would not be a valid offer if it read "Price to be determined within 30 days."

Then, as to method of payment, the purchaser is given four choices with boxes to check indicating the choice made. The boxes *not* chosen will not be a part of this agreement, so we can ignore them.

A. **All Cash at Closing:** This choice means the offer is not contingent upon obtaining a loan. It also says the buyer will pay all closing costs (another sentence the buyer might want altered and initialed.) This is not our buyer's choice.

B. **Loan To Be Assumed:** See "Exhibit ___." Another form (not shown here) is available for attachment to cover the details of a loan assumption. This is not our buyer's choice.

C. **New Loan To Be Obtained:** This is the box we did check and it makes the offer contingent upon the buyer being able to obtain the desired financing. A contingency is, in effect, a loophole, so it is important to be specific about the loan the buyer is seeking.

We chose 7 percent as an interest rate because it was approximately the going rate at the time and selected 30 years because that is the most popular choice.

(1) **Loan Type:** We checked Conventional.

(2) **Rate Type:** We checked Fixed Rate Mortgage Loan.

(3) **Closing Costs and Discount Points:** It might have been confusing to fit our buyer's intentions for closing costs into the printed language here so we chose to cross out this paragraph and add "See Special stipulation #1."

(4) **Closing Attorney:** The name of the law firm that the buyer chooses to close the sale should be inserted here.

(5) **Loan Obligations:** The buyer is agreeing to apply for the loan within five days, to pursue it diligently, and to let the seller know the name of the lender. This paragraph also specifies that the buyer could change his mind and seek a different type of loan as long as it did not affect any obligations the seller might have. The buyer cannot deliberately change the financial condition to avoid approval for the loan. If the buyer's loan is rejected, the buyer must provide a copy of the lender's turn-down letter.

D. Second Loan to be Obtained: see Exhibit "____." This, too, can be detailed in an exhibit form, but it is not our buyer's choice.

---

3. <u>Earnest Money</u>. Buyer has paid to _____**Southland Realty**_____ ("Holder") earnest money of $_____**3,000.00**_____ check, OR $_____**N/A**_____ cash, which has been received by Holder. The earnest money shall be deposited in Holder's escrow/trust account (with Holder retaining the interest if the account is interest bearing) within five banking days from the

Binding Agreement Date and shall be applied toward the purchase price of the Property at the time of closing. In the event any earnest money check is not honored, for any reason, by the bank upon which it is drawn, Holder shall promptly notify Buyer and Seller. Buyer shall have three banking days after notice to deliver good funds to Holder. In the event Buyer does not timely deliver good funds, the Seller shall have the right to terminate this Agreement upon written notice to the Buyer. Holder shall disburse earnest money only as follows: (a) upon the failure of the parties to enter into a binding agreement; (b) at closing; (c) upon a subsequent written agreement signed by all parties having an interest in the funds; (d) upon order of a court or arbitrator having jurisdiction over any dispute involving the earnest money; or (e) upon a reasonable interpretation of this Agreement by Holder.   Prior to disbursing earnest money pursuant to a reasonable interpretation of this Agreement, Holder shall give all parties fifteen days notice, stating to whom the disbursement will be made. Any party may object in writing to the disbursement, provided the objection is received by Holder prior to the end of the fifteen-day notice period. All objections not raised in a timely manner shall be waived. In the event a timely objection is made, Holder shall consider the objection and shall do one or more of the following: (a) hold the earnest money for a reasonable period of time to give the parties an opportunity to resolve the dispute; (b) disburse the earnest money and so notify all parties; and/or (c) interplead the earnest money into a court of competent jurisdiction. Holder shall be reimbursed for and may deduct from any funds interpleaded its costs and expenses, including reasonable attorneys' fees. The prevailing party in the interpleader action shall be entitled to collect from the other party the costs and expenses reimbursed to Holder. No party shall seek damages from Holder (nor shall Holder be liable for the same) for any matter arising out of or related to the performance of Holder's duties under this earnest money paragraph. If Buyer breaches Buyer's obligations or warranties herein, holder may pay the earnest money to Seller by check, which if accepted and deposited by Seller, shall constitute liquidated damages in full settlement of all claims of Seller. It is agreed to by the parties that such liquidated damages are not a penalty and are a good faith estimate of Seller's actual damages, which damages are difficult to ascertain.

---

3. Earnest Money

Line #1 of the Earnest Money section specifies who will hold the earnest money, how much it is, and in what form. It also specifies that it be deposited by the holder in a trust account (which can be an interest-bearing account as long as the contract states to whom the interest will go) within five days. Provisions in case the check bounces are also outlined.

The earnest money is not the consideration in this contract. It is not essential that there be any at all. It is customary, though, for a buyer to put up some "good faith" money with an offer, saying in effect, "If I don't do what this offer says I will do, you can keep my deposit." How much it should be depends on the circumstances of the transaction, but the more there is, the more impressed a seller will be with the offer. It is usually in the form of cash or a check, but anything of measurable value can be used—including even labor, such as an agreement to repair a roof or paint a fence, as long as a value for those services is specified in case the seller defaults and the buyer is entitled to have the earnest money returned.

The rest of this paragraph spells out how the earnest money might be disbursed as follows:

(a)   Returned to the buyer if no binding agreement is reached
(b)   Credited to the buyer at closing
(c)   According to a written agreement signed by all parties
(d)   Upon a court order (in the event of a dispute)
(e)   Upon a reasonable interpretation of the contract by the broker holding the money

---

4. **Closing and Possession**.

    A. **Property Condition:** Seller warrants that at the time of closing or upon the granting of possession if at a time other than at closing, the Property will be in substantially the same condition as it was on Binding Agreement Date, except for normal wear and tear, and changes made to the condition of the Property pursuant to the written agreement of Buyer and Seller. Seller shall deliver Property clean and free of debris at time of possession. If the Property is destroyed or substantially damaged prior to closing, Seller shall promptly notify Buyer of the amount of insurance proceeds available to repair the damage and whether Seller will complete repairs prior to closing. Buyer may terminate this Agreement not later than five days after receiving such notice by giving written notice to Seller. If Buyer does not terminate this Agreement, Buyer shall receive at closing such insurance proceeds as are paid on the claim which are not spent to repair the damage.

    B. **Taxes:** Real estate taxes on said Property for the calendar year in which the sale is closed shall be prorated as of the date of closing. Seller shall pay State of Georgia property transfer tax.

    C. **Timing of Closing and Possession:** This transaction shall be closed on _____**June 5**_____, 20 **02** or on such other date as may be agreed to by the parties in writing, provided, however, that: (1) in the event the loan described herein is unable to be closed on or before said date; or (2) Seller fails to satisfy valid title objections, Buyer or Seller may, by notice to the other party (which notice must be received on or before the closing date), extend this Agreement's closing date and the date for surrender of occupancy if later than the closing date, up to seven days from the above-stated closing date. Buyer agrees to allow Seller to retain possession of the Property through: *[Select sections A, B, or C below. The sections not marked are not a part of this Agreement.]*

           [X] A. the closing; or [ ] B. _____ hours after the closing; or [ ] C. _____ days after the closing at _____m. o'clock

    D. **Warranties Transfer:** Seller agrees to transfer to Buyer, at closing, subject to Buyer's acceptance thereof, Seller's interest in any manufacturer's warranties, service contracts, termite bond or treatment guarantee and/or other similar warranties which, by their terms, may be transferable to Buyer.

    E. **Prorations:** Seller and Buyer agree to prorate all utility bills between themselves, as of the date of closing (or the day of possession of the Property by the Buyer, whichever is the later) which are issued after closing and include service for any period of time the Property was owned/occupied by Seller or any other person prior to Buyer.

    F. **Closing Certifications:** Buyer and Seller shall execute and deliver such certifications, affidavits, and statements as are required at closing to meet the requirements of the lender and of federal and state law.

---

4. Closing and Possession

In the Closing and Possession section, several important seller/buyer obligations are spelled out.

    A. **Property Condition:** The seller is promising to deliver the property at closing in clean condition, free of debris, and in the same condition it was in at time of contract. (It doesn't say perfect.) The paragraph also provides some options in the event the property is destroyed or substantially damaged before the closing.

    B. **Taxes:** The parties agree to prorate the property tax bill, and the seller agrees to pay the state transfer tax.

    C. **Timing of Closing and Possession:** We fill in the dates desired, but note that, in the event that more time is needed for loan funding or for settling a title problem, either party, with written notice to the other, has the right to extend the closing for seven days. Licensees should recommend a closing date that represents a reasonable time frame for closing. If occupancy before closing by the buyer or after closing by the seller is to be allowed, the shortest possible time limit is best. "Agreement to Occupy" forms (not shown here) for this purpose specify that this is *not* a landlord-tenant relationship because, if it was and the party refused to vacate, the eviction process could be difficult.

    D. **Warranties Transfer:** The seller is obligated to transfer to the buyer any relevant warranties or service contracts that are transferable.

    E. **Prorations:** The parties agree to adjust at closing for any costs that require adjustment.

    F. **Closing Certifications:** The parties are agreeing to provide any certificates that the lender or the law requires.

5. <u>Title</u>.
   A. **Warranty:** Seller warrants that, at the time of closing, Seller will convey good and marketable title to said Property by general warranty deed subject only to: (1) zoning; (2) general utility, sewer, and drainage easements of record on the Acceptance Date upon which the improvements do not encroach; (3) subdivision and/or condominium declarations, covenants, restrictions, and easements of record on the Acceptance Date; and (4) leases and other encumbrances specified in this Agreement. Buyer agrees to assume Seller's responsibilities in any leases specified in this Agreement.
   B. **Examination:** Buyer may, prior to closing, examine title and furnish Seller with a written statement of objections affecting the marketability of said title. If Seller fails to satisfy valid title objections prior to closing or any extension thereof, then Buyer may terminate the Agreement upon written notice to Seller, in which case Buyer's earnest money shall be returned. Good and marketable title as used herein shall mean title which a title insurance company licensed to do business in Georgia will insure at its regular rates, subject only to standard exceptions.
   C. **Survey:** Any survey of the Property attached hereto by agreement of the parties prior to the Binding Agreement Date shall be a part of this Agreement. Buyer shall have the right to terminate this Agreement upon written notice to Seller if a new survey performed by a surveyor licensed in Georgia is obtained which is materially different from any attached survey with respect to the Property, in which case Buyer's earnest money shall be returned. The term Amaterially different@ shall not apply to any improvements constructed by Seller in their agreed-upon locations subsequent to Binding Date Agreement. Matters revealed in said survey shall not relieve the warranty of title obligations of Seller referenced above.

5. Title   A.   **Warranty:** The seller in this paragraph is promising to provide *marketable title* and to convey this title with a *general warranty deed* (see Chapter 4). The buyer is agreeing to honor any existing lease on the property.

Many corporations, notably banks and third party relocation companies, will not use a general warranty deed. They will only provide a special warranty deed. So, if a corporation is the seller, we might have to cross out the word "general" and substitute "special."

B.   **Examination:** The buyer has a right to examine the title evidence before the closing. If the search has revealed problems that cannot be rectified, the buyer has a right to cancel the contract and have the earnest money refunded.

C.   **Survey:** There may or may not be a survey attached to this contract and made a part of it. If it is attached and then before the closing the buyer acquires a new survey that shows some material difference, the buyer may cancel the contract and have the earnest money refunded.

6. <u>Seller's Property Disclosure</u>. Seller's Property Disclosure Statement is attached hereto and incorporated herein. Seller warrants that to the best of Seller's knowledge and belief, the information contained therein is accurate and complete as of the Binding Agreement Date.

7. <u>Termite Letter</u>. An official Georgia Wood Infestation Report ("Report") prepared by a licensed pest control operator, covering each dwelling and garage on the Property and dated within one hundred eighty days of the acceptance date is ☐ **OR,** is not ☒ attached to this Agreement as an exhibit. If the Report is not attached, Seller shall provide such a Report to Buyer within seven days from the Binding Agreement Date. Buyer shall have the right to terminate this Agreement within ten days from the Binding Agreement Date if either of the following events occur: (a) the Report is not timely provided to Buyer; or (b) the Report provided after the Binding Agreement Date indicates present infestation of, or damage to, the Property from termites or other wood destroying organisms. If Buyer does not timely give Seller notice of Buyer's decision to terminate this Agreement, Buyer's right to terminate the Agreement pursuant to this paragraph shall be waived. Notwithstanding the above, Buyer shall continue to have whatever other rights to terminate this Agreement, if any, that exist elsewhere in this Agreement. Unless otherwise noted on the Seller's Property Disclosure Statement, to the best of Seller's knowledge, the information contained in any attached or later provided Report is accurate and complete, and no other termite inspections have been performed or reports issued, the findings of which are inconsistent with the Report attached hereto. Prior to closing, Seller shall treat active infestation of termites and other wood destroying organisms, if any. At closing, Seller shall provide Buyer with a Report prepared by a licensed pest control operator dated within thirty days of the closing, stating that each dwelling and garage has been found to be free from active infestation of termites and other wood destroying organisms. This paragraph shall not limit Buyer's right to request that Seller repair and/or replace defects resulting from termites and other wood destroying organisms if the Property is sold with the right to request repairs in accordance with the Inspection Paragraph herein.

6. Seller's Property Disclosure

This affirms that the offeror has seen the seller's Property Disclosure Statement. In Georgia the disclosure is not a legal requirement.

There are times when a seller will not provide the Property Disclosure Statement. If that were the case, we would have had to cross out this paragraph.

7. Termite Letter

Sentence #1 of this paragraph contains two boxes to check, noting whether a termite inspection certificate, no more than 180 days old at time of acceptance, is **OR** is not included. If not, the seller has seven days from the binding agreement date to provide it. The buyer has ten days from the binding agreement date to terminate the agreement, if the report is not presented in a timely fashion or if the report indicates infestation or damage. The buyer can choose to deal with damage, if any, under the next paragraph concerning the inspection.

In essence, failure to provide the termite report with this offer creates another contingency.

---

8. **Inspection**. Buyer and/or Buyer's representatives shall have the right to enter the Property at Buyer's expense and at reasonable times (including immediately prior to closing) to thoroughly inspect, examine, test and survey the Property. This shall include the right to inspect and test for lead-based paint and lead-based paint hazards for not less than ten days from the Binding Agreement Date. Seller shall cause all utility services and any pool, spa, and similar items to be operational so that Buyer may complete all inspections under this Agreement. The Buyer agrees to hold the Seller and all Brokers harmless from all claims, injuries, and damages arising out of or related to the exercise of these rights.

[Select section A or B below. The section not marked shall not be part of this Agreement.]

Buyer(s)
Initials
☐

A. **Property Sold With Right to Request Repairs.**
    (1) Buyer shall have the right to request that Seller repair and/or replace only defects in the Property identified by Buyer's representative(s) by providing Seller, within ___**eight (8)**___ days from Binding Agreement Date, with a copy of inspection report(s) and a signed written amendment to this Agreement setting forth the defects noted in the report which Buyer requests be repaired and/or replaced. The term "defects" shall mean any portion of or item in the Property which: (a) is not in good working order and repair (normal wear and tear excepted); (b) constitutes a violation of applicable laws, governmental codes or regulations and is not otherwise grandfathered; or (c) is in a condition which represents a significant health risk or an unreasonable risk of injury or damage to persons or property. If Buyer does not timely present the written amendment and inspection report, Buyer shall be deemed to have accepted the Property "as is" in accordance with paragraph B below.
    (2) If Buyer timely submits the inspection report and the written amendment, Buyer and Seller shall have ___**fifteen (15)**___ days (hereinafter "Defect Resolution Period") from the Binding Agreement Date to negotiate through written offers and counteroffers the defects to be repaired and/or replaced by Seller.
    (3) Neither party may terminate this Agreement prior to the end of the Defect Resolution Period due to the failure to agree on the repair and/or replacement of defects without the written consent of the other party.
    (4) If Seller at any time during the Defect Resolution Period notifies Buyer that Seller will repair and/or replace all of the defects listed in the initial amendment submitted by Buyer, an agreement on the repair and/or replacement of defects shall be deemed to have been reached and all parties shall execute an amendment to that effect.
    (5) If Buyer and Seller have not within the Defect Resolution Period agreed on the defects to be repaired and/or replaced by signing a written amendment to this Agreement, Buyer may either accept the last unexpired counteroffer of Seller or accept the Property "as is" in accordance with paragraph B below, by giving notice to Seller within three days after the end of the Defect Resolution Period. If Buyer fails to timely give this notice, this Agreement shall terminate immediately, and Buyer's earnest money shall be returned in accordance with the Earnest Money paragraph above. All agreed-upon repairs and replacements shall be completed in a good and workmanlike manner prior to closing.

Buyer(s)
Initials
☐

OR

B. **Property Sold "As Is."** All parties agree that the Property is being sold "as is," with all faults including but not limited to lead-based paint and lead-based paint hazards and damage from termites and other wood destroying organisms. The Seller shall have no obligation to make repairs to the Property.

8. Inspection   First, the buyer is assured of the right to enter the property at reasonable times for the purpose of inspecting or testing. And the seller must see that all systems are operational for this purpose. Then the buyer makes a choice by initialing either box A or box B.

A. **Property Sold With Right to Request Repairs.** This paragraph sets up another contingency. The steps are as follows:
- The buyer, within ___ days, has the property inspected and files an amendment with the seller, specifying defects to be repaired or replaced. (This does not include cosmetic flaws but does include things that are out of order, code violations, or risks to health or safety.)
- If no amendment is filed or it is not timely, the contingency is removed.
- If the amendment is filed, buyer and seller have ____ days from the binding agreement date to negotiate their differences, if any. This is the "Repair Resolution Period."
- If negotiations fail, buyer can choose to take the best offer the seller has made or to terminate the contract and receive a refund of the earnest money.

B. **Property Sold "As Is."** With this choice, the buyer agrees to forego the inspection contingency. The seller is not obligated to make any repairs.

---

9. Other Provisions.

A.   Binding Effect, Entire Agreement, Modification, Assignment: This Agreement shall be for the benefit of, and be binding upon, Buyer and Seller, their heirs, successors, legal representatives and permitted assigns. This Agreement constitutes the sole and entire agreement between the parties hereto and no modification or assignment of this Agreement shall be binding unless signed by all parties to this Agreement. No representation, promise, or inducement not included in this Agreement shall be binding upon any party hereto. Any assignee shall fulfill all the terms and conditions of this Agreement.

B.   Survival of Agreement: All conditions or stipulations not fulfilled at time of closing shall survive the closing until such time as the conditions or stipulations are fulfilled.

C.   Governing Law: This Agreement may be signed in multiple counterparts, is intended as a contract for the purchase and sale of real property and shall be interpreted in accordance with the laws of the State of Georgia.

D.   Time of Essence: Time is of the essence of this Agreement.

E.   Terminology: As the context may require in this Agreement: (1) the singular shall mean the plural and vice versa; and (2) all pronouns shall mean and include the person, entity, firm, or corporation to which they relate.

F.   Responsibility to Cooperate: All parties agree to timely take such actions and produce, execute, and/or deliver such information and documentation as is reasonably necessary to carry out the responsibilities and obligations of this Agreement.

G.   Notices. Except as otherwise provided herein, all notices, including offers, counteroffers, acceptances, amendments and demands, required or permitted hereunder shall be in writing, signed by the party giving the notice and delivered either: (1) in person, (2) by an overnight delivery service, prepaid, (3) by facsimile transmission (FAX) (provided that an original of the notice shall be promptly sent thereafter if so requested by the party receiving the same) or (4) by the United States Postal Service, postage prepaid, registered or certified return receipt requested. The parties agree that a faxed signature of a party constitutes an original signature binding upon that party. Notice shall be deemed to have been given as of the date and time it is actually received. Notwithstanding the above, notice by FAX shall be deemed to have been given as of the date and time it is transmitted if the sending FAX produces a written confirmation with the date, time and telephone number to which the notice was sent. Receipt of notice by the Broker representing a party as a client shall be deemed to be notice to that party for all purposes herein, except in transactions where the Broker is practicing designated agency, in which case, receipt of notice by the designated agent representing a party as a client shall be required to constitute notice. All notice requirements referenced herein shall be strictly construed.

---

9. Other Provisions   Standard legal clauses appear in section #9 that would rarely be altered. They relate to the following:

A. **Binding Effect, Entire Agreement, Modification, Assignment:** Explains the fact that the agreement is binding on heirs and that it cannot be modified or assigned without permission of both parties.

B. **Survival of Agreement:** Promises that any conditions that cannot be fulfilled until after the closing will still be binding even though the sales agreement in effect ceases to exist when the deed is signed. (This is called a *survival clause.*)

C. **Governing Law:** The laws of Georgia will apply in interpreting this agreement.
D. **Time of Essence:** Time limits in the agreement are to be strictly observed.
E. **Terminology:** Explains how pronouns are used in the agreement.
F. **Responsibility to Cooperate:** This agreement says all parties will cooperate in producing any documentation needed.
G. **Notices:** The required notices can be delivered in person, by overnight service, by FAX, and by U.S. mail. Notices are deemed to have been given when they are received, except for FAX messages that are deemed "delivered" when sent. A FAXED signature constitutes an original signature.

---

10. <u>Disclaimer.</u> Buyer and Seller acknowledge that they have not relied upon any advice, representations or statements of Brokers and waive and shall not assert any claims against Brokers involving the same. Buyer and Seller agree that Brokers shall not be responsible to advise Buyer and Seller on any matter including but not limited to the following: any matter which could have been revealed through a survey, title search or inspection of the Property; the condition of the Property, any portion thereof, or any item therein; building products and construction techniques; the necessity or cost of any repairs to the Property; hazardous or toxic materials or substances; termites and other wood destroying organisms; the tax or legal consequences of this transaction; the availability and cost of utilities or community amenities; the appraised or future value of the Property; any condition(s) existing off the Property which may affect the Property; the terms, conditions and availability of financing; and the uses and zoning of the Property whether permitted or proposed. Buyer and Seller acknowledge that Brokers are not experts with respect to the above matters and that, if any of these matters or any other matters are of concern to them, they should seek independent expert advice relative thereto. Buyer further acknowledges that in every neighborhood there are conditions which different buyers may find objectionable. Buyer shall therefore be responsible to become fully acquainted with neighborhood and other off site conditions which could affect the Property.

---

10. Disclaimer Licensees disclaim any liability for having given technical or professional counsel to the buyers that was outside of their areas of knowledge. This paragraph also states that the buyer is responsible for becoming acquainted with the neighborhood and observing any off-site conditions that could affect the property.

11. Agency and Brokerage Licensees might pay special attention to the Agency and Brokerage section because it covers material of much importance to them.

A. **Agency.**
(1) The term "Broker" in this section refers to any licensee. It also states that no licensee owes a duty to a buyer or seller greater than what is outlined in BRRETA.
(2) States that if a broker does not represent the buyer or seller, they are responsible for protecting their own interests.
(3) Here we find two more boxes. The broker working with the seller must check whether or he or she is **OR** is **NOT** representing the seller.
(4) The two boxes in this line are where the broker working with the buyer checks that he or she is **OR** is **NOT** representing the buyer.
(5) If both buyer and seller are represented by the same broker, we now check two more boxes to note whether this is *dual* or *designated* agency.

Under #5, the section labeled **(a) Dual Agency Disclosure** is only applicable if there is a single-agent dual agency, and it provides for the necessary informed consent.

Under #5, the section labeled **(b) Designated Agency Assignment** is only used if that is in fact what is occurring, and the blanks are for naming the designated agents. If it is not designated agency, skip this part.

There is also a blank for noting any material relationship the broker might have with one party or the other—another required BRRETA disclosure.

B. **Brokerage.** This paragraph provides that the seller will pay the listing broker for valuable services and the listing broker will compensate the selling broker. The closing attorney is instructed to pay these commissions out of the closing proceeds. It also provides that, if the sale fails to close, the nonperforming party owes both brokers a full commission.

---

11. <u>**Agency and Brokerage.**</u>
    A. **Agency.**
      (1) In this Agreement, the term ABroker@ shall mean a licensed Georgia real estate broker or brokerage firm and where the context would indicate the broker's affiliated licensees. No Broker in this transaction shall owe any duty to Buyer or Seller greater than what is set forth in their brokerage engagements and the Brokerage Relationships in Real Estate Transactions Act, O.C.G.A. § 10-6A-1 et .seq.;
      (2) Seller and Buyer acknowledge that if they are not represented by a Broker they are each solely responsible for protecting their own interests, and that Broker's role is limited to performing ministerial acts for that party.
      (3) The Broker, if any, working with the Seller is identified on the signature page as the "Listing Broker"; and said Broker is ☒ **OR,** is **NOT** ☐ representing the Seller;
      (4) The Broker, if any, working with the Buyer is identified on the signature page as the ASelling Broker@,and said Broker is ☒ **OR,** is **NOT** ☐ representing the Buyer; and
      (5) If Buyer and Seller are both being represented by the same Broker, a relationship of either designated agency ☐ **OR,** dual agency ☐ shall exist.
        (a) **Dual Agency Disclosure.** [*Applicable only if dual agency has been selected above*] Seller and Buyer are aware that Broker is acting as a dual agent in this transaction and consent to the same. Seller and Buyer have been advised that:
          1 - In serving as a dual agent the Broker is representing two clients whose interests are or at times could be different or even adverse;
          2 - The Broker will disclose all adverse, material facts relevant to the transaction and actually known to the dual agent to all parties in the transaction except for information made confidential by request or instructions from another client which is not otherwise required to be disclosed by law;
          3 - The Buyer and Seller do not have to consent to dual agency; and
          4 - The consent of the Buyer and Seller to dual agency has been given voluntarily and the parties have read and understood their brokerage engagement agreements.
          5 - Notwithstanding any provision to the contrary contained herein, Seller and Buyer each hereby direct Broker, while acting as a dual agent, to keep confidential and not reveal to the other party any information which could materially and adversely affect their negotiating position.
        (b) **Designated Agency Assignment.** [*Applicable only if the designated agency has been selected above*] The Broker has assigned _____N/A_____ to work exclusively with Buyer as Buyer's designated agent and _____N/A_____ to work exclusively with Seller as Seller's designated agent. Each designated agent shall exclusively represent the party to whom each has been assigned as a client and shall not represent in this transaction the client assigned to the other designated agent.
        (c) **Material Relationship Disclosure.** The Broker and/or affiliated licensees have no material relationship with either client except as follows:_____N/A_____.
          (A material relationship means one actually known of a personal, familial or business nature between the Broker and affiliated licensees and a client which would impair their ability to exercise fair judgment relative to another client.)

    B. **Brokerage.** The Broker(s) identified herein have performed valuable brokerage services and are to be paid a commission pursuant to a separate agreement or agreements. Unless otherwise provided for herein, the Listing Broker will be paid a commission by the Seller, and the Selling Broker will receive a portion of the Listing Broker's commission pursuant to a cooperative brokerage agreement. The closing attorney is directed to pay the commission of the Broker(s) at closing out of the proceeds of the sale. If the sale proceeds are insufficient to pay the full commission, the party owing the commission will pay any shortfall at closing. If more than one Broker is involved in the transaction, the closing attorney is directed to pay each Broker their respective portion of said commission. In the event the sale is not closed because of Buyer's and/or Seller's failure or refusal to perform any of their obligations herein, the non-performing party shall immediately pay the Broker(s) the full commission the Broker(s) would have received had the sale closed, and the Selling Broker and Listing Broker may jointly or independently pursue the non-performing party for their portion of the commission.

---

12.   <u>Time Limit of Offer</u>. This instrument shall be open for acceptance until ____**10**____ o'clock ____**A**____M. on the __**14th**__ day of _____**May**_____, 20__**02**___.

13.   <u>Exhibits and Addenda</u>. All exhibits and/or addenda attached hereto, listed below, or referenced herein are made a part of this Agreement. If any such exhibit or addendum conflicts with any preceding paragraph, said exhibit or addendum shall control:

SPECIAL STIPULATIONS: The following Special Stipulations, if conflicting with any exhibit, addendum, or preceding paragraph, shall control.

    1. Sellers and Buyer agree that each will pay half of the closing costs. Sellers will provide a current survey at their expense. Buyer will pay half of the closing costs, applicable loan discount points, insurance premiums and escrow deposits.

    2. Refrigerator and laundry equipment (washer and dryer) to be included in the purchase at a value of $300 (see Exhibit).

    3. Undersigned Buyer is licensed real estate broker representing himself.

---

12. Time Limit of Offer

A time limit is not essential to this agreement, but it is included, if the seller is expected to respond within a specified time frame. If the seller waited until the time limit had passed and then decided to accept the offer, there would be no contract unless the buyer then agreed to extend the time limit. On the other hand, it is not binding on the buyer, who can withdraw the offer any time up to the point where it has become a binding agreement. We elected to give our seller 48 hours to respond.

13. Exhibits and Addenda

It is important to note in this space any additional pages that are being added to the contract. In addition to the Seller's Property Disclosure form, we are adding a Personal Property Agreement (not shown here) to cover the refrigerator and laundry equipment.

Special Stipulations

There is no "standard" language for special stipulations, but licensees may have lists of "suggested language" for the most common situations.

In general, the following suggestions apply:

- The goal is that there be a clear understanding and no possibility of ambiguity; therefore, use simple language and be specific.
- When possible, have someone else review the stipulations to see if the reader interprets them in the way you intended.
- For clarity, keep each item in a separate paragraph and number the items.
- Take as much space as is needed. It is always possible to add an addendum, if space does not prove ample.
- When in doubt about whether to disclose something in a special stipulation, it is probably a good idea. For example, perhaps the buyer already knows that the roof needs repair, but including that in writing in the contract is prudent.
- If faced with very lengthy and complex special stipulations, the licensee is in some danger of practicing law without a license. So in this case the broker should be consulted.

There are three special stipulations we have added to the contract we prepared from the narrative given, reading as follows:

1. Sellers and buyer agree that each will pay half of the closing costs. Sellers will provide a current survey at their expense. Buyer will pay

half of the closing costs, applicable loan discount points, insurance premiums, and escrow deposits.

2. Refrigerator and laundry equipment (washer and dryer) to be included in the purchase at a value of $300 (see Exhibit).
3. Undersigned Buyer is a licensed real estate broker representing himself.

Signatures

The offer is now signed by the buyer and by the buyer's agent if any, and the Seller's Property Disclosure form (not shown here) is attached. The Personal Property Agreement (not shown here) is filled out and attached. Now, the agreement is ready to be delivered to the listing broker for presentation to the sellers.

Acceptance Date and Binding Agreement Date

Note: The important box at the bottom of the page is not to be filled in until all negotiations are over and the last person has agreed. It then becomes a binding agreement when notice of this is received by the other party.

Narrative (continued) *When Franc's Fisher presents the offer to the Palmers at 2:00 P.M. on May 13th, they decide that it is not entirely acceptable. They want to receive at least $173,000 for their house, and they prefer to close on July lst. The buyer accepted this counteroffer the following morning.*

Negotiating the Purchase and Sale Agreement

Had Mr. Altman's offer been acceptable without any changes, the Palmers would have signed under the purchaser's signature. (For the seller, the agreement *does* require the signatures of anyone and everyone who is on the title to the property.) Then as soon as the buyer was given written notice of the acceptance, it would have become a binding agreement.

Because the offer was not acceptable, the sellers in this case had three choices. (1) They could simply reject it; (2) they could let the time limit expire, and it would cease to exist; or (3) they could make a counteroffer. They made a counteroffer.

It is important for licensees to make sure that any proposal made by one party to the other during a negotiation period, before a final agreement is reached, be made in writing. The Statute of Frauds would render any verbal agreement unenforceable.

Following are the two ways to prepare a counteroffer:

1. Licensee Franc's Fisher, on behalf of the Palmers, can cross out the price offered and substitute $173,000. She will also cross out the closing date and substitute July 1st. Then in both places where changes were made, the Palmers will each write their initials plus the time and date in the margin. They now sign the amended contract, and it goes back to the buyer. If Mr. Altman is also agreeable to making those two changes, he also places his initials, plus time and date beside them.

The Palmers or their agent are informed that Altman has accepted, and the contract has now become a binding agreement.

Note: The buyer, when presented with a counteroffer, also has choices. If he is not willing to accept the changes that the seller has proposed, he is under no obligation to continue negotiating and is entitled to the return of any earnest money. Or, he can present his own counteroffer, again crossing out the terms that did not suit him and initialing with time and date the changes. It then goes back to the seller.

Now that the ball is back in the sellers' court, the sellers might initial the last changes the buyer made, with time and date, and now we have an agreement. Or, the sellers can reject this latest effort out of hand, or they can make another counteroffer by the same crossing-out and initialing method described above.

It is possible for the offers and counteroffers to go back and forth any number of times, and one can easily see that all this crossing out, adding new words, with initials, time and date can soon make the form unreadable. At this point it is advisable to start over with a new agreement form.

2. Another method of making a counteroffer is in use where counteroffer forms are available. In this case, (referring again to the narrative), Franc's Fisher would *not* have the sellers sign on the original form and would add "See attached counteroffer form." to the special stipulations section.

We have numbered as #1 the counteroffer in Figure 11.1, noted the time and date (to show that we are still negotiating within the time limit that was placed on the offer), checked the box indicating it is from seller to buyer, and filled in the date and address of the original offer to make this, then, a part of that contract. Then, in the blank space we note the following:

*   The offered price is changed from $170,000 to $173,000.
*   The closing date is changed from June 15th to July 1st.

Placing a new time limit at this point is optional, and our sellers sign at the bottom of the counteroffer form, and the whole package goes back to the buyer for his signature. When the buyer signs, he also fills in the acceptance date and promptly notifies the sellers so the agreement has now become binding. If the buyer had *not* wished to accept the counteroffer, he might have taken a new copy of the same form and labeled it #2 and made a counter-counteroffer.

Note: The process of negotiating to reach a point where buyer and seller are in complete agreement can sometimes be very complex, no matter which method is used. It will demand the close and meticulous attention on the part of licensees representing either party. Once the agreement has become a binding contract, nothing can be added or changed on the form. If buyer and seller later agree to some further change, an amendment must be prepared.

The next step will be to deal with the contingencies. When those have been resolved, the transaction can move toward a closing.

Figure 11.1   Counteroffer

COUNTEROFFER #____1____

____2____ o'clock __P__ m. on the ____13th____ day of _____May_____, 20__02__ .

2002 Printing

This is a Counteroffer from: *[Select A or B below. The one not selected is not a part of this Agreement.]*

☒ **A. Seller to Buyer**   OR   ☐ **B. Buyer to Seller**

The following is a counteroffer to that certain offer to purchase or sell set forth in the Purchase and Sale Agreement dated _____**May**_____, 20__02__ ("Agreement") for the purchase and sale of real property located at:

1445 Grove Road, Atlanta   , Georgia   **30001**   .

All terms and conditions of the Agreement are agreed to and accepted by the undersigned with the express exception of the following:

    1. **Offered priced is changed to $173,000.00**
    2. **Closing date is changed to July 1, 2002.**

☐ **(Mark box if additional pages are attached.)**

The provisions set forth in this counteroffer shall control over any conflicting or inconsistent provisions set forth in the Agreement or any prior counteroffer. By signing below, all parties agree and acknowledge that they are accepting the Agreement subject to the terms and conditions set forth herein. While Buyer and Seller need to sign only this counteroffer for there to be an offer and acceptance of the Agreement (subject to the terms and conditions set forth herein), each party agrees if so requested by the other party, to promptly sign a conformed copy of the Agreement incorporating therein the terms and conditions set forth in this counteroffer.

Time Limit of Offer.
This instrument shall be regarded as an offer by the Buyer or Seller who first signs to the other and is open for acceptance until:
_____ o'clock _____M. on the _____ day of _____, 20_____ .

Francis Fisher	( )	**Arthur Altman**	
Selling Broker	MLS Office Code	Buyer's Signature:	SS/FEI#

By: _____
   Broker or Broker's Affiliated Licensee

Print or Type Name: **Francis Fisher**

Buyer's Signature: SS/FEI#

Print or Type Name:

Bus. Phone:_____ FAX #_____

Buyer's Signature: SS/FEI#

Print or Type Name:_____

Multiple Listing #

Peter Palmer
Seller's Signature: SS/FEI#

_____ (_____)
Listing Broker   MLS Office Code

Print or Type Name: **Peter Palmer**

By: _____

Patsy Palmer
Seller's Signature: SS/FEI#

   Broker or Broker's Affiliated Licensee

Print or Type Name: _____

Print or Type Name: **Patsy Palmer**

Bus. Phone:_____ FAX# _____

Acceptance Date
The above proposition is hereby accepted,   o'clock   M. on the day of   , 20

Binding Agreement Date
This instrument shall become a binding agreement on the date ("Binding Agreement Date") when notice of the acceptance of this Agreement has been received by offeror. The offeror shall promptly notify offeree when acceptance has been received.

CLOSING THE TRANSACTION

The closing of a real estate transaction is the procedure of finalizing the contract. Customs for this process differ quite widely from state to state but, in general, the party responsible for the closing must make sure that all of the terms and conditions of the contract have been met; must have the title searched to be sure that the seller is in a position to deliver marketable title; must prepare the documents that are to be signed, which might include loan documents, affidavits, and deeds; and must prepare the closing statement showing the final cost to the purchaser and the final net due to the seller.

In some states, closings are handled in *escrow* by a disinterested third party, who performs the necessary duties according to an *escrow agreement,* which is prepared and signed by the parties to the contract after their agreement has been finalized. In a few states, brokers might perform this escrow role, but in most cases the escrow agent is connected with an independent, licensed escrow company, or is associated with a law firm, a lender, or a title company. When the escrow agent has everything ready, the buyer and seller are called in (usually at separate times) to review the closing statement, sign documents, and, in the seller's case, deliver the deed, in the buyer's case, present the check.

In other states, it is customary to bring buyer and seller together to a closing in the office of a broker, a lender, or an attorney. In Georgia, for example, an attorney who represents the lender financing the buyer's purchase typically performs closing functions. It is important to note that this attorney does not represent either the seller or the buyer, and that they are entitled to have their own legal counsel on hand, if they wish.

To see a full Purchase and Sale Agreement or Counteroffer form, go to Appendix A.

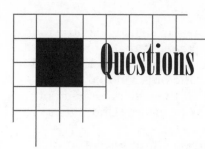

Questions

1. A broker holding an earnest money deposit
    a. holds the money to guarantee commission.
    b. is a trustee for the principal.
    c. must refund it to the purchaser on demand.
    d. may keep the money in a personal checking account.

2. Acceptance of an offer will not create a binding contract if the acceptance is
    a. absolute.
    b. complete.
    c. unconditional.
    d. qualified.

3. Johnson made an offer to Quick to purchase Quick's land. Quick accepted the offer but died before notifying Johnson. Under these circumstances, Johnson
    a. may enforce the contract.
    b. is protected by the statute of frauds.
    c. is protected by supervening illegality.
    d. will have to renegotiate the contract with Quick's heirs.

4. After the signing of a valid sales contract, purchaser Bob Clark discovered the land he was buying had no oil underneath it as he had thought. He may
    a. rescind because of his mistake.
    b. have to complete the transaction.
    c. sue for damages.
    d. make a counteroffer to the seller.

5. Which of the following would not be legally sufficient to support the consideration in a sales contract?
    a. Money
    b. Property
    c. Service
    d. Love and affection

6. Smith enters into a contract with Jones to buy Jones's land. Before closing, Smith changes her mind. When Brown, an acquaintance of Smith, says he would like to buy the land, Smith transfers her rights and obligations under the contract to Brown. Smith's actions are
    a. legal if not restricted by the contract.
    b. illegal whether mentioned in the contract or not.
    c. a novation.
    d. a breach of contract.

7. In a real estate purchase, the contract must include as an essential element
    a. the type of deed to be given.
    b. consideration.
    c. all encumbrances and liens of record.
    d. earnest money.

8. Robert made an offer to Dan who immediately made a counteroffer. Which of the following statements is false?
    a. Dan's counteroffer was a qualified acceptance.
    b. Robert may make yet another offer to Dan.
    c. Robert may call the whole thing off without penalty.
    d. If Robert refuses Dan's counteroffer, then Dan may accept the original offer and bind Robert to the contract.

9. The phrase "time is of the essence" in the contract means
    a. the contract is executed.
    b. the parties have reasonable leeway.
    c. each party gets one time out.
    d. time limits must be strictly observed.

10. If a purchaser breaches a valid and enforceable sales contract, the seller may at his or her option
    a. declare the contract forfeited and retain as liquidated damages any payments received from the buyer.
    b. affirm the contract and keep any payments received from the buyer.
    c. sue for special presentation.
    d. sue for the commission.

11. Which of the following will normally control the contents of a deed?
    a. The listing agreement
    b. The contract for sale
    c. The verbal representations of seller and broker
    d. The requests of the purchaser made to his/her attorney

12. If an offer is mailed to the seller, a contract exists when
    a. the buyer receives the acceptance in the mail.
    b. the agent receives the acceptance in the mail.
    c. the seller mails the acceptance.
    d. the seller calls the agent to inform the agent of the acceptance.

13. When there is a conflict between the wordings of portions of a sales contract, which of the following takes precedence over all other wording?
    a. Typewritten
    b. Printed
    c. Standard
    d. Handwritten

14. Seller Evans, having signed a contract for the sale of her home, verbally promised the buyer that the living room would be freshly painted. When the buyer moved in, the buyer discovered that the room had not been painted as promised. Under these circumstances
    a. the seller breached the sales contract.
    b. the buyer has no legal recourse.
    c. the seller must reimburse the buyer a reasonable amount for failure to paint the room.
    d. the buyer has a legal basis for a suit for damages.

15. Before being notified of the seller's acceptance, the prospective purchaser may
    a. withdraw the offer and receive a full refund of the earnest money deposit.
    b. not withdraw the offer until the seller has had a reasonable time to consider it.
    c. withdraw the offer and receive a full refund of the earnest money deposit unless the offer had a time limit which has not yet expired.
    d. withdraw the offer but forfeit the earnest money.

12 Property Management

Property management is one of the many specialized fields in the real estate business. It has become essential to the successful operation of many properties. The demand for professional property management services has grown enormously due to the increase in absentee ownership; the necessity for specialized knowledge; and the increase in the size of office buildings, apartment complexes, industrial parks, shopping centers, and mixed-use developments. Some firms work exclusively in property management. In other brokerage companies, management services are a separate department.

The National Association of REALTORS® has established the Institute of Real Estate Management (IREM) to improve the skills, ethical standards, and trade practices in the management field. Members must meet stringent educational and experience requirements to earn the highly respected professional designation of Certified Property Manager (CPM).

THE PROPERTY MANAGER

The professional property manager is much more than a rent collector, a building manager, or a person who shows apartments and handles complaints. Property management is an agency relationship. The property owner is the principal or client.

The manager is an agent with an agent's responsibility of absolute loyalty in seeking to maintain, preserve, and enhance the owner's investment in the property and to generate the highest possible net return from the property over its economic life. The complexities of the job require an understanding of business administration, accounting, income taxation, insurance, advertising, marketing, credit, purchasing, repairs and maintenance, the standards for evaluating income properties, and public relations. The manager must also be familiar with laws governing agency, leases, landlord/tenant relationships, and fair housing.

THE MANAGEMENT CONTRACT

The management contract establishes the agency relationship, giving the manager the authority to act on the owner's behalf. Georgia License Law requires it be established with a written agreement that contains as a minimum the following five items:

1. *Names of the Parties.* This would include the exact names of all owners of record and of the firm responsible for management.
2. *Property Description.* A precise description is needed.
3. *Manager's Authority and Responsibility.* The agreement should be specific as to the manager's authority in such areas as collecting rents, paying bills, hiring, firing, and supervising employees, and making necessary repairs. For example, is the owner's consent needed before authorizing repairs? Does the manager have the authority to set rental rates or offer rental incentives?
4. *Reporting.* The frequency and content of needed reports should be stated. The manager's most important report to the owner is the "operating statement." This report is an accounting of income and expense for a given period of time. It assists the owner in monitoring the manager's performance and serves as a basis for formulating management policy.
5. *Management Fee.* The management fee is negotiable. It can be a percentage of rents collected, a fixed dollar amount, or be calculated on any other basis agreed upon. Sometimes, additional fees are paid for new leases or for overseeing major repairs and alterations.

FUNCTIONS OF THE PROPERTY MANAGER

The goals of property owners are diverse. Some are mainly interested in income, some in tax shelter, and others in appreciation. The manager must clearly understand the owner's objectives in formulating a program for the property. The management functions may include the following:

Developing a Plan After signing a contract, the property manager's first step might be a thorough inspection of the property and of its operating statements in an attempt to answer the following questions:

- Are the premises attractive or are repairs needed?
- Is the vacancy rate high? If so, why?
- Is the vacancy rate low? Should the rents be higher?
- Has the building been well managed?

The next step would be to establish a rent schedule based on the supply and demand factors in the area. How important is the competition? Would an investment in upgrading, in remodeling, or in providing amenities make good economic sense?

The plan must also include an *operating budget* for the next 12 months, including

- projected rental income with allowances for vacancies and collection losses;
- fixed operating expenses such as taxes, insurance, and salaries;

- variable operating expenses such as utilities, maintenance, and management; and
- reserves for items that do not have to be replaced each year, such as carpet, furniture, and appliances.

Note: A budget is a guideline and must be adjusted from time to time on the basis of actual experience.

Marketing—Renting the Space

Marketing begins with the appearance of the property. Its condition must be appealing to the type of tenant desired. Then prospects are sought through any type of advertising or through using the services of a real estate broker. Sometimes rental incentives are offered. A sales center and staff might be needed.

Establishing some criteria for tenant selection is critical because it is a well-known fact that empty space is preferable to an unreliable or incompatible tenant. A manager will usually insist upon a credit report and references. Checking with the prospective tenant's present and former landlord can be enlightening. If the prospect proves to have the necessary qualifications, the final step is to enter into a lease agreement.

Collecting Rents

A lease will usually specify that rent must be paid in advance; will state the amount, the time, and the place of payment; and will provide for late payment penalties. If the rent is not paid when due, most managers use a system of payment notices to remind the tenant of the delinquent account. A firm collection policy helps to minimize past-due accounts, so the manager must be prepared to take the necessary legal action to collect the rent and/or evict the tenant.

Rents collected by a property manager are deposited in a trust account from which bills are paid in connection with the management of the property (utilities, repairs, maintenance, etc.). The balance of the rents less the management fee is remitted to the owner. Security deposits are also kept in a trust account and must remain untouched until the leases end.

Keeping Tenants

One of the best measures of a manager's performance is the ability to keep tenants. Turnover is costly. When a tenant moves out, there is not only loss of income in the interim but also the cost of reconditioning the space, advertising for a new tenant, and possibly paying a brokerage commission for leasing. In keeping tenants happy, management must provide and enforce appropriate rules, carry out a well-managed program of preventive and corrective maintenance, and be responsive to complaints.

Property Maintenance

A good maintenance program is one of the manager's most important functions. Regular inspections must be made to identify needed repairs and to make sure that essential systems such as heating and cooling operate continuously. The best maintenance programs stress preventive measures rather than dealing with remedial action. The manager's task includes hiring employees or contractors as needed and buying necessary materials and supplies. As consumer demands change, the manager must recognize that renovations might be in order to modernize the building and will supervise those renovations.

Kickbacks or commissions to property managers from suppliers and sub-contractors are prohibited unless authorized in writing by the owner.

Accounting and Reporting

As agent for the owner, the property manager is accountable for all rents and security deposits received and must keep them in a trust account. Periodic operating statements are prepared and furnished to the owner. At this time there are a number of software programs that facilitate the bookkeeping task. The manager is also responsible for obtaining insurance to cover losses from fire, casualty, and public liability.

Sale of the Property

If the property is sold, the management contract is terminated. If the new owner wishes to retain the same property manager, a new contract must be signed.

THE PROPERTY MANAGEMENT AGREEMENT

The Leasing/Management agreement is an agency contract in which a property owner, the principal, employs a broker, the agent. All of the aspects of agency law apply. It is important that the terms of this agreement be in writing to be enforceable and to prevent any misunderstandings.

We are using a form that serves two purposes. It authorizes the agent to find tenants, and then it also authorizes the agent to take care of the day-to-day oversight of the property. It could be used for one or the other or both.

Narrative *Two brothers, Bill and Bob Benson, have bought and remodeled an apartment building with 12 2-bedroom units. It will be ready for occupancy on July 1st of this year, so on June 1st they are entering into an agreement with Broker Charles Tracy to find tenants and also to oversee the operation of the building on their behalf. The building is located at 1111 Legion Way, Atlanta, Georgia, 30077. The legal description is Land Lot 444 of the 22nd District, 1st Section of Fulton County Georgia, and is Lot 1 in Block A of the Fairweather Subdivision as shown in Plat Book 765 on Page 321 in the Fulton County records.*

The agreement is to last for 18 months starting June 1st of this year, and Broker Tracy is to be paid 8 percent of rents collected as well as a $250 one-time fee for each new lease signed within 90 days of the beginning of this agreement. Tenants must sign a one-year lease, paying $1,100 per month for each apartment. A $1,000 security deposit is to be held in Broker Tracy's trust account. Broker Tracy is to pay authorized expenses and his compensation out of rents received and remits the balance to the owners each month at their office address, 9988 Broad Street, Atlanta, Georgia, 30022. The owners' approval will be required for any repairs costing in excess of $250. Owner will deposit $500 in the trust account for emergency repairs.

Pets are not to be prohibited. Two parking spaces will be allotted to each apartment, to be used for operative passenger vehicles only. It is Broker Tracy's policy to represent landlords, tenants, and to practice dual agency on occasion.

EXCLUSIVE LEASING/MANAGEMENT AGREEMENT

2002 Printing

State law prohibits Broker from representing Owner as a client without first entering into a written agreement with Owner under O.C.G.A. § 10-6A-1 et. seq.

This Agreement, made and entered into this _____**1st**_____ day of _____**June**_____, 20___**02**___, by and between _____**Bill and Bob Benson**_____ (hereinafter referred to as "Owner") and_____**Charles Tracy**_____ (hereinafter referred to as "Broker");

WHEREAS, Owner owns that certain real estate property described as follows:
All that tract of land lying and being in Land Lot _____**444**_____ of the _____**22nd**_____ District, _____**1st**_____ Section of _____**Fulton**_____ County, Georgia, and being known as Address _____**1111 Legion Way**_____ _____, City _____**Atlanta, Georgia**_____, Zip Code _____**30077**_____, according to the present system of numbering in and around this area, being more particularly described as Lot _____**1**_____, Block _____**A**_____, Unit ___**N/A**___, Phase/Section ___**N/A**___ of _____**Fairweather**_____ subdivision, as recorded in Plat Book _____**756**_____, Page ___**321**___, _____**Fulton**_____ County, Georgia, records together with all fixtures, landscaping, improvements, and appurtenances, all being hereinafter collectively referred to as the "Property." The full legal description of the Property is the same as is recorded with the Clerk of the Superior Court of the county in which the Property is located and is made a part of this Agreement by reference.

WHEREAS, Owner desires to retain Broker as Owner's agent to exclusively rent, lease, operate, and manage the property for and in behalf of the Owner;

NOW THEREFORE, in consideration of the premises and mutual covenants herein set forth, the parties agree as follows:

Opening Paragraph   In line #1, we note the date of reaching the agreement and the names of the owners and of the broker. Then follows the legal description. It states that the owners are retaining the broker's services to rent, lease, and/or manage the property on behalf of the owners.

1.   **Term.** Broker shall have the exclusive right to lease and manage the Property for the period of _____**18 months**_____ beginning on the ___**1st**___ day of _____**June**_____, ___**2002**___. If Owner terminates this Agreement, Owner shall pay Broker all fees which would be due both from the present and future months by virtue of any unexpired rental agreement in effect at the time of termination. Broker may deduct the full amount of such fees from any monies coming to Broker which would be due Owner.

2.   **Leases.** Broker is authorized to enter into a lease of the Property on Owner's behalf if it is for a term of no more than _____**12**_____ months or less than _____**12**_____ months at a monthly rental of at least $_____**1,100.00**_____. The Property may be occupied by a tenant obtained by Broker as of _____**July 1**_____, 20 ___**02**___. Any such lease will be in writing on Broker's standard lease form then in use.

1. Term   Paragraph #1 sets forth the term of this agreement and protects the broker's right to be compensated if the landlord should terminate the agreement before the end of the term.

2. Leases   In paragraph #2, it is stated that tenants are to be given one-year leases starting on July 1st, at a monthly rental of at least $1,100.

3. **Broker's Authority.** The Owner hereby gives the Broker the following authority and powers and agrees to assume the expenses in connection with:

A. To exclusively advertise the Property for rental and to display "for rent" signs thereon; to sign, renew, and cancel leases for the Property; to collect rents due or to become due and give receipts therefor; to terminate tenancies and to sign and serve in the name of the Owner such notices as are appropriate; to institute and prosecute actions; to evict tenants and to recover possession of the Property; to sue in the name of the Owner and recover rents and other sums due; and when expedient, to settle, compromise, and release such actions or lawsuits or reinstate such tenancies.

B. To make or cause to be made and supervise repairs and alterations, and to do decorating on the Property; to purchase supplies and pay bills therefor; the Broker agrees to secure the prior approval of the Owner on all expenditures in excess of $ __250__ for any one item, except monthly or recurring operating charges and/or emergency repairs in excess of the maximum, if in the opinion of the Broker such repairs are necessary to protect the Property from damage or to maintain services to the tenants as called for in their leases.

C. To hire, discharge and supervise all contractors and/or employees required for the operation and maintenance of the Property; it being agreed that any employees hired shall be deemed employees of the Owner and not the Broker, and that the Broker may perform any of its duties through Owner's attorneys, agents, or employees and shall not be responsible for their acts, defaults, or negligence if reasonable care has been exercised in their appointment and retention.

D. To make contracts for electricity, gas, fuel, water, telephone, window cleaning, trash or rubbish hauling and other services as the Broker shall deem advisable; the Owner to assume the obligations of any contract so entered into the termination of this Agreement.

E. To contract with others, including affiliates of broker or companies owned by broker, to perform services including, but not limited to, repairs, maintenance, accounting, data processing, record keeping, legal fees and court costs. Any such arrangement with affiliates or companies owned by Broker will be on terms fair and reasonable to the Owner and no less favorable than could reasonably be realized with unaffiliated persons or companies. The Owner is hereby aware that Broker may deduct these expenses from the monies coming to Broker that are due to the Owner.

F. To institute and prosecute legal actions and proceedings in Owner's name and behalf to terminate leases for cause, to remove tenants from Property, to recover from damage to the Property, and for such purposes, Broker may employ attorneys and incur court costs and litigation costs at Owner's expense any and all of these things. Broker in his discretion is also authorized to settle or compromise any such legal actions or proceedings.

4. **Compensation.** Broker shall be compensated on the following basis:

A. For Leasing: $ __250.00__ or __N/A__ % of monthly rent.

B. For Management: $ __N/A__ or __8__ % of monthly rent.

C. For Refinancing: $ __N/A__ .

D. For Modernization: $ __N/A__ plus _____ % of expenditures

    For Restoration: $ __N/A__ plus _____ % of expenditures

    For Repairs: $ _____ plus _____ % of expenditures

E. Other:_____

3. Broker's Authority

Paragraph #3 outlines the broker's authority as follows:

A. To represent the owner in advertising the property, signing, renewing, and canceling leases, collecting rents, evicting tenants, and bringing suit in the owner's name when necessary.

B. To make repairs and alterations as needed. Costs in excess of $250 are to be approved by the owner except in an emergency.

C. To hire, fire, and supervise employees and contractors as needed.

D. To contract for needed utilities and services.

E. To contract with outside parties for such things as repairs, accounting, and legal advice.

F. To institute and prosecute legal actions, or to settle or compromise disputes.

4. Compensation

Paragraph #4 sets forth the broker's compensation. In our narrative there are only two fees noted, one for leasing and one for management.

5. **Sale of Property**. If Owner sells the Property to a tenant (or spouse or roommate of such tenant) obtained by Broker, either during the term of the lease or thereafter, Owner will pay Broker a commission of **N/A** % of the price for which the Property is sold. This obligation shall survive the expiration or termination of this Agreement.

6. **Non-Discrimination**. Owner and Broker are subject to state and federal civil rights and discrimination laws, which prohibit discrimination on the basis of race, color, religion, sex, familial status, handicap, or national origin. Neither Owner nor Broker will perform any act which would have the effect of discriminating against any person in violation of law.

7. **Emergency Repairs**. Broker is authorized to make such emergency repairs to the Property as Broker reasonably believes to be necessary to protect the Property from damage or to maintain services to a tenant for which a lease provides. Owner has paid to and will maintain with Broker the sum of $ **500.00** as a deposit for the cost of such emergency, but expenditures of such repairs are not limited to that amount if for reasons of necessity Broker must spend more. The deposit money shall be deposited in Broker's escrow account with Broker retaining the interest if the account is interest-bearing. In the event any deposit money check is not honored, for any reason, by the bank upon it is drawn, Owner shall deliver good funds to Holder within three days of the bank's notice to Broker. In the event Owner does not timely deliver good funds, the Tenant, in his sole discretion, shall have the right to terminate this Agreement by giving written notice to the Owner. In that event, Owner shall promptly reimburse Broker for the cost of all other emergency repairs which Broker pays for or for which Broker is obligated, but Owner understands that Broker is under no duty to make expenditures in excess of the amount of the deposit.

8. **Condition of Property**. Owner certifies that unless provided otherwise herein, all systems and furnished appliances are in working condition. Owner certifies that the Property is in good and habitable condition now and Owner, will at all times, be responsible for the maintenance of the Property in a good habitable condition, and in compliance with all applicable laws, ordinances and regulations of all government authorities. Upon the execution of this agreement Owner will provide two sets of keys for the Property and ensure that the Property is clean and the grounds are in good condition.
Owner shall maintain adequate fire and extended insurance coverage on the Property, and Owner will, at all times, maintain landlord's liability insurance for Owner and will cause Broker to be named as additional insured under such liability insurance. Owner will provide Broker with evidence of such insurance coverage prior to date of occupancy of tenant.
Has your property flooded three or more times in the last five years?   ☐Yes ☒No

9. **Receipt and Payment of Funds**. Broker is authorized to deposit all rent received from the Property in a trust account maintained by Broker for that purpose. However, Broker will not be held liable in event of bankruptcy or failure of a depository. Broker shall render Owner, on a monthly basis, a detailed accounting of funds received and disbursed in Owner's behalf and shall remit to Owner the balance of such funds, if any, remaining after Broker deducts any and all commissions, Management fees and other charges due Broker or other parties in Owner's behalf. In the event the disbursements shall be in excess of the rents collected by the Broker, the Owner hereby agrees to pay such excess promptly upon demand of the Broker. Broker to prepare IRS Form 1099 and any other tax related forms or documents as may be required by law. Broker is further authorized to make the following payments for Owner on a monthly basis; however, Broker shall be under no obligation to make such payments if there are insufficient funds on hand in Owner's account with Broker, it being understood that Broker will promptly notify Owner if such funds are not on hand. The Broker is hereby instructed and authorized to pay mortgage indebtedness, property and employees taxes, special assessments, and to place fire, liability, steam boiler, pressure vessel, or any other insurance required, and the Broker is hereby directed to accrue and pay for same from the Owner's funds, with the following exceptions:_____**None**_____

5. Sale of Property

Paragraph #5 provides for a commission for the broker if the landlord sells the property to the tenant. (Our narrative did not contain any such agreement.)

6. Non-Discrimination

Paragraph #6 obliges both owner and broker to abide by all the fair housing laws.

7. Emergency Repairs

Paragraph #7 gives the broker the right to make repairs in an emergency and provides for the owner to place a deposit in the trust account to cover this expense.

8. Condition of Property

In Paragraph #8 the owner is attesting that the property is in good condition, free of environmental hazards; and that the owner will be responsible for keeping it that way. The tenant is to receive two sets of keys. Owner will keep the property insured and attests that it has not flooded three or more times in the past five years.

9. Receipt and Payment of Funds

Paragraph #9 obligates the broker to keep receipts in a trust account, to disburse the balance to the owner monthly as long as the balance in the account is sufficient, and to pay out of the account carrying charges such as the mortgage payment and the taxes.

---

10. <u>Miscellaneous Charges</u>. Broker is authorized to charge and collect from the tenant for Broker's own account, charges of late payment of rent, bad check processing, credit reports, and such other matters as Broker may deem necessary, and to deposit any security deposits into an interest-bearing account for Broker's own behalf.

11. <u>Indemnity</u>. Owner agrees to save the Broker harmless from all damage suits in connection with the leasing and management of the Property and from liability from injury suffered by an employee or other person whomsoever, and to carry, at his own expense, necessary public liability and worker's compensation insurance adequate to protect the interest of the parties hereto, which policies shall be so written as to protect the Broker in the same manner and to the same extent they protect the Owner, and will name the Broker as coinsured. The Broker shall not be liable for any error of judgement or for any mistake, fact of law, or for anything which it may do or refrain from doing hereinafter, except in cases of willful misconduct or gross negligence. Notwithstanding any other provisions to the contrary, Broker shall under no circumstances have any liability greater than the compensation actually paid to Broker hereunder including commissions.

12. <u>Other Provisions</u>.
    A. **Binding Effect, Entire Agreement, Modification, Assignment:** This Agreement shall be for the benefit of, and be binding upon, the parties hereto, their heirs, successors, legal representatives and permitted assigns. This Agreement constitutes the sole and entire agreement between the parties hereto and no modification or assignment of this Agreement shall be binding unless signed by all parties to this Agreement. No representation, promise, or inducement not included in this Agreement shall be binding upon any party hereto. Any assignee shall fulfill all the terms and conditions of this Agreement.
    B. **Survival of Agreement:** All conditions or stipulations not fulfilled at time of closing shall survive the closing until such time as the conditions or stipulations are fulfilled.
    C. **Governing Law:** This Agreement is intended as a contract for the purchase and sale of real property and shall be interpreted in accordance with the laws of the State of Georgia.
    D. **Time of Essence:** Time is of the essence of this Agreement.
    E. **Terminology:** As the context may require in this Agreement: (1) the singular shall mean the plural and vice versa; and (2) all pronouns shall mean and include the person, entity, firm, or corporation to which they relate.
    F. **Responsibility to Cooperate:** All parties agree to timely take such actions and produce, execute, and/or deliver such information and documentation as is reasonably necessary to carry out the responsibilities and obligations of this Agreement.
    G. **Notices.** Except as otherwise provided herein, all notices, including demands, offers, counteroffers, acceptances, and amendments required or permitted hereunder shall be in writing, signed by the party giving the notice and delivered to the party at the address set forth below (or such other address as the party may provide in writing) either: (1) in person, (2) by an overnight delivery service, prepaid, (3) by facsimile transmission (FAX) (provided that an original of the notice shall be promptly sent thereafter if so requested by the party receiving the same) or (4) by the United States Postal Service, postage prepaid, registered or certified return receipt requested. The parties agree that a faxed signature of a party constitutes an original signature binding upon that party. Notice shall be deemed to have been given as of the date and time it is actually received. Notwithstanding the above, notice by **FAX** shall be deemed to have been given as of the date and time it is transmitted if the sending FAX produces a written confirmation with the date, time and telephone number to which the notice was sent. Receipt of notice by the Broker representing a party as a client shall be deemed to be notice to that party for all purposes herein, except in transactions where the Broker is practicing designated agency, in which case, receipt of notice by the designated agent representing a party as a client shall be required to constitute notice. All references to any notice required to be given or due dates for rent payments shall be strictly construed.

    Owner's address: _____   Broker's Address: _____

    _____   _____

    _____   _____

    _____   _____

    Fax #:_____   Fax #:_____

13. <u>Disclaimer.</u> Owner acknowledges that Owner has not relied upon any advice, representations or statements of Broker and waives and shall not assert any claims against Broker involving advice, representations or statements not specifically referenced in the Special Stipulations. Owner agrees that Broker shall not be responsible to advise Owner on any matter, including but not limited to the following: insurance, any matter which could have been revealed through a survey, title search or inspection of the Property; the condition of the Property, any portion thereof, or any item therein; the necessity or cost of any repairs to the Property; hazardous or toxic materials or substances; the tax or legal consequences of any lease transaction; the appraised or future value of the Property; any condition(s) existing off the Property which may affect the Property; the creditworthiness of prospective tenants; the uses and zoning of the Property whether permitted or proposed; and any matter relating to crime and security in and around the Property. Owner acknowledges that Broker is not an expert with respect to the above matters and that, if any of these matters or any other matters are of concern to Owner, Owner should seek independent expert advice relative thereto.

10. Miscellaneous Charges
Paragraph #10 authorizes the broker to collect certain charges for his own account and to keep security deposits in interest-bearing accounts with the interest accruing to the broker.

11. Indemnity
In Paragraph #11 the owners are agreeing to indemnify the broker if any claim arises out of this agreement. It also limits the broker's liability.

12. Other Provisions
Paragraph #12 contains the standard legal language to the effect that this is the entire agreement, binding on both parties; that it cannot be assigned without consent; that the time limits are to be strictly interpreted; and as to language.

It also outlines the acceptable means for sending notices, in person, by overnight delivery, by FAX, or by U.S. Post Office registered and certified mail.

13. Disclaimer
Paragraph #13 is the disclaimer, holding that the owner cannot sue the broker for matters outside of the broker's expertise.

---

14. **Broker's Policy on Agency.** Unless Broker indicates below that Broker is not offering a specific agency relationship, the types of agency relationships offered by Broker are seller agency, buyer agency, designated agency, dual agency, Owner agency, and tenant agency.

The agency relationship(s), if any, **NOT** offered by Broker include the following_____

Dual Agency Disclosure: [*Applicable only if Broker's agency policy is to practice dual agency*] Owner does hereby consent to Broker acting in a dual agency capacity in transactions in which Broker is representing as clients both the Owner and a tenant interested in or leasing the Property, and Broker is not acting in a designated agency capacity. By entering this Agreement, Owner acknowledges that Owner understands that Owner does not have to consent to dual agency, is doing so voluntarily, and that this brokerage engagement has been read and understood. In serving as a dual agent, Broker is representing two parties as clients whose interests are or at times could be different or even adverse. As a dual agent, Broker will disclose to both parties all adverse material facts relevant to the transaction actually known to the dual agent except for information made confidential by request or instructions from client and which is not required to be disclosed by law. Owner hereby directs Broker, while acting as a dual agent to keep confidential and not reveal to the tenant any information which would materially and adversely affect the tenant's negotiating position. Broker or Broker's affiliated licensees will timely disclose to each client the nature of any material relationship the broker and the broker's affiliated licensees have with the other client or clients, other than that incidental to the transaction. A material relationship shall mean any actually known personal, familial, or business relationship between Broker and a client which would impair the ability of Broker to exercise fair and independent judgment relative to another client. The other party whom Broker may represent in the event of dual agency may or may not be identified at the time Owner enters into this Agreement. If any party is identified after the Agreement and has a material relationship with Broker, then Broker shall timely provide to Owner a disclosure of the nature of such relationship.

15. **Limits on Broker's Authority and Responsibility.** Owner acknowledges and agrees that Broker: (a) may show other properties to prospective tenants who are interested in Owner's Property; (b) is not an expert with regard to matters that could be revealed through a survey, title search, or inspection; the condition of property; the necessity, or cost of repairs; hazardous or toxic materials; the availability and cost of utilities or community amenities; conditions existing off the property that may affect the property; uses and zoning of the property; the appraised or future value of the property; termites and wood-destroying organisms; building products and construction techniques; the tax or legal consequences of a contemplated transaction; and matters relating to financing (and if these matters are of concern to Owner, Owner is hereby advised to seek independent expert advice on any of these matters of concern to Owner); (c) shall owe no duties to Owner nor have any authority to act on behalf of Owner other than what is set forth in this Agreement; (d) may make all disclosures required by law; (e) may disclose all information about the Property to others; and (f) shall, under no circumstances, have any liability greater than the amount of the real estate commission paid hereunder to Broker (excluding any commission amount, paid to a cooperating real estate broker, if any).

16. **Required State Law Disclosures.** (a) Broker agrees to keep all information which Owner asks to be kept confidential by express request or instruction unless the Owner permits such disclosure by subsequent work or conduct or such disclosure is required by law; (b) Broker may not knowingly give customers false information; (c) In the event of a conflict between Broker's duty not to give customers false information and the duty to keep the confidences of Owner, the duty not to give customers false information shall prevail; (d) Unless specified below, Broker has no other known agency relationships with other parties which would conflict with any interests of Owner (with the exception that Broker may represent other tenants, and Owners, buyers and sellers in buying, selling or leasing property).

14. Broker's Policy on Agency

Paragraph #14 contains the required agency disclosure.

15. Limits on Broker's Authority and Responsibility

Paragraph #15 limits both the broker's authority and liability.

16. Required State Law Disclosures

Paragraph #16 contains the following three disclosures required by BRRETA:

1. The duty of confidentiality
2. The obligation to avoid giving false information
3. The requirement that any conflict of interest be disclosed by the broker

---

SPECIAL STIPULATIONS: The following Special Stipulations, if conflicting with any preceding paragraph, shall control.

1. Owner's approval required for repairs exceeding $250.00.
2. Pets are allowed.
3. 2 parking spaces alloted to each apartment.

☐ **(Mark box if additional pages are attached.)**

BY SIGNING THIS AGREEMENT, OWNER ACKNOWLEDGES THAT: (1) OWNER HAS REAL ALL PROVISIONS MADE HEREIN; (2) OWNER UNDERSTANDS ALL SUCH PROVISIONS AND DISCLOSURES AND HAS ENTERED INTO THIS AGREEMENT VOLUNTARILY; AND (3) OWNER IS NOT SUBJECT TO A CURRENT LEASING/MANAGEMENT AGREEMENT WITH ANY OTHER BROKER.

> RECEIPT OF A COPY OF THIS AGREEMENT IS HEREBY ACKNOWLEDGED BY OWNER.
>
> The above proposition is hereby accepted, _____ o'clock _____ M., on the _____ day of _____, 20_____.

I certify that I have read and understand the above printed matter. This __**1st**__ day of _____**June**_____, 20__**02**__.

_____**Charles Tracy**_____ (_____)
Listing Broker   MLS Office Code

By:_____
   Broker or Broker's Affiliated Licensee

Print or Type Name:_____

Bus. Phone:_____ FAX #_____

_____

Bill Benson
Owner Signature   SS/FEI #
Print or Type Name:_____

_____
Address

_____

Bill Benson
Owner Signature   SS/FEI #
Print or Type Name: _____

Address_____

Special Stipulations   The special stipulation space is for adding anything that was not already made clear in the form. If more space is needed one just writes, "See attached," and incorporates another sheet of paper into the contract. In this case we have added three stipulations, having to do with repairs needed authorization, the pet prohibition, and the parking spaces.

Now when both parties sign on the lines indicated, the contract has become a binding agreement.

To see a full Exclusive Leasing/Management Agreement, go to Appendix A.

Questions

1. When real estate under a property management contract is sold, the contract
   a. expires with the conveyance.
   b. binds the new owner.
   c. is subject to termination at the option of either party with proper notice.
   d. is valid but unenforceable.

2. The property manager has the right to enter the leased premises
   a. at reasonable times to make necessary repairs.
   b. upon reasonable notice to the tenant.
   c. at reasonable times and upon reasonable notice.
   d. only with the tenant's permission, unless the lease provides otherwise.

3. As part of the property manager's regular duties, the manager should develop a rent schedule based upon
   a. the highest rent in the market.
   b. the rental level the tenant says he can pay.
   c. the rental history of the premises.
   d. what landlords are charging for rent in other cities.

4. To insure against a tenant proving to be unsatisfactory, it is a good idea to
   a. check with former employers.
   b. ask for a credit report.
   c. ask for a police report.
   d. check with former wives.

13 Writing Leases

THE LEASE

In this chapter we are using a lease form that contains considerable detail because misunderstandings are best avoided by making sure that there is a meeting of the minds on as many points as possible. Even so, this form would not be adequate for a more complex commercial transaction. The parties to that type of lease would probably use the services of an attorney. Even though an oral lease for one year or less might be legally binding, it is always a prudent idea to have the lease in writing.

Narrative *On the 10th of July, Manuel and Lola Chavez are working with a sales agent at the Crestview Ravine Apartments and are planning to enter into a one-year lease beginning on August 1st. The three-bedroom apartment they have chosen is number 514 in Building A, located at 1400 Crestview Ravine Drive in Atlanta, Georgia. The zip code is 30555. They agree to pay $1,100 per month and also to pay for all utilities except for sewer, water, and garbage disposal. They will not be responsible for lawn care.*

George Hopkins, the sales agent for Crestview Ravine Apartments, is a salaried employee of Crestview Realty, Inc., that has a contract to manage the apartments for the Crestview Ravine Apartments Corp. Crestview Realty, Inc., is paid a flat fee of $800 for each new lease signed. Mr. Hopkins informs the prospective tenants of the following:

A security deposit equal to one month's rent is required. (The security deposit will be kept in the managing broker's trust account at the SouthSide Bank, account #44556). Rent payments are due in advance. A tenant who is not in default on rent payments may have early termination for a fee equal to one month's rent. If the rent payment is late, a fee of $100 is charged, effective five days after rent is due. The fee for a returned check is $25.

A $150 re-key fee is charged if all keys are not returned upon termination of the lease. No more than five persons can occupy the apartment. (The Chavez family includes three children.) No pets are permitted.

The legal address of the apartment is Land Lot 111, 7th District, Crestview County, Georgia, being Lot 11, Block A, Building A, Unit 514 in the Crestview

Ravine Apartments, Inc., recorded in Plat Book 444, page 9 of the Crestview County records.

LEASE FOR
RESIDENTIAL PROPERTY
(NOT TO BE USED FOR LEASE/PURCHASE TRANSACTIONS)

[To be Used When Broker is Managing Property]

2002 Printing

In consideration of the mutual covenants set forth herein, this Lease is entered into this __10th__ day of _____July_____ , 20 __02__ between __Crestview Ravine Apts. Inc.__ , (hereinafter "Landlord") and _____Manuel & Lola Chavez_____ , (hereinafter "Tenant") Landlord leases to Tenant, and Tenant leases from Landlord, the Property described as follows:
All that tract of land lying and being in Land Lot __111__ of the __7th__ District, __N/A__ Section of **Crestview** County, Georgia, and being known as Address _____1400 Crestview Ravine Drive_____ , City, ____Atlanta____ , Georgia, Zip Code __30555__ , according to the present system of numbering in and around this area, being more particularly described as Lot __11__ , Block __A__ , Unit __514__ , Building __A__ , of __Crestview Ravine Apartments__ subdivision, as recorded in Plat Book __444__ , Page __9__ , __Crestview__ County, Georgia, records together with all fixtures, landscaping, improvements, and appurtenances, all being hereinafter collectively referred to as the "Property." The full legal description of the Property is the same as is recorded with the Clerk of the Superior Court of the county in which the Property is located and is made a part of this Lease by reference.

1. **TERM.** The initial term of this Lease shall be __12__ months __N/A__ days beginning on __August 1__ , 20 __02__ ("Commencement Date"), through and including __July 31__ , 20 __02__ .

Opening Paragraph

The date we have entered on line #1 is not the day that the lease is to begin, but the date when the contract is being written. Following that, we have entered the names of the landlord and of the tenants. The legal description of the property and street address are entered as given, always remembering to put "N/A" on lines where we have nothing else to enter. The use of just the street address is insufficient.

---

2. **POSSESSION.** If Landlord is unable to deliver possession of the Property on the Commencement Date, rent shall be abated on a daily basis until possession is granted. If possession is not granted within seven days of the Commencement Date, Tenant may terminate this Lease in which event Landlord shall promptly refund all deposits to Tenant. Landlord shall not be liable for delays in the delivery of possession to Tenant.

3. **RENT.** Tenant shall pay rent in advance in the sum of _____Eleven hundred_____ Dollars ($__1,100.00__) per month on the first day of each month during the Lease Term, at the address set forth in the Other Provisions Paragraph (or at such other place as may be designated from time to time by Landlord in writing). If the Commencement Date begins on the 2nd day through the last day of any month, the rent shall be prorated for that portion of the month and shall be paid at the time of leasing the Property.

4. **LATE PAYMENT; SERVICE CHARGE FOR RETURNED CHECKS.** Rent not paid in full by the fifth day of the month shall be late. Landlord has no obligation to accept any rent not received by the fifth of the month. If late payment is made and Landlord accepts the same, the payment must be in the form of cash, cashier's check or money order and must include a late charge of $__100.00__ and, if applicable, a service charge for any returned check of $__25.00__ . Landlord reserves the right to refuse to accept personal checks from Tenant after one or more of Tenant's personal checks have been returned by the bank unpaid.

---

1. Term

In paragraph #1 we note the term of the lease, one year beginning August 1st.

2. Possession

In paragraph #2 the tenant is guaranteed possession when the lease begins; and rent will be prorated on a daily basis if there is a delay. The tenant can cancel the lease and receive a refund of deposits, if the occupancy is delayed for seven days or more. The landlord is not accountable for delay in giving possession.

3. Rent   Paragraph #3 specifies the amount of rent due and the fact that it is in default if not received within five days of the due date. The language in this paragraph relating to prorating rent, if the lease begins on any day except the 1st of the month, does not apply. (The landlord likes to have all rent coming in on the 1st of the month.)

4. Late Payment; Service Charge for Returned Checks   Paragraph #4 shows the late fee to be charged and the fee for a returned check.

5. Security Deposit To Be Held by Landlord or Broker   Paragraph #5 relates to the security deposit.

A. Landlord holding security deposit. This paragraph does not apply since the deposit is not being turned over to the landlord.

B. Broker holding security deposit. We must fill in the amount of security deposit the tenant is paying on line #1 and show that the broker is holding the security deposit, not the landlord. This paragraph also describes the broker's duties regarding the refund of the deposit.

6. Move-In/Move-Out Inspection   Paragraph #6 provides for inspections to be made when the tenant moves in and again when the tenant moves out. This protects the tenant from being charged for damages that might have already occurred before the lease began.

7. Repairs and Maintenance   In Paragraph #7 the landlord agrees to make "major repairs" (electrical, plumbing, heating, cooling, built-in appliances, and structural defects) within a reasonable time. The tenant is responsible for "incidental" repairs.

---

5. <u>SECURITY DEPOSIT TO BE HELD BY LANDLORD OR BROKER</u>. *[Select Section A or B below. The Section not marked shallnot be part of this Agreement]*

☐   A. <u>Landlord Holding Security Deposit</u>.

(1) Tenant agrees to deposit _____ Dollars ($_____) cash, money order and/or check with Landlord before taking possession of the Property as security for Tenant's fulfillment of the conditions of this Lease ("Security Deposit"). The Security Deposit shall be held by Landlord as follows: *[Select Section (a) or (b) below. The section not marked shall not be part of this Agreement.]*

☐   (a) <u>Ten or fewer units owned by Landlord or Landlord's spouse or minor children</u>. The Security Deposit is to be deposited in *[check one]* (___) Landlord's escrow/trust bank account or (___) in the general account of Landlord at _____bank, and not in a separate escrow/trust account. If the Security Deposit is to be deposited in the Landlord's general account, Tenant acknowledges and agrees that Landlord shall have the right to use such funds for whatever purpose Landlord sees fit, and such funds will not be segregated or set apart in any manner. Interest earned on such account(s) shall accrue to and be retained by Landlord.

☐   (b) <u>More than ten units owned by Landlord or Landlord's spouse or minor children</u>. The Security Deposit shall be deposited in Landlord's escrow/trust account (Account#_____) at _____ bank. Interest earned from such account(s), if any, shall accrue to and be retained by Landlord.

(2) Tenant recognizes and accepts the risk of depositing the Security Deposit with Landlord. Tenant acknowledges that Tenant has not relied upon the advice of Broker or Broker's Affiliated Licensees in deciding to pay such security deposit to Landlord. Landlord and Tenant acknowledge and agree that:

    (a) Broker has no responsibility for, or control over, the Security Deposit deposited with Landlord;

    (b) Broker has no ability or obligation to insure that the Security Deposit is properly applied or deposited;

    (c) The disposition of the Security Deposit is the sole responsibility of Landlord and Tenant as herein provided; and

    (d) Broker has no knowledge of the financial condition or financial stability of Landlord. Landlord and Tenant agree to indemnify and hold harmless Broker and Broker's affiliated licensees against all claims, damages, losses, expenses or liability arising from the handling of the Security Deposit by Landlord.

(3) The Security Deposit will be returned to Tenant within thirty days after Property is vacated if:

    (a) Lease term has expired or Lease has been terminated in writing by the mutual consent of both parties;

    (b) All monies due Landlord by Tenant have been paid;

    (c) Property is not damaged and is left in its original condition, normal wear and tear excepted;

    (d) All keys have been returned; and

    (e) Tenant is not in default under any of the terms of this Lease.

(4) Within one month after termination of this Lease or Tenant's vacating of the property, whichever is later, Landlord shall return Security Deposit to Tenant, after deducting any sum which Tenant owes Landlord hereunder, or any sum which Landlord may expend to repair arising out of or related to Tenant's occupancy hereunder, abandonment of the Property or default in this Lease (provided Landlord attempts to mitigate such actual damages), including but no limited to any repair, replacement, cleaning or painting of the Property reasonably necessary due to the negligence, carelessness, accident, or abuse of Tenant or invitee, guests, or members of Tenant's household. In the event Landlord elects to retain any part of the Security Deposit, Landlord shall provide Tenant with a written statement setting forth the reasons for the retention of any portion of the Security Deposit, including the damages for which any portion of the Security Deposit is retained. The use and application of the Security Deposit by Landlord shall be at the discretion of the Landlord. Appropriation by Landlord of all or part of the Security Deposit shall not be an exclusive remedy for Landlord, but shall be cumulative, and in addition to all remedies of Landlord at law or under this Lease. The Tenant may not apply the Security Deposit to any rent payment.

☐   **B. Broker Holding Security Deposit**.

(1) Tenant has paid $_____**1,100**_____ cash, money order, and/or check, as security deposit, to the following Real Estate Broker _____**Crestview Realty, Inc.**_____ ("Holder"), which has been received by Holder. The Security Deposit shall be deposited in Holder's escrow/trust account (with Holder retaining the interest if the account is interest bearing) within five banking days from the Binding Agreement Date. In the event any Security Deposit check is not honored, for any reason, by the bank upon which it is drawn, Holder shall promptly notify Tenant and Landlord. Tenant shall have three banking days after notice to deliver good funds to Holder. In the event Tenant does not timely deliver good funds, the Landlord shall have the right to terminate this Agreement upon written notice to the Tenant.

(2) Holder shall disburse the Security Deposit only as follows: (a) upon the failure of the parties to enter into a binding lease; (b) upon a written agreement signed by all parties having an interest in the funds; (c) upon order of a court or arbitrator having jurisdiction over any dispute involving the security deposit; (d) upon a reasonable interpretation of this Agreement by Holder; or (e) upon the termination of the agency relationship between Landlord and Holder, in which event Holder shall only disburse the Security Deposit, to another licensed Georgia Real Estate Broker selected by Landlord unless otherwise agreed to in writing by Landlord and Tenant after notice to Holder and Tenant. Prior to disbursing the Security Deposit pursuant to a reasonable interpretation of this Agreement; Holder shall give all parties fifteen days notice, stating to whom the disbursement will be made. Any party may object in writing to the disbursement, provided the objection is received by Holder prior to the end of the day notice period. All objections not raised in a timely manner, shall be waived. In the event a timely objection is made, Holder shall consider the objection and shall do any or a combination of the following: (a) hold the Security Deposit for a reasonable period of time to give the parties an opportunity to resolve the dispute; (b) disburse the Security Deposit and so notify all parties; and/or (c) interplead the Security Deposit into a court of competent jurisdiction. Holder shall be reimbursed for and may deduct from any funds interpleaded its costs and expenses, including reasonable attorney's fees. The prevailing party in the interpleader action shall be entitled to collect from the other party the costs and expenses reimbursed to Holder. No party shall seek damages from Holder (nor shall Holder be liable for the same) for any matter arising out of or related to the performance of Holder's duties under this Security Deposit paragraph.

6.   **MOVE-IN/MOVE-OUT INSPECTION**. Prior to Tenant tendering a Security Deposit, Landlord shall provide Tenant with a list of any existing damages to the Property using the form entitled "Move-In, Move-Out Inspection Form" which form is attached hereto and incorporated herein by this reference. Prior to taking occupancy, Tenant will be given the right to inspect the Property to ascertain the accuracy of the list. Both Landlord and Tenant shall sign the Move-In, Move-Out Form. Tenant shall be entitled to retain a copy of the Move-In/Move-Out Form. Within three business days after the date of termination of occupancy, Landlord will inspect the Property and compile a comprehensive list of any damage to the Property during Tenant's occupancy using the Move-In/Move-Out Form. Tenant shall have the right to inspect the Property within five business days after termination of Tenant's occupancy at a reasonable time mutually agreeable to Landlord and Tenant. To ascertain the accuracy of the list, Landlord and Tenant shall sign the list. Tenant must sign the list or sign a written statement listing the items of damage which Tenant disputes.

7.   **REPAIRS AND MAINTENANCE.** Tenant acknowledges that Tenant has inspected the Property and that it is fit for residential occupancy. Upon receipt of written notice from Tenant, Landlord shall, within a reasonable time period thereafter, repair the following (a) all defects in the Property which create unsafe living conditions or render the Property uninhabitable, and (b) to the extent required by state law, such other defects which, if not corrected, will leave the Property in a state of disrepair. Except as provided above, the Tenant agrees to maintain the Property in the neat and clean condition presented at the time of rental, reasonable wear and tear excepted.

8. **LEAD-BASED PAINT – DWELLINGS BUILT PRIOR TO 1978.** For any dwelling located on the Property built prior to 1978, Tenant acknowledges that Tenant has received, read, and signed the Lead-Based Paint Exhibit attached hereto and incorporated herein by reference.

9. **NOTICE OF PRIOR FLOODING OF PREMISES.** Landlord hereby notifies Tenant as follows: Some portion or all of the living space on the Property has ☐ or has not ☒ been flooded at least three times within the last five years immediately preceding the execution of this Lease.

10. **RENEWAL TERM**. Either party may terminate this Lease at the end of the term by giving the other party thirty days written notice prior to the end of the term. If neither party gives notice of termination, the Lease will automatically be extended on a month-to-month basis with all terms remaining the same. Thereafter, Tenant may terminate this Lease upon thirty days written notice to Landlord and Landlord may terminate this Lease upon sixty days written notice to Tenant, except that Landlord reserves the right to increase the amount of rent upon delivery of written notice to Tenant sixty days prior to the effective date of any increase.

11. **SUBLET AND ASSIGNMENT.** Tenant may not sublet the Property in whole or in part or assign this Lease without the prior written consent of Landlord. This Lease shall create the relationship of Landlord and Tenant between the parties hereto; no estate shall pass out of Landlord and this Lease shall create a usufruct only.

12. **RIGHT OF ACCESS, SIGNAGE.** Landlord and Landlord's agents shall have the right of access to the Property for inspection, repairs and maintenance during reasonable hours. In the case of emergency, Landlord may enter the Property at any time to protect life and prevent damage to the Property. Landlord and/or Landlord's agents may place a "for rent" or "for sale" sign in the yard or on the exterior of any dwelling on the property in whole or in part, may install a lockbox and may show the Property to prospective tenants or purchasers during reasonable hours. Tenant agrees to cooperate with Landlord, Landlord's agent and Brokers (as defined in Agency and Brokerage herein) who may show the Property to prospective Tenants. In the event a lockbox is installed, Tenant shall secure jewelry and other valuables and agrees to hold Landlord and/or Landlord's Agent harmless for any loss thereof. For each occasion where the access rights described above are denied, Tenant shall pay Landlord the sum of $_____N/A_____ as liquidated damages; it being acknowledged that Landlord shall be damaged by the denial of access, that Landlord's actual damages are hard to estimate, and that the above amount represents a reasonable pre-estimate of Landlord's damages rather than a penalty.

13. **USE.** The Property shall be used for residential purposes only and shall be occupied only by the _____5_____ (#) persons listed as follows_____**Manuel & Lola Chavez and Three Children**_____.
The Property shall be used so as to comply with all federal, state, county, and municipal laws and ordinances and any applicable declaration of condominium; declaration of covenants, conditions, and restrictions ;all rules and regulations pursuant thereto; and any community association bylaws; and rules and regulations. Tenant shall not use or permit the Property to be used for any disorderly or unlawful purpose; nor shall Tenant engage in any activity on the Property which would endanger the health and safety of other Tenants or which otherwise creates a nuisance.

8. Lead-Based Paint— Dwellings Built Prior to 1978

Paragraph #8 relates only to buildings built before 1978. A federal law requires that the tenant be given a pamphlet relating to lead-based paint and a disclosure of any known presence of lead-based paint in the structure.

9. Notice of Prior Flooding of Premises

Paragraph #9 contains the state law mandated notice of flooding three times in the last five years.

10. Renewal Term

Paragraph #10 states that this lease will be automatically renewed on a month-to-month basis unless the tenant gives 30 days notice of their desire to terminate it. The landlord must give 60 days notice to terminate or to raise the rent.

11. Sublet and Assignment

In Paragraph #11, the tenant is denied the right to sublet or assign this lease.

12. Right of Access, Signage

Paragraph #12 gives the landlord the right of access at reasonable hours or in any emergency. The landlord can post a "For Rent" or "For Sale" sign, put a lockbox on the apartment, and show it at reasonable times to prospects.

13. Use

Paragraph #13 limits occupancy to the number of persons specified, and it provides that no illegal uses are permitted.

14. **PROPERTY LOSS**. Storage of personal property by Tenant shall be at Tenant's risk and Landlord shall not be responsible for any loss or damage. Tenant shall be responsible to insure Tenant's personal property against loss or damage. Landlord shall not be responsible for any damage to Tenant's property, unless such damage is caused by Landlord's gross negligence.

15. **DEFAULT**.
   A. If Tenant defaults under any term, condition or provision of this Lease, including, but not limited to, failure to pay rent or failure to reimburse Landlord for any damages, repairs or costs when due, Landlord shall have the right to terminate this Lease by giving written notice to Tenant and to pursue all available legal and equitable remedies to remedy the default. Such termination shall not release Tenant from any liability for any amount due under this Lease.
   B. If Tenant abandons the Property or violates any of the Rules and Regulations set forth herein, or otherwise fails to abide by and perform any of the obligations, terms, conditions or provisions of this Lease, each and any such breach shall constitute a default under this Lease. If any such default continues for three calendar days after Landlord delivers written notice of said default to Tenant, Landlord may, at his option, terminate this Lease by delivering written notice thereof to Tenant.
   C. All rights and remedies available to Landlord by law or in this Lease shall be cumulative and concurrent.

14. Property Loss

In Paragraph #14 the tenant is required to insure personal possessions. The landlord will not be responsible for any tenant losses unless the loss was caused by the landlord's gross negligence.

15. Default

Paragraph #15 deals with the landlord's rights in the case of the tenant failing to pay the rent due or in any other way defaulting on terms of this lease.

A. In case of default, the landlord may, upon written notice, end the lease or, without ending the lease, re-occupy the property and remove the tenant and his or her possessions. The tenant still owes all of the rent due to the end of the lease minus whatever the landlord might get from re-renting the space.

B. If the tenant defaults or abandons the premises, the landlord may end the lease three days after giving written notice of this intention.

C. The landlord's right are current and cumulative.

Note: This paragraph notwithstanding, the landlord has to abide by the state's landlord/tenant code in pursuing an eviction.

16. Rules and Regulations

The rules and regulations in Paragraph #16 should be carefully studied.

A. Prohibits the tenant from changing locks. We have added our re-keying charge.

B. States that non-operating vehicles are prohibited.

C. Prohibits the storing of anything that is a fire hazard.

D. Outlines what can and what cannot be attached to a wall.

E. Sates that there will be no pets unless a special exhibit is attached to this lease.

F. Obligates the tenant to keep the property in good repair. Has to do with care of the grounds, and we have entered N/A.

17. Utilities

In Paragraph #17 the tenant initials the lines opposite the utilities for which he or she does accept responsibility.

16. **RULES AND REGULATIONS**.
   A.   Tenant is prohibited from adding, changing or in any way altering locks installed on the doors of Property without prior written permission of Landlord. If all keys to the Property are not returned when Tenant vacates the Property, Landlord may charge a re-key charge in the amount of $_____**150.00**_____ .
   B.   Non-operative vehicles are not permitted on the Property. Any such non-operative vehicle may be removed by Landlord at the expense of Tenant, for storage or, for public or private sale, at Landlord's option, and Tenant shall have no right or recourse against Landlord thereafter.
   C.   Other than for normal household use, no goods or materials of any kind or description which are combustible or would increase fire risk shall be kept in or placed on the Property.
   D.   No nails, screws or adhesive hangers except standard picture hooks, shade brackets and curtain rod brackets maybe placed in walls, woodwork or any part of the Property.
   E.   No pets are allowed unless the exhibit entitled "Pet Exhibit" is attached to this Lease.
   F.   Lawn and Exterior Maintenance: *[Select one. The section not marked shall not be a part of this Agreement].*
   ☐ (1) Tenant shall keep the lawn mowed, shrubs trimmed, gutters cleaned out, trash and grass clippings picked up on a regular basis (minimum of once every two weeks in growing season and fall leaf season) and shall keep the Property, including yard, lot, grounds, house, walkways and driveway clean and free of rubbish.
   ☐ (2) Partial maintenance by tenant - Tenant shall maintain the following: _____**N/A**_____
   ☐ (3) Landlord or Landlord's designated agent shall provide all yard/exterior maintenance.

17. **UTILITIES.** Applicable utilities and/or service to be paid by Tenant:

UTILITY	INITIALS	UTILITY	INITIALS
( ) Water		( ) Sewer	
(**X**) Electricity	**MC/LC**	(**X**) Natural Gas	**MC/LC**
( ) Garbage		(**X**) Cable Television	**MC/LC**
(**X**) Telephone	**MC/LC**	( ) Other _____	

Tenant must provide proof of payment of final bills for all utilities or service termination (cutoff) slips. Landlord may, at landlord's option, pay utilities and be reimbursed by Tenant along with next month's rent.

18. Abandonment

Paragraph #18 gives the landlord the right, when it seems that the tenant has moved out while still owing rent, to consider the premises abandoned. The landlord can store or dispose of any personal property the tenant leaves behind.

19. Disclaimer

Paragraph #19 contains the standard disclaimer of responsibility for the landlord and property manager. They are not to be held accountable for matters outside of their expertise.

18. **ABANDONMENT**. If Tenant removes or attempts to remove personal property from the Property other than in the usual course of continuing occupancy, without having first paid Landlord all monies due, the Property may be considered abandoned, and Landlord shall have the right, without notice, to store or dispose of any personal property left on the Property by Tenant. Landlord shall also have the right to store or dispose of any of Tenant's personal property remaining on the Property after the termination of this Lease. Any such personal property shall become Landlord's personal property.

19. **DISCLAIMER**. Tenant and Landlord acknowledge that they have not relied upon any advice, representations or statements of Brokers and waive and shall not assert any claims against Brokers involving the same. Tenant and Landlord agree that Brokers shall not be responsible to advise Tenant and Landlord on any matter, including but not limited to the following: any matter which could have been revealed through a survey, title search or inspection of the Property; the condition of the Property, any portion thereof, or any item therein; building products and construction techniques; the necessity or cost of any repairs to the Property; hazardous or toxic materials or substances; termites and other wood destroying organisms; the tax or legal consequences of this transaction; the availability and cost of utilities or community amenities; the appraised or future value of the Property; any condition(s) existing off the Property which may affect the Property; the terms, conditions and availability of financing; and the uses and zoning of the Property whether permitted or proposed. Tenant and Landlord acknowledge that Brokers are not experts with respect to the above matters and that, if any of these matters or any other matters are of concern to them, they should seek independent expert advice relative thereto. Tenant further acknowledges that in every neighborhood there are conditions which different tenants may find objectionable. Tenant shall therefore be responsible to become fully acquainted with neighborhood and other off site conditions which could affect the Property.

20. <u>OTHER PROVISIONS</u>.
  A. **Time of Essence:** Time is of the essence of this Lease.
  B. **No Waiver:** Any failure of Landlord to insist upon the strict and prompt performance of any covenants or conditions of this Lease or any of the rules and regulations set forth herein shall not operate as a waiver of any such violation or of Landlord's right to insist on prompt compliance in the future of such covenant or condition, and shall not prevent a subsequent action by Landlord for any such violation. No provision, covenant or condition of this Lease may be waived by Landlord unless such waiver is in writing and signed by Landlord.
  C. **Definitions:** "Landlord" as used in this Lease shall include its representatives, heirs, agents, assigns, and successors in title to Property. For the purposes herein, Broker shall be the authorized agent of Landlord and shall have the full and complete authority to act on behalf of Landlord under this Lease including without limitation the right to execute this Lease in a representative capacity on behalf of Landlord. "Tenant" shall include Tenant's heirs and representatives. The terms "Landlord" and "Tenant" shall include singular and plural, and corporations, partnerships, companies or individuals, as may fit the particular circumstances.
  D. **Entire Agreement:** This Lease and any attached addenda constitute the entire Agreement between the parties and no oral statement or amendment not reduced to writing and signed by both parties shall be binding.
  E. **Attorney's Fees and Costs of Collection:** Whenever any sums due hereunder are collected by law, or by attorney at law to prosecute such an action, then both parties agree that the prevailing party will be entitled to reasonable attorney's fees, plus all costs of collection.
  F. **Indemnification:** Tenant releases Landlord and Broker from liability for and agrees to indemnify Landlord and Broker against all losses incurred by Landlord or Broker as a result of: (a) Tenant's failure to fulfill any condition of this Lease; (b) any damage or injury happening in or about the Property to Tenant or Tenant's invitee or licensees or such persons' property, except where such damage or injury is due to gross negligence or willful misconduct of Landlord or Broker; (c) Tenant's failure to comply with any requirements imposed by any governmental authority; and (d) any judgment, lien or other encumbrance filed against the Property as a result of Tenant's actions.
  G. **Notices:** Except as otherwise provided herein, all notices, including demands, required or permitted hereunder shall be in writing and delivered either: (1) in person; (2) by an overnight delivery service, prepaid; (3) by facsimile transmission (FAX); or (4) by the United States Postal Service, postage prepaid, registered or certified return receipt requested. Notwithstanding the above, notice by FAX shall be deemed to have been given as of the date and time it is if the sending FAX produces a written confirmation with the date, time and telephone number to which the notice was sent. Receipt of notice by the Broker representing a party as a client shall be deemed to be notice to that party for all purposes herein except in transactions where the Broker is practicing designated agency, receipt of notice by the designated agent representing a party as a client shall be required to constitute notice to that party. Notices shall be sent to Landlord at:_____
  _____.
  All references to any notice required to be given or due dates for rental payments shall be strictly construed.
  H. **Waiver of Homestead Exemption:** Tenant for himself and his family waives all exemptions or benefits under the homestead laws of Georgia.
  I. **Governing Law:** This Agreement may be signed in multiple counterparts and shall be governed by and interpreted pursuant to the laws of the State of Georgia.

20. Other Provisions

Paragraph #20 provides for the following:

  A. **Time of essence:** The time frames stated in this contract are to be strictly enforced.
  B. **No Waiver:** In case the landlord is softhearted and accepts a late rent payment, or an inadequate payment, or overlooks a violation of the rules, that does not mean the landlord has waived the right to enforce the requirements later.
  C. **Definitions:** The term "landlord" shall include heirs, agents, assigns, and successors; and the term "tenant" shall include heirs and representatives. (This means the lease will not end if either party dies.)
  D. **Entire Agreement:** That this form constitutes the entire agreement.
  E. **Attorney's Fees and Cost of Collection:** States that attorney's fees or collection costs arising out of any litigation under this lease shall be paid to the prevailing party.
  F. **Indemnification:** The landlord is indemnified from any liability for any injury or damages the tenant or the tenant's guest might suffer, unless it was the result of the landlord's gross negligence.
  G. **Notices:** Lists the acceptable manners in which written notices can be delivered: in person, by overnight delivery, by FAX, and by registered mail. Notices are considered to have been delivered when they are received, except for FAX transmissions that are delivered when sent.

H. **Waiver of Homestead Exemption:** Tenant gives up their rights to Homestead.

I. **Governing Law:** Makes the entire contract subject to the law of Georgia.

---

21. AGENCY AND BROKERAGE.

  A. Agency.

    (1) In this Agreement, the term "Broker" shall mean a licensed Georgia real estate broker or brokerage firm and where the context would indicate the broker's affiliated licensees. No Broker in this transaction shall owe any duty to Tenant or Landlord greater than what is set forth in their brokerage engagement and the Brokerage Relationships in Real Estate Transactions Act, O.C.G.A. § 10-6A-1 et. seq.

    (2) Landlord and Tenant acknowledge that if they are not represented by a Broker they are each solely responsible for protecting their own interests, and that Broker's role is limited to performing ministerial acts for either party.

    (3) The Broker, if any, working with the Landlord is identified on the signature page as the "Listing Broker"; and said Broker is ☒ **OR**, is **NOT** ☐ representing the Landlord;

    (4) The Broker, if any, working with the Tenant is identified on the signature page as the "Leasing Broker", and said Broker is ☐ **OR**, is **NOT** ☒ representing the Tenant; and

    (5) If Tenant and Landlord are both being represented by the same Broker, a relationship of either designated agency ☐, **OR**, dual agency ☐ shall exist.

      (a) Dual Agency Disclosure. [*Applicable only if dual agency has been selected above*] Landlord and Tenant are aware that Broker is acting as a dual agent in this transaction and consent to the same. Landlord and Tenant have been advised that:

        1 - In serving as a dual agent the Broker is representing two clients whose interests are or at times could be different or even adverse;

        2 - The Broker will disclose all adverse, material facts relevant to the transaction and actually known to the dual agent to all parties in the transaction except for information made confidential by request or instructions from another client which is not otherwise required to be disclosed by law;

        3 - The Tenant and Landlord do not have to consent to dual agency; and

        4 - The consent of the Tenant and Landlord to dual agency has been given voluntarily and the parties have read and understood their brokerage engagement agreements.

        5 - Notwithstanding any provision to the contrary contained herein Landlord and Tenant each hereby direct Broker, while acting as a dual agent, to keep confidential and not reveal to the other party all information which could materially and adversely affect the negotiating position of the party.

      (b) Designated Agency Assignment. [*Applicable only if the designated agency has been selected above*] The Broker has assigned _____ to work exclusively with Tenant as Tenant's designated agent and _____ to work exclusively with Landlord as Landlord's designated agent. Each designated agent shall exclusively represent the party to whom each has been assigned as a client and shall not represent in this transaction the client assigned to the other designated agent.

      (c) Material Relationship Disclosure. The Broker and/or affiliated licensees have no material relationship with either client except as follows: _____. (A material relationship means one actually known of a personal, familial or business nature between the Broker and affiliated licensees and a client which would impair their ability to exercise fair judgment relative to another client.)

  B. Brokerage. The Brokers listed below have performed a valuable service in this transaction and are made parties hereunder to enforce their commission rights. Payment of commission to a Broker shall not create an agency or subagency relationship between Leasing Broker and either Landlord or Landlord's Broker. Landlord agrees to pay the Broker listed below and representing Landlord to lease and/or manage the Property ("Listing Broker") a commission (which commission has already been negotiated in a separate agreement) of $_____**800.00**_____ or ____**N/A**____% of the Lease amount, which shall be due and payable upon occupancy. In the event the Lease is made in cooperation with another Broker listed below as the Leasing Broker, the Listing Broker shall receive ____**N/A**____% of the total real estate commission paid hereunder and the Leasing Broker shall receive ____**N/A**____% of the total real estate commission paid hereunder. In the event Tenant and/or Landlord fail or refuse to perform any of their obligations herein, the non-performing party shall immediately pay the Listing Broker and the Leasing Broker their full commissions. The Listing Broker and Leasing Broker may jointly or independently pursue the non-performing party for that portion of the commission which they would have otherwise received under the Lease.

---

21. Agency and Brokerage

Paragraph #21 defines the duties of the brokers involved in this transaction.

Crestview Realty represents the landlord and will be paid $800. Because there is no cooperating agent, other blanks are not applicable. Landlord and tenant affirm that the disclosures required by the Georgia's BRRETA law have been made.

Under BROKER working with LANDLORD (3), we check the box *is*.

Under BROKER working with TENANT (4), we check *is not* because Manuel and Lola Chavez have no agent.

The Dual Agency Disclosure and Transaction Agency Disclosure paragraphs are not a part of this lease, because this transaction was neither a dual agency nor a transaction brokerage.

---

22.   **MILITARY ACTIVATION.** If Tenant is called to active duty during the term of this Lease, Tenant shall present to Landlord official orders activating Tenant; then and in that event, this Lease shall be controlled by the Soldiers' and Sailors' Civil Relief Act of 1940 as amended in 50 U.S.C.A. §§ 50-590 and O.C.G.A. §§ 44-7-37 as amended.

23.   **EXHIBITS.** All exhibits attached hereto, listed below or referenced herein are made a part of this Lease. If any such exhibit conflicts with any preceding paragraph, said exhibit shall control:

24.   **SPECIAL STIPULATIONS.** The following Special Stipulations, if conflicting with any exhibit or preceding paragraph, shall control:

☐ **(Mark box if additional pages are attached.)**

IN WITNESS WHEREOF, the parties hereto have set their hand and seal the day and year first written above.

_____**Crestview Realty**_____ (_____)	_____**Manuel Chavez**_____
Leasing Broker MLS Office Code	Tenant's Signature SS/FEI #
	Print or Type Name:_____
By: _____**George Hopkins**_____	_____**Lola Chavez**_____
Broker or Broker's Affiliated Licensee	Tenant's Signature SS/FEI #
Print or Type Name:_____	Print or Type Name:_____
Bus. Phone:_____ FAX #_____	**Crestview Apartments, Inc by George Hopkins**
	Landlord's Signature (or Authorized Agent for Landlord)
_____ (_____)	
Listing Broker MLS Office Code	Print or Type Name:_____
Multiple Listing # _____	
	Landlord's Signature (or Authorized Agent for Landlord)
By: _____	Print or Type Name:_____
Broker or Broker's Affiliated Licensee	
Print or Type Name: _____	TELEPHONE # for Emergency Repairs
Bus. Phone:_____ FAX #_____	Landlord's address for notices and mailing of rent:
	_____
	_____, _____

22. Military Activation   Paragraph #22 confirms that military personal on active duty can terminate a lease without any penalty when transferred.

23. Exhibits   Paragraph #23 provide space for listing any Exhibits attached.

24. Special Stipulations   The space provided in Paragraph #24 is for writing in any special stipulations that were not covered in the other portions of the form. We had none.

Signatures   Finally, we have the signatures of the landlord and of the tenant. The authorized agent may sign for the landlord.

To see a full Lease for Residential Property, go to Appendix A.

Questions

1. Under a lease, the leasehold estate is a right belonging to the
   a. landlord.
   b. tenant.
   c. remainderman.
   d. reversioner.

2. Tenant Kelly read her lease very carefully and could find no restrictive covenant regarding the use of the property. Because zoning permitted, Kelly changed her business from a shoe store to a fish market. Landlord Hines objected. What is the probable outcome?
   a. Kelly may operate her fish market for the duration of the lease.
   b. Kelly may not change the business purpose of her lease without permission from Hines.
   c. Kelly may operate her fish market until she receives written notice from Hines of his intent to terminate the lease.
   d. While Hines may not evict Kelly, he may file suit for damages resulting from the unauthorized use of the property.

3. A lease is all of the following EXCEPT
   a. a conveyance.
   b. an option.
   c. a contract.
   d. an agreement.

4. A valid written lease does not require
   a. legal capacity of both parties.
   b. an offer and acceptance.
   c. valuable consideration.
   d. the signatures of both parties.

5. In the absence of an agreement to the contrary, a tenant may
   a. use the property for any purpose.
   b. mortgage the leasehold estate.
   c. sublease the property to a drug pusher.
   d. remove the house to another lot.

6. A lease provision which prohibits using certain premises for a drugstore is called a
   a. protective covenant.
   b. use covenant.
   c. restrictive covenant.
   d. condemnation covenant.

7. Which of the following is incorrect about leasehold improvements?
   a. Leasehold improvements are made by the tenant.
   b. Leasehold improvements belong to the landlord at the end of the lease, unless agreed otherwise by the parties.
   c. Leasehold improvements are made by the landlord because of one's implied duty to keep the premises habitable.
   d. Leasehold improvements must be specifically authorized in the lease or otherwise agreed to by the parties.

8. A one-year lease for a single family home requires
   a. only a street address and apartment number for a legal description.
   b. a physical description of the unit.
   c. a legal description by reference to a recorded plat.
   d. a complete legal description of the premises.

9. Although desirable, it is not necessary that a lease be in writing if it is to be
   a. for commercial property.
   b. for a period of one year or less.
   c. for a religious order leasing church space.
   d. a ground lease.

10. Salesperson with XYZ Realty has arranged a lease that has now expired. The tenant is demanding a return of the security deposit, and the landlord is refusing to return it. The salesperson should
    a. explain to the tenant that the landlord is probably within his or her rights.
    b. explain to the landlord that the tenant is entitled to the money.
    c. make an inspection to determine which party is correct.
    d. refer the matter to the broker.

11. The typical form lease contract is probably inappropriate for arranging
    a. a residential tenancy for years.
    b. a month-to-month lease on an apartment.
    c. a condominium lease.
    d. a commercial lease.

12. Which of the following statements about the security deposit is true?
    a. A security deposit is essential to a lease.
    b. Interest earned on a security deposit always accrues to the benefit of the tenant.
    c. A licensed salesperson should turn the security deposit over to the broker for deposit in the trust account.
    d. The security deposit is returned in full at the end of the lease.

13. A tenant who has a one-year lease on an apartment, commencing on January 1st, must
    a. give 30 days notice when he or she plans to vacate.
    c. vacate the premises by December 31st.
    d. vacate the premises within 30 days after expiration of lease.
    d. give 10 days notice before vacating.

14 Community Association Management

A community association is an association of homeowners in a subdivision, planned development, townhouse development, condominium complex, or cooperative, organized for the purpose of preserving, improving, maintaining, and enhancing their homes and property.

Community association management differs from property management in that the property manager has one client, the owner or ownership entity, and little day-to-day contact with tenants. The community association manager is continuously interacting with multiple owners.

Community associations have become popular because:

- Today's living environments often include common recreational facilities—some very elaborate—that must be maintained and operated. For example, there might be swimming pools, tennis courts, lakes, playgrounds, and landscaped areas.
- Developers may impose protective covenants, prohibiting certain uses or requiring performance of other duties. Owners, in effect, give up some rights in order to maintain an attractive community and to protect property value. In enforcing covenants, the community association management is somewhat like a private government, except that the association's power derives, not from statutes, but from contracts in the form of covenants and deed restrictions.

Covenants can regulate placement of satellite dishes, changes to the exterior of the house, whether or not a business can be operated on the premises, etc. They can also create a duty to pay dues or assessments.

SUBDIVISION HOMEOWNER ASSOCIATIONS (HOAs)

In Georgia, the following three types of homeowner associations (HOAs) are recognized:

1. **Subdivision with No Governing Homeowner Association.** This type may seem appealing to the owners in that they have the protection of covenants but no obligation to pay assessments. If one owner violates

the covenants, it is up to one or more other owners to take action at their expense. Since legal actions are expensive, the covenants may go unenforced.

2. **Subdivision with a Voluntary Homeowner Association.** In this format the owner who has no desire to use the amenities can elect not to join the association. The association, however, has the obligation to enforce the covenants and maintain the amenities. Voluntary participation may be strong enough to work effectively at first, but it tends to fall off as the community ages. Money becomes scarcer just when the common property requires more maintenance and repair. Disrepair of the amenities affects every owner's home value.

3. **Subdivision with a Mandatory Association Membership.** In a community with mandatory membership, the association has the mechanism to ensure that the facilities are maintained and the covenants enforced—namely, the power to levy assessments against the owners. A disadvantage may lie in the fact that a lender will take a mandatory association fee into account in qualifying a buyer for a home loan. However, it is generally thought to provide the best means of maintaining an appealing community.

THE GEORGIA PROPERTY OWNERS ASSOCIATION ACT OF 1994

As indicated, HOAs have been established under the concept that restrictions on ownership may be imposed by contract. They have evolved out of the common law concept of deed restrictions. However, the Georgia Property Owners Association Act (POA) of 1994 provides the option to create an HOA or submit it to a statutory scheme of development that provides significant collection and enforcement powers. This is not mandatory.

CONDOMINIUMS

Georgia state law regulates condominium formation. The condominium owner automatically becomes a mandatory member of a community association and is bound by the declaration and bylaws of the condominium association.

Condominium Management

Management of a condominium complex is similar to the management of a subdivision HOA except that

- there is usually more commonly owned area to maintain in a condominium complex, including the land under the buildings and the exteriors of buildings; and
- due to the fact that occupants live in close proximity and share many common areas, covenants contained in condominium documents are usually much more pervasive, which means that owners sacrifice more individual rights and freedom of choice. Rules often regulate such things as parking, pets, leasing of units, business use of units, and modifications of building exteriors and grounds.

The Condominium Association's Power

The condominium association generally has the power to

- tax owners in the form of regular and/or special assessments;
- adopt reasonable rules governing use of the units and common elements;
- fine owners for violations of the covenants or the rules;
- take legal action to enforce obligations; and
- approve or disapprove alterations to building exteriors or common elements.

COOPERATIVES

Cooperative ownership is generally found in subsidized housing or, at the opposite end of the economic scale, in high-priced, upscale apartments. In effect, a corporation is registered under state law to own new or existing property; and occupancy is granted to prospects who subscribe to a stock purchase and sign a proprietary lease on the unit of their choice. All owners contribute to paying the common expenses, called "carrying charges."

Cooperatives differ from condominiums in that owners, who are technically tenants, often do not have responsibility for the repair and maintenance of their units; and in that membership can be terminated and members dispossessed for nonpayment of carrying charges.

FUNDAMENTALS OF COMMUNITY ASSOCIATION MANAGEMENT

Role of Officers and Directors

The board of directors is the decision-making authority in a community association, responsible for operating and conducting the business affairs of the association on behalf of all owners. In typical bylaws, the board is elected for staggered terms at an annual meeting of all owners, and then the board selects the officers.

There is usually a president, vice-president, secretary, and treasurer, who have specific functions similar to those of officers in any nonprofit corporation. All must be board members, except that in some bylaws the treasurer does not necessarily have to be a director. Officers are administrators and serve at the pleasure of the board.

Role of the Community Association Manager

More and more associations are realizing the benefit of delegating administrative tasks to professional management. The tasks of a community association manager may vary with the size and complexity of the community. Familiarity with the documents used in creating the association, the declaration, and the bylaws is essential. In general, the manager will work closely with contractors, association employees, board members, and committee volunteers as well as having frequent interaction with the owners.

The manager works within guidelines established by the board of directors and, as a result, can serve as a buffer between the directors and various individuals who compete for their time and attention. The manager also gives a degree of stability to an ever-changing community.

Managerial Duties That Might Be Delegated

Duties the directors might delegate include

- preparing and submitting a budget;
- keeping financial records, including journals and a ledger;
- collecting assessments and depositing them;
- paying the association's bills;
- contacting the accountant for statements and audits as needed;
- contacting the attorney regarding delinquent accounts;
- sending notices of meetings;
- attending director's meetings;
- conducting the membership meeting;
- conducting elections;
- hiring and supervising clerical help;
- purchasing insurance for the association;
- keeping minutes of meetings;
- administering architectural rules and standards;
- enforcing the association's rules;
- preserving and maintaining equipment;
- ensuring adequate garbage and trash disposal;
- securing pest control services as needed;
- obtaining security services as needed; and
- providing a newsletter or other communication to owners.

Duties the Manager Does Not Undertake

Normally the manager is not accountable for

- repairing an individual homeowner's property unless it is the responsibility of the association;
- taking direction from anyone other than a person or persons designated by the board of directors;
- providing owners with legal advice, accounting advice, or other professional advice;
- making structural changes to association property unless authorized to do so by the board of directors; and
- loaning money to the association or borrowing from the association for any purpose.

The Management Agreement

The management agreement typically should include the following 13 items:

1. Identification of the parties and the date of the agreement
2. Definitions of "association documents," "fiscal year," "common areas"
3. Term of the agreement
4. The role management is to play
5. Details of financial management responsibilities
6. Details of physical management responsibilities
7. Policies for on-site employees and contracting procedures for contract services
8. Insurance and bonding requirements
9. How books and records are to be kept and auditing procedures
10. Required reports and government filings
11. Procedures for notice of meetings and conduct of meetings
12. Compensation of management
13. Provisions for termination of the agreement

Any other matters deemed appropriate can, of course, be added to the basic 13.

FIDELITY INSURANCE

Georgia license law requires that each manager who handles any community association funds be covered by a fidelity bond or fidelity insurance to protect the associations against loss due to mishandling of funds. Only brokers who at no time handle more than $60,000 are exempt.

The fidelity bond or insurance shall

- be written by an insurance company authorized to write such bonds by the state;
- cover the maximum amount of funds the broker ever handles;
- name the community association as additional insured;
- cover the broker, partners, officers, affiliates, and employees of the broker, as well as any other person handling the funds; and
- provide that the insurance company may not cancel the coverage without 30 days notice.

The broker must have a separate fidelity bond or policy for each association managed and must provide the association with a copy of such bond or policy. The required insurance does not cover directors who have check-signing authority, but most association policies will include them under the association's employee dishonesty policy if requested to do so.

COMMUNITY ASSOCIATION LICENSING POLICIES

Changes in the Georgia real estate license law, effective in 1997, require that any person engaged in community association management must hold a real estate license. At the same time a new category of license was added, the community association management or CAM license. Unlike the salesperson's license, the CAM license holder is not authorized to list or sell property but only to work in community association management. Like the salesperson, the CAM license holder must work only as an agent of a broker. Only a broker is authorized to enter into a contract to provide management services to a community association for a fee.

The CAM license is acquired by completing 25 hours of approved study and passing an examination.

While licensing is generally required for brokers and for community association managers, certain individuals are exempt from the licensing requirement even though they may perform the same services as a broker or community association manager. The six exemptions include

1. any person who, as owner or through another person engaged by such owner on a full-time basis, provides community management services;
2. any person employed on a full-time basis by the owner of property for the purpose of providing community association management services;

3. any person employed on a full-time basis by a community association for the purpose of providing management services;

4. any member of the community association who provides management services only to that one association of which that person is a member;

5. anyone performing physical maintenance of the property; and

6. any licensed certified public accountant acting solely as an incident to the practice of public accounting.

Questions

1. A community association may include homeowners in all the following EXCEPT a
   a. subdivision.
   b. condominium.
   c. cemetery.
   d. town house.

2. A broker who manages a community association must have fidelity insurance unless she or he at no time handles more than
   a. $25,000.
   b. $40,000.
   c. $60,000.
   d. $75,000.

3. A person who wants to get a community association management license must take a prelicense course of
   a. 25 hours.
   b. 40 hours.
   c. 60 hours.
   d. 75 hours.

Appendix A: Georgia Real Estate Forms

EXCLUSIVE SELLER LISTING AGREEMENT
(ALSO REFERRED TO AS EXCLUSIVE SELLER BROKERAGE AGREEMENT)

2002 Printing

State law prohibits Broker from representing Seller as a client without first entering into a written agreement with Seller under O.C.G.A. § 10-6A-1 et. seq.

For and in consideration of the mutual promises contained herein and other good and valuable consideration, _____ as seller (hereinafter referred to as "Seller"), and _____ as broker and its licensees (hereinafter collectively referred to as "Broker") do hereby enter into this Agreement, this _____ day of _____, 20_____.

1. **Exclusive Listing Agreement**. Seller hereby grants to Broker the exclusive right and privilege as the Agent of the Seller to show and offer for sale the following described property as the real estate broker for Seller: All that tract of land lying and being in Land Lot _____ of the _____ District, _____ Section of _____ County, Georgia, and being known as Address _____, _____ City, Georgia Zip Code _____, according to the present system of numbering in and around this area, being more particularly described as Lot ___, Block _____, Unit _____, Phase/Section _____ of _____ subdivision, as recorded in Plat Book _____, Page _____, _____ County, Georgia records together with all fixtures, landscaping, improvements, and appurtenances, all being hereinafter collectively referred to as the "Property." The full legal description of the Property is the same as is recorded with the Clerk of the Superior Court of the county in which the Property is located and is made a part of this Agreement by reference. The term of this Agreement shall begin on _____, 20_____ and shall continue through _____, 20_____ (hereinafter referred to as "Listing Period").

2. **Broker's Duties To Seller**. Broker's sole duties to Seller shall be to: (a) use Broker's best efforts to procure a buyer ready, willing, and able to purchase the Property at a sales price of at least $_____ (including commission) or any other price acceptable to Seller; (b) assist to the extent requested by Seller, in negotiating the terms of and filling out a pre-printed real estate purchase and sale agreement; and (c) comply with all applicable laws in performing its duties hereunder including the Brokerage Relationships in Real Estate Transaction Act, O.C.G.A. § 10-6A-1 et. seq.

3. **Seller's Duties**. Seller represents that Seller: (a) presently has title to the Property or has full authority to enter into this Agreement; (b) will cooperate with Broker to sell the Property to prospective buyers and will refer all inquiries concerning the sale of the Property to the Broker during the terms of this agreement; (c) will make the Property available for showing at reasonable times as requested by Broker; and (d) will provide Broker with accurate information regarding the Property (including information concerning all adverse material facts pertaining to the physical condition of the Property).

4. **Marketing**.
   A. **Advertisements:** Broker may advertise the Property for sale in all media and may photograph and/or videotape and use the photographs and/or videotapes in connection with Broker's marketing efforts. Seller agrees not to place any advertisements on the property or to advertise the property for sale in any media except with the prior written consent of Broker. Broker is also hereby authorized to place Broker's "For Sale" sign on the Property. Broker is authorized to procure buyers to purchase the Property in cooperation with other real estate brokers and their affiliated licensees. Broker may distribute listing and sales information (including the sales price) to them and other members of the multiple listing service(s), and said cooperating brokers and their licensees may republish such information on their Internet web sites. Broker and other real estate brokers and their affiliated licensees may show the Property without first notifying the Seller.
   B. **Lockboxes:** A lockbox may be used in connection with the marketing of the Property. There have been isolated instances of reported burglaries of homes on which lockboxes have been placed and for which the lockbox has been alleged to have been used to access the home. In order to minimize the risk of misuse of the lockbox, Broker recommends against the use of lockboxes on door handles that can be unscrewed from the outside or on other parts of the home from which the lockbox can be easily removed. Since others will have access to the Property, Seller agrees to either remove all valuables or put them in a secure place.
   C. **Multiple Listing Service(s):** Seller acknowledges that Broker is a member of the following multiple listing service(s): _____ ("Service(s)").

   Broker agrees that Broker will file this listing with said Service(s) within forty eight hours after Seller signs the same (excepting weekends, federal holidays and postal holidays).

   Seller acknowledges that the Service(s) is/are not a party to this Agreement and is/are not responsible for errors or omissions on the part of Seller or of Broker. Seller agrees to indemnify the Service(s) from and against any and all claims, liabilities, damages or losses arising out of or related to the listing and sale of the Property.

5. **Commission**. Seller agrees to pay Broker no later than at closing a real estate commission of _____ percent (_____%) of the purchase price of the Property or $_____ in the event that during the term of this Agreement, (1) Broker procures a buyer ready, willing, and able to purchase the Property at the price described above; or (2) Seller enters into an enforceable contract for the

sale or exchange of the Property with any buyer, whether through the efforts of Broker or any other person, including Seller. Broker shall share this commission with a cooperating broker, if any, who procures the buyer of the Property by paying such cooperating broker _____% of Broker's commission or $ _____. Cooperating brokers are expressly intended to be third-party beneficiaries under this Agreement. In the event that Seller sells or contracts to sell the Property to any buyer introduced to the Property by Broker within _____ days after the expiration of the Listing Period, then Seller shall pay the commission referenced above to Broker at the closing of the sale or exchange of the Property. Notwithstanding the above, in the event that the Property is sold to the prospective buyer by or through another licensed broker with whom Seller has signed an exclusive right to sell listing agreement, then no commission shall be owed to Broker by virtue of this Agreement. The commission obligations set forth herein shall survive the termination of this Agreement.

6. **Limits on Broker's Authority and Responsibility.** Seller acknowledges and agrees that Broker: (a) may show other properties to prospective buyers who are interested in Seller's Property; (b) is not an expert with regard to matters that could be revealed through a survey, title search, or inspection; the condition of property; the necessity or cost of repairs; hazardous or toxic materials; the availability and cost of utilities or community amenities; conditions existing off the property that may affect the property; uses and zoning of the property; the appraised or future value of the property; termites and wood-destroying organisms; building products and construction techniques; the tax or legal consequences of a contemplated transaction; or matters relating to financing (and if these matters are of concern to Seller, Seller is hereby advised to seek independent expert advice on any of these matters of concern to Seller); (c) shall owe no duties to Seller nor have any authority to act on behalf of Seller other than what is set forth in this Agreement; (d) may make all disclosures required by law; (e) may disclose all information about the Property to others; and (f) shall, under no circumstances, have any liability greater than the amount of the real estate commission paid hereunder to Broker (excluding any commission amount paid to a cooperating real estate broker, if any).

Seller agrees to hold Broker harmless from any and all claims, causes of action, or damages arising out of or relating to: (a) Seller providing Broker incomplete and/or inaccurate information; (b) the handling of earnest money by anyone other than Broker; or (c) any injury to persons on the Property and/or loss of or damage to the Property or anything contained therein.

7. **Extension.** If during the term of this Agreement, Seller and a prospective buyer enter into a real estate sales contract which is not consummated for any reason whatsoever, then the original expiration date of this Agreement shall be extended for the number of days that the Property was under contract.

8. **Seller's Property Disclosure Statement and Official Georgia Wood Infestation Report.** Within ____ days of the date of this Agreement, Seller agrees to provide Broker with a current, fully executed Seller's Property Disclosure Statement. Additionally, within _____ days of the date of this Agreement, Seller agrees to provide Broker with an Official Georgia Wood Infestation Report dated not more than one hundred eighty days prior to the date of this Agreement. Broker is hereby authorized to distribute the same to prospective buyers interested in the Property.

9. **Required State Law Disclosures.** (a) Broker agrees to keep all information which Seller asks to be kept confidential by express request or instruction unless the Seller permits such disclosure by subsequent word or conduct or such disclosure is required by law. (b) Broker may not knowingly give customers false information. (c) In the event of a conflict between Broker's duty not to give customers false information and the duty to keep the confidences of Seller, the duty not to give customers false information shall prevail. (d) Unless specified below, Broker has no other known agency relationships with other parties which would conflict with any interests of Seller (except that Broker may represent other buyers, sellers, landlords, and tenants in buying, selling or leasing property).

10. **Broker's Policy on Agency.** Unless Broker indicates below that Broker is not offering a specific agency relationship, the types of agency relationships offered by Broker are: seller agency, buyer agency, designated agency, dual agency, landlord agency, and tenant agency.

The agency relationship(s), if any, **NOT** offered by Broker is/are the following:_____

Dual Agency Disclosure: *[Applicable only if Broker's agency policy is to practice dual agency]* Seller does hereby consent to Broker acting in a dual agency capacity in transactions in which Broker is representing as clients both the Buyer and Seller and Broker is not acting in a designated agency capacity. By entering this Agreement, Seller acknowledges that Seller understands that Seller does not have to consent to dual agency, is doing so voluntarily, and that this brokerage engagement has been read and understood. In serving as a dual agent, Broker is representing two parties as clients whose interests are or at times could be different or even adverse. As a dual agent, Broker will disclose to both parties all adverse material facts relevant to the transaction actually known to the dual agent except for information made confidential by request or instructions from client and which is not required to be disclosed by law. Seller hereby directs Broker, while acting as a dual agent to keep confidential and not reveal to the Buyer any information which would materially and adversely affect the Seller's negotiating position. Broker or Broker's affiliated licensees will timely disclose to each client the nature of any material relationship the broker and the broker's affiliated licensees have with the other client or clients, other than that incidental to the transaction. A material relationship shall mean any actually known personal, familial, or business relationship between Broker and a client which would impair the ability of Broker to exercise fair and independent judgment relative to another client. The other party whom Broker may represent in the event of dual agency may or may not be identified at the time Seller enters into this Agreement. If any party is identified after the Agreement and has a material relationship with Broker, then Broker shall timely provide to Seller a disclosure of the nature of such relationship.

11. **Entire Agreement.** This Agreement constitutes the sole and entire agreement between the parties hereto, and no modification of this

Agreement shall be binding unless signed by all parties. No representation, promise, or inducement not included in this Agreement shall be binding upon any party hereto.

12. <u>Governing Law</u>. This Agreement shall be governed by and interpreted pursuant to the laws of the State of Georgia.

SPECIAL STIPULATIONS: The following Special Stipulations, if conflicting with any preceding paragraph, shall control.

☐ **(Mark box if additional pages are attached.)**

BY SIGNING THIS AGREEMENT, SELLER ACKNOWLEDGES THAT: (1) SELLER HAS READ ALL PROVISIONS AND DISCLOSURES MADE HEREIN; (2) SELLER UNDERSTANDS ALL SUCH PROVISIONS AND DISCLOSURES AND HAS ENTERED INTO THIS AGREEMENT VOLUNTARILY; AND (3) SELLER IS NOT SUBJECT TO A CURRENT LISTING AGREEMENT WITH ANY OTHER BROKER.

RECEIPT OF A COPY OF THIS AGREEMENT IS HEREBY ACKNOWLEDGED BY SELLER.

The above proposition is hereby accepted, _____ o'clock _____ M., on the _____ day of _____, 20_____.

Company _____

By: _____
    Broker or Broker's Affiliated Licensee

Print/Type Name: _____

Phone #: _____

Fax #: _____

Seller _____ SS/FEI#

Seller _____ SS/FEI#

Print/Type Name(s): _____

Phone #: _____

Fax #: _____

Address: _____

_____

      F1, Exclusive Seller Listing Agreement, Page 3 of 3 01/01/02

Reprinted with permission from the Georgia Association of REALTORS®

ESTIMATE OF NET TO SELLER

Georgia
Association of
REALTORS®

2002 Printing

Seller: _____ Date Prepared: _____, 20_____

Address: _____ Projected Closing Date: _____, 20_____

County: _____ Month Tax Bill Paid: _____

Sales Price $_____

Present Loan Pay-Off Expenses:

1st mortgage principal balance after last payment $_____

Failure to notify bank penalty + $_____

Pre-payment penalty + $_____

Accrued Interest (Principal Balance $_____
    x Rate_____% ÷ 365 x # of days to closing _____) + $_____

2nd mortgage/home equity loan principal balance
    after last payment + $_____

Accrued Interest (Principal Balance $_____
    x Rate_____% ÷ 365 x # of days to closing _____) + $_____

Subtotal Present Loan Pay-Off Expenses -$_____

Costs of Sale:

Real Estate Brokerage Fee $_____

Termite Letter + $_____

Unpaid Property Taxes (Annual taxes $_____
    ÷ 365 x # of days from January 1 to closing _____) + $_____

Special Assessments (i.e., Association Fees) + $_____

Repairs/Clean-Up + $_____

Survey + $_____

State of Georgia Property Transfer Tax + $_____

Seller's Contribution to Closing Costs + $_____

Other_____ + $_____

Other_____ + $_____

Subtotal Costs of Sale - $_____

Credits:

Pre-Paid Property Taxes (Annual taxes $_____
    ÷ 365 x # of days from closing to December 31_____) + $_____

Escrow Refund of Taxes & Insurance (Usually received
    30 days after closing) + $_____

Other_____ + $_____

Subtotal Credits + $_____

TOTAL ESTIMATE OF NET TO SELLER $_____

The above information is based on data available as of this date. Additional monthly payments and accrued interest may reduce the loan payoff. Fees such as warehouse fees, tax service, lender inspection, photos, document preparation, handling fees, courier fees, etc. may also appear on the closing statement. No representation is made as to the accuracy or completeness of this form. This is an estimate only.

F72, Estimate of Net to Seller 01/01/02

EXCLUSIVE BUYER BROKERAGE AGREEMENT

2002 Printing

State law prohibits Broker from representing Buyer as a client without first entering into a written agreement with Buyer under O.C.G.A. § 10-6A-1 et. seq.

For and in consideration of the mutual promises contained herein and other good and valuable consideration, _____
_____ as buyer (hereinafter referred to as "Buyer"), and _____
_____ as broker and its licensees (hereinafter collectively referred to as "Broker") do hereby enter into this
Agreement, this _____ day of _____, 20_____.

1. **Exclusive Brokerage Agreement.** Buyer hereby hires Broker to act as Buyer's exclusive real estate broker and agent to assist Buyer in locating and negotiating the purchase or exchange of real property. Buyer has not entered into a buyer brokerage agreement with any other real estate broker or any previous buyer brokerage agreement has been terminated. The term of this Agreement shall begin on _____, 20_____ and shall continue through _____, 20_____.

2. **Broker's Duties To Buyer.** Broker's sole duties to Buyer shall be to: (a) attempt to locate property suitable to Buyer for purchase; (b) assist to the extent requested by Buyer in negotiating the terms of and filling out a pre-printed real estate purchase and sale agreement; and (c) comply with all applicable laws in performing its duties hereunder including the Brokerage Relationships in Real Estate Transactions Act, O.C.G.A. § 10-6A-1 et. seq.

3. **Buyer's Duties.** Buyer agrees to: (a) work with only Broker (and not with any other real estate broker or licensee) in identifying, previewing, and seeing property for purchase by Buyer; (b) be available to meet with Broker to see property; (c) provide Broker with accurate information as requested by Broker (including financial information about Buyer's financial ability to complete the transaction and written authorization to obtain verification of funds); and (d) inspect and otherwise become familiar with any potentially adverse conditions relating to the physical condition of any property in which Buyer becomes interested, any improvements located on such property and the neighborhood surrounding such property.

4. **Limits on Broker's Authority and Responsibility.** Buyer acknowledges and agrees that Broker: (a) may show property in which Buyer is interested to other prospective buyers; (b) is not an expert with regard to matters which could have been revealed through a survey, title search or inspection of the property; the condition of property, any portion thereof, or any item therein; building products and construction techniques; the necessity or cost of any repairs to property; hazardous or toxic materials; termites and other wood destroying organisms; the tax and legal consequences of any real estate transaction; the availability and cost of utilities and community amenities; the appraised or future value of the property; conditions existing off the property that may affect the property; and the uses and zoning of property and matters relating to financing (and if these matters are of concern to Buyer, Buyer is hereby advised to seek independent expert advice relative thereto); (c) shall owe no duties to Buyer nor have any authority on behalf of Buyer other than what is set forth in this Agreement; (d) may make all disclosures required by law; and (e) shall, under no circumstances, have any liability greater than the amount of the real estate commission paid hereunder to Broker (excluding any commission amount retained by the listing broker, if any).

   Buyer agrees to hold Broker harmless from any and all claims, causes of action, or damages arising out of or relating to: (a) Buyer providing Broker incomplete and/or inaccurate information; or (b) the handling of earnest money or other considerations by anyone other than Broker.

5. **Early Termination.** Broker or Buyer shall have the right to terminate this Brokerage Agreement at any time by giving the other party written notice; however this shall not limit Broker's remedies under the commission paragraph.

6. **Commission.** Broker shall seek to be paid a commission from the listing broker under a cooperative brokerage arrangement or from the seller if there is no listing broker. In the event the seller or listing broker does not pay Broker a commission, then Buyer shall pay Broker at time of closing, a commission of $_____ or _____% of the purchase price of all real property in Georgia which Buyer purchases during the term of this Agreement whether or not the property has been identified to Buyer by Broker. In addition, if Buyer leases property or enters into a lease/purchase contract during this Agreement, and the landlord does not agree to pay Broker a leasing commission, Buyer shall also pay Broker for the duration of the lease and any renewal or extension thereof a commission of _____% of each rental payment paid by Buyer to Landlord thereunder. Furthermore, in the event that during the _____ day period following termination of this Brokerage Agreement, Buyer purchases, contracts to purchase, leases or lease purchases any property identified to Buyer by Broker during the term of this Brokerage Agreement, then Buyer shall pay Broker at closing or the commencement of any lease, if applicable, the commission or commissions set forth above. The commission obligations set forth above shall survive the termination of this Agreement.

F4, Exclusive Buyer Brokerage Agreement, Page 1 of 3 01/01/02

7. <u>Extension</u>. If during the term of this Brokerage Agreement, Buyer and a seller enter into a real estate sales contract which is not consummated for any reason whatsoever, then the original expiration date of this Agreement shall be extended for the number of days that the property was under contract.

8. <u>Entire Agreement</u>. This Brokerage Agreement constitutes the sole and entire agreement between the parties hereto, and no modification of this Brokerage Agreement shall be binding unless signed by all parties. No representation, promise, or inducement not included in this Brokerage Agreement shall be binding upon any party hereto.

9. <u>Required State Law Disclosures</u>. (a) Broker agrees to keep all information which Buyer asks to be kept confidential by express request or instruction unless the Buyer permits such disclosure by subsequent word or conduct or such disclosure is required by law; (b) Broker may not knowingly give customers false information; (c) In the event of a conflict between Broker's duty not to give customers false information and the duty to keep the confidences of Buyer, the duty not to give customers false information shall prevail; (d) Unless specified below, Broker has no other known agency relationships with other parties which would conflict with any interests of Buyer (with the exception that Broker may represent other buyers, sellers, tenants and landlords in buying, selling or leasing property).

10. <u>Broker's Policy on Agency</u>. Unless Broker indicates below that Broker is not offering a specific agency relationship, the types of agency relationships offered by Broker are seller agency, buyer agency, designated agency, dual agency, landlord agency, and tenant agency.

    The agency relationship(s), if any, **NOT** offered by Broker is/are the following:_____.

11. <u>Dual Agency Disclosure</u>. [*Applicable only if Broker's agency policy is to practice dual agency*] Buyer does hereby consent to Broker acting in a dual agency capacity in transactions in which the Broker is representing as clients both the Buyer and a seller of real property in which Buyer is interested in purchasing and the Broker is not acting in a designated agency capacity. By entering into this Agreement, Buyer acknowledges that Buyer does not have to consent to dual agency, is doing so voluntarily, and that this brokerage engagement has been read and understood. In serving as a dual agent, Broker is representing two parties as clients whose interests are or at times could be different or even adverse. As a dual agent, Brokers will disclose to both parties all adverse material facts relevant to the transaction actually known to the dual agent except for information made confidential by request or instructions from either client and which is not required to be disclosed by law. Buyer hereby directs Broker, while acting as a dual agent to keep confidential and not reveal to the seller any information which would materially and adversely affect the Buyer's negotiating position. Broker or Broker's affiliated licensees will timely disclose to each client the nature of any material relationship the Broker and the Broker's affiliated licensees have with the other client or clients, other than that incidental to the transaction.   A material relationship shall mean any actually known personal, familial, or business relationship between Broker and a client which would impair the ability of Broker to exercise fair and independent judgment relative to another client. The other party whom Broker may represent in the event of dual agency may or may not be identified at the time Buyer enters into this Agreement. If any party is identified after the Agreement and has a material relationship with Broker, then Broker shall timely provide to Buyer a disclosure of the nature of such relationship.

12. <u>Governing Law</u>. This Agreement shall be governed by and interpreted pursuant to the laws of the State of Georgia.

SPECIAL STIPULATIONS: The following Special Stipulations, if conflicting with any exhibit, addendum, or preceding paragraph, shall control.

Reprinted with permission from the Georgia Association of REALTORS®

☐ **(Mark box if additional pages are attached.)**

BY SIGNING THIS AGREEMENT, BUYER ACKNOWLEDGES THAT: (1) BUYER HAS READ ALL PROVISIONS AND DISCLOSURES MADE HEREIN; (2) BUYER UNDERSTANDS ALL SUCH PROVISIONS AND DISCLOSURES AND HAS ENTERED INTO THIS AGREEMENT VOLUNTARILY; AND (3) BUYER IS NOT SUBJECT TO A CURRENT BUYER BROKERAGE ENGAGEMENT WITH ANY OTHER BROKER.

RECEIPT OF A COPY OF THIS AGREEMENT IS HEREBY ACKNOWLEDGED BY BUYER.

The above proposition is hereby accepted, _____ o'clock _____ M., on the _____ day of _____, 20_____.

Company _____

By: _____
    Broker or Broker's Affiliated Licensee

Print/Type Name: _____

Phone #: _____

Fax #: _____

Buyer _____ SS/FEI#

Buyer _____ SS/FEI#

Print/Type Name(s): _____

Phone #: _____

Fax #: _____

Address: _____

_____

ESTIMATE OF COST TO BUYER

Georgia
Association of
REALTORS®

2002 Printing

Buyer: _____ Date Prepared: _____ , 20_____

Address: _____ Projected Closing Date: _____ , 20_____

Purchase Price: $_____ Loan Amount: $_____

Loan Type: _____ Interest Rate: _____(%) Term (Years): _____

Financing Costs:

Down Payment	$_____
Closing Costs	+ $_____
Loan Discount (Points)	+ $_____

Escrow Establishment Charges:

Taxes (_____ months @ $_____/month)	+ $_____
Homeowner's Insurance (2 Months)	+ $_____
Mortgage Insurance (2 Months)	+ $_____
Prepaid Interest (____ days @ $_____/day)	$_____

Miscellaneous Charges:

Homeowner's Insurance (First Year's Premium)	+ $_____
Loan Transfer Fee	+ $_____
Purchase of Seller's Escrow Account	+ $_____
Proration of Property Taxes (County and City)	+ $_____
Other: _____	+ $_____

Credits:

Proration of Property Taxes (County and City)	- $_____
Earnest Money Deposit	- $_____
Other: _____	- $_____
TOTAL ESTIMATE OF COST TO BUYER	$_____

Estimated Monthly Payment:

Principal and Interest	+ $_____
Homeowner's Insurance	+ $_____
Mortgage Insurance	+ $_____
Property Taxes	+ $_____
Other: _____	+ $_____
Other: _____	+ $_____
Total	$_____

Projected Due Date of First Payment:

_____ , 20_____

The above information is based on data available as of this date. Additional monthly payments and accrued interest may reduce the loan payoff. Fees such as warehouse fees, tax service, lender inspection, photos, document preparation, handling fees, courier fees, etc. may also appear on the closing statement. No representation is made as to the accuracy or completeness of this form. This is an estimate only.

F73, Estimate of Cost to Buyer 01/01/02

PURCHASE AND SALE AGREEMENT

Date:_____, 20_____

2002
Printing

1. <u>Purchase and Sale</u>. The undersigned buyer ("Buyer") agrees to buy and the undersigned seller ("Seller") agrees to sell all that tract or parcel of land, with such improvements as are located thereon, described as follows: All that tract of land lying and being in Land Lot _____ of the _____ District, _____ Section of _____ County, Georgia, and being known as Address _____, City_____, Georgia Zip Code __ _____, according to the present system of numbering in and around this area, being more particularly described as Lot _____, Block_____, Unit _____, Phase/Section _____of _____Subdivision, as recorded in Plat Book _____, Page _____, _____ County, Georgia records together with all fixtures, landscaping, improvements, and appurtenances, all being hereinafter collectively referred to as the "Property." The full legal description of the Property is the same as is recorded with the Clerk of the Superior Court of the county in which the Property is located and is made a part of this Agreement by reference.

2. <u>Purchase Price and Method of Payment</u>. Buyer warrants that Buyer will have sufficient cash at closing, which when combined with the loan(s), if any, referenced herein, will allow Buyer to complete the purchase of the Property. Buyer does not need to sell or lease other real property in order to complete the purchase of the Property. The purchase price of the Property to be paid by Buyer at closing is: _____ U.S. Dollars, $_____ subject to the following: *[Select sections A, B, C, and/or D below. The sections not marked are not a part of this Agreement.]*

☐ **A**. **All Cash At Closing:** Buyer shall pay the purchase price to Seller in cash, or its equivalent. Buyer's obligation to close shall not be subject to any financial contingency. Buyer shall pay all closing costs.

☐ **B**. **Loan To Be Assumed**: See Exhibit "_____."

☐ **C**. **New Loan To Be Obtained:** This Agreement is made conditioned upon Buyer's ability to obtain a loan (except if the loan is denied because Buyer lacks sufficient cash to close excluding the amount of the loan and/or because Buyer has not sold or leased other real property) in the principal amount of _____% of the purchase price listed above, with an interest rate at par of not more than _____% per annum on the unpaid balance, to be secured by a first lien security deed on the Property; the loan to be paid in consecutive monthly installments of principal and interest over a term of not less than _____ years. "Ability to obtain" as used herein means that Buyer is qualified to receive the loan described herein based upon lender's customary and standard underwriting criteria. The loan shall be of the type selected below: *[The sections not marked are not a part of this Agreement.]*

  (1) **Loan Type:** ☐**Conventional**; ☐ **FHA** (see attached exhibit); ☐**VA** (see attached exhibit) ; ☐**Other** (see attached exhibit)
  (2) **Rate Type:** ☐**Fixed Rate Mortgage Loan**; ☐**Adjustable Rate Mortgage ("ARM") Loan**;
  (3) **Closing Costs and Discount Points:** Seller shall, at the time of closing, contribute a sum not to exceed $_____ to be used by Buyer to pay for: (a) preparation of the warranty deed and owner's affidavit by the closing attorney; (b) at Buyer's discretion, closing costs, loan discount points, survey costs, and insurance premiums (including flood insurance, if applicable) relating to the Property and/or loan; and (c) at Buyer's discretion, other costs to close including escrow establishment charges and prepaid items, if allowed by lender. Buyer shall pay all other costs, fees, and amounts for the above referenced items and to fulfill lender requirements to otherwise close this transaction.
  (4) **Closing Attorney:** This transaction shall be closed by the law firm of_____ _____, provided the firm is approved to close loans for Buyer's lender.
  (5) **Loan Obligations:** Buyer agrees to: (a) make application for the loan within _____ days from the Binding Agreement Date; (b) immediately notify Seller of having applied for the loan and the name of the lender; and (c) pursue qualification for and approval of the loan diligently and in good faith. Should Buyer not timely apply for the loan, Seller may terminate the Agreement if Buyer does not, within five days after receiving written notice thereof, cure the default by providing Seller with written evidence of loan application. Buyer agrees that a loan with terms consistent with those described herein shall satisfy this loan contingency. Buyer may also apply for a loan with different terms and conditions and close the transaction provided all other terms and conditions of this Agreement are fulfilled, and the new loan does not increase the costs charged to the Seller. Buyer shall be obligated to close this transaction if Buyer has the ability to obtain a loan with terms as described herein and/or any other loan for which Buyer has applied and been approved. From the Binding Agreement Date until closing, Buyer shall not intentionally make any material changes in Buyer's financial condition which would adversely affect Buyer's ability to obtain a loan. In the event any application of Buyer for a loan is denied, Buyer shall promptly provide Seller with a letter from the lender denying the loan stating the basis for the loan denial.

☐ **D**. **Second Loan to be Obtained**, see Exhibit "_____."

3. <u>Earnest Money</u>. Buyer has paid to _____ ("Holder") earnest money of $_____ check, OR $_____ cash, which has been received by Holder. The earnest money shall be deposited in Holder's escrow/trust account (with Holder retaining the interest if the account is interest bearing) within five banking days from the

Reprinted with permission from the Georgia Association of REALTORS®

Binding Agreement Date and shall be applied toward the purchase price of the Property at the time of closing. In the event any earnest money check is not honored, for any reason, by the bank upon which it is drawn, Holder shall promptly notify Buyer and Seller. Buyer shall have three banking days after notice to deliver good funds to Holder. In the event Buyer does not timely deliver good funds, the Seller shall have the right to terminate this Agreement upon written notice to the Buyer. Holder shall disburse earnest money only as follows: (a) upon the failure of the parties to enter into a binding agreement; (b) at closing; (c) upon a subsequent written agreement signed by all parties having an interest in the funds; (d) upon order of a court or arbitrator having jurisdiction over any dispute involving the earnest money; or (e) upon a reasonable interpretation of this Agreement by Holder. Prior to disbursing earnest money pursuant to a reasonable interpretation of this Agreement, Holder shall give all parties fifteen days notice, stating to whom the disbursement will be made. Any party may object in writing to the disbursement, provided the objection is received by Holder prior to the end of the fifteen-day notice period. All objections not raised in a timely manner shall be waived. In the event a timely objection is made, Holder shall consider the objection and shall do one or more of the following: (a) hold the earnest money for a reasonable period of time to give the parties an opportunity to resolve the dispute; (b) disburse the earnest money and so notify all parties; and/or (c) interplead the earnest money into a court of competent jurisdiction. Holder shall be reimbursed for and may deduct from any funds interpleaded its costs and expenses, including reasonable attorneys' fees. The prevailing party in the interpleader action shall be entitled to collect from the other party the costs and expenses reimbursed to Holder. No party shall seek damages from Holder (nor shall Holder be liable for the same) for any matter arising out of or related to the performance of Holder's duties under this earnest money paragraph. If Buyer breaches Buyer's obligations or warranties herein, holder may pay the earnest money to Seller by check, which if accepted and deposited by Seller, shall constitute liquidated damages in full settlement of all claims of Seller. It is agreed to by the parties that such liquidated damages are not a penalty and are a good faith estimate of Seller's actual damages, which damages are difficult to ascertain.

4. **Closing and Possession**.
   A. **Property Condition:** Seller warrants that at the time of closing or upon the granting of possession if at a time other than at closing, the Property will be in substantially the same condition as it was on Binding Agreement Date, except for normal wear and tear, and changes made to the condition of the Property pursuant to the written agreement of Buyer and Seller. Seller shall deliver Property clean and free of debris at time of possession. If the Property is destroyed or substantially damaged prior to closing, Seller shall promptly notify Buyer of the amount of insurance proceeds available to repair the damage and whether Seller will complete repairs prior to closing. Buyer may terminate this Agreement not later than five days after receiving such notice by giving written notice to Seller. If Buyer does not terminate this Agreement, Buyer shall receive at closing such insurance proceeds as are paid on the claim which are not spent to repair the damage.
   B. **Taxes:** Real estate taxes on said Property for the calendar year in which the sale is closed shall be prorated as of the date of closing. Seller shall pay State of Georgia property transfer tax.
   C. **Timing of Closing and Possession:** This transaction shall be closed on _____, 20____or on such other date as may be agreed to by the parties in writing, provided, however, that: (1) in the event the loan described herein is unable to be closed on or before said date; or (2) Seller fails to satisfy valid title objections, Buyer or Seller may, by notice to the other party (which notice must be received on or before the closing date), extend this Agreement's closing date and the date for surrender of occupancy if later than the closing date, up to seven days from the above-stated closing date. Buyer agrees to allow Seller to retain possession of the Property through: *[Select sections A, B, or C below. The sections not marked are not a part of this Agreement.]*
   ☐ A. the closing; or ☐ B. _____ hours after the closing; or ☐ C. _____ days after the closing at _____m. o'clock
   D. **Warranties Transfer:** Seller agrees to transfer to Buyer, at closing, subject to Buyer's acceptance thereof, Seller's interest in any manufacturer's warranties, service contracts, termite bond or treatment guarantee and/or other similar warranties which, by their terms, may be transferable to Buyer.
   E. **Prorations:** Seller and Buyer agree to prorate all utility bills between themselves, as of the date of closing (or the day of possession of the Property by the Buyer, whichever is the later) which are issued after closing and include service for any period of time the Property was owned/occupied by Seller or any other person prior to Buyer.
   F. **Closing Certifications:** Buyer and Seller shall execute and deliver such certifications, affidavits, and statements as are required at closing to meet the requirements of the lender and of federal and state law.

5. **Title**.
   A. **Warranty:** Seller warrants that, at the time of closing, Seller will convey good and marketable title to said Property by general warranty deed subject only to: (1) zoning; (2) general utility, sewer, and drainage easements of record on the Acceptance Date upon which the improvements do not encroach; (3) subdivision and/or condominium declarations, covenants, restrictions, and easements of record on the Acceptance Date; and (4) leases and other encumbrances specified in this Agreement. Buyer agrees to assume Seller's responsibilities in any leases specified in this Agreement.
   B. **Examination:** Buyer may, prior to closing, examine title and furnish Seller with a written statement of objections affecting the marketability of said title. If Seller fails to satisfy valid title objections prior to closing or any extension thereof, then Buyer may terminate the Agreement upon written notice to Seller, in which case Buyer's earnest money shall be returned. Good and marketable title as used herein shall mean title which a title insurance company licensed to do business in Georgia will insure at its regular rates, subject only to standard exceptions.
   C. **Survey:** Any survey of the Property attached hereto by agreement of the parties prior to the Binding Agreement Date shall be a part of this Agreement. Buyer shall have the right to terminate this Agreement upon written notice to Seller if a new survey performed by a surveyor licensed in Georgia is obtained which is materially different from any attached survey with respect to the Property, in which case Buyer's earnest money shall be returned. The term Amaterially different@ shall not apply to any improvements constructed by Seller in their agreed-upon locations subsequent to Binding Date Agreement. Matters revealed in said survey shall not relieve the warranty of title obligations of Seller referenced above.

6. <u>Seller's Property Disclosure.</u> Seller's Property Disclosure Statement is attached hereto and incorporated herein. Seller warrants that to the best of Seller's knowledge and belief, the information contained therein is accurate and complete as of the Binding Agreement Date.

7. <u>Termite Letter.</u> An official Georgia Wood Infestation Report ("Report") prepared by a licensed pest control operator, covering each dwelling and garage on the Property and dated within one hundred eighty days of the acceptance date is ☐ **OR,** is not ☐ attached to this Agreement as an exhibit. If the Report is not attached, Seller shall provide such a Report to Buyer within seven days from the Binding Agreement Date. Buyer shall have the right to terminate this Agreement within ten days from the Binding Agreement Date if either of the following events occur: (a) the Report is not timely provided to Buyer; or (b) the Report provided after the Binding Agreement Date indicates present infestation of, or damage to, the Property from termites or other wood destroying organisms. If Buyer does not timely give Seller notice of Buyer's decision to terminate this Agreement, Buyer's right to terminate the Agreement pursuant to this paragraph shall be waived. Notwithstanding the above, Buyer shall continue to have whatever other rights to terminate this Agreement, if any, that exist elsewhere in this Agreement. Unless otherwise noted on the Seller's Property Disclosure Statement, to the best of Seller's knowledge, the information contained in any attached or later provided Report is accurate and complete, and no other termite inspections have been performed or reports issued, the findings of which are inconsistent with the Report attached hereto. Prior to closing, Seller shall treat active infestation of termites and other wood destroying organisms, if any. At closing, Seller shall provide Buyer with a Report prepared by a licensed pest control operator dated within thirty days of the closing, stating that each dwelling and garage has been found to be free from active infestation of termites and other wood destroying organisms. This paragraph shall not limit Buyer's right to request that Seller repair and/or replace defects resulting from termites and other wood destroying organisms if the Property is sold with the right to request repairs in accordance with the Inspection Paragraph herein.

8. <u>Inspection.</u> Buyer and/or Buyer's representatives shall have the right to enter the Property at Buyer's expense and at reasonable times (including immediately prior to closing) to thoroughly inspect, examine, test and survey the Property. This shall include the right to inspect and test for lead-based paint and lead-based paint hazards for not less than ten days from the Binding Agreement Date. Seller shall cause all utility services and any pool, spa, and similar items to be operational so that Buyer may complete all inspections under this Agreement. The Buyer agrees to hold the Seller and all Brokers harmless from all claims, injuries, and damages arising out of or related to the exercise of these rights.

[Select section A or B below. The section not marked shall not be part of this Agreement.]

Buyer(s)

Initials

A. Property Sold With Right to Request Repairs.

    (1) Buyer shall have the right to request that Seller repair and/or replace only defects in the Property identified by Buyer's representative(s) by providing Seller, within _____ days from Binding Agreement Date, with a copy of inspection report(s) and a signed written amendment to this Agreement setting forth the defects noted in the report which Buyer requests be repaired and/or replaced. The term "defects" shall mean any portion of or item in the Property which: (a) is not in good working order and repair (normal wear and tear excepted); (b) constitutes a violation of applicable laws, governmental codes or regulations and is not otherwise grandfathered; or (c) is in a condition which represents a significant health risk or an unreasonable risk of injury or damage to persons or property. If Buyer does not timely present the written amendment and inspection report, Buyer shall be deemed to have accepted the Property "as is" in accordance with paragraph B below.

    (2) If Buyer timely submits the inspection report and the written amendment, Buyer and Seller shall have _____ days (hereinafter "Defect Resolution Period") from the Binding Agreement Date to negotiate through written offers and counteroffers the defects to be repaired and/or replaced by Seller.

    (3) Neither party may terminate this Agreement prior to the end of the Defect Resolution Period due to the failure to agree on the repair and/or replacement of defects without the written consent of the other party.

    (4) If Seller at any time during the Defect Resolution Period notifies Buyer that Seller will repair and/or replace all of the defects listed in the initial amendment submitted by Buyer, an agreement on the repair and/or replacement of defects shall be deemed to have been reached and all parties shall execute an amendment to that effect.

    (5) If Buyer and Seller have not within the Defect Resolution Period agreed on the defects to be repaired and/or replaced by signing a written amendment to this Agreement, Buyer may either accept the last unexpired counteroffer of Seller or accept the Property "as is" in accordance with paragraph B below, by giving notice to Seller within three days after the end of the Defect Resolution Period. If Buyer fails to timely give this notice, this Agreement shall terminate immediately, and Buyer's earnest money shall be returned in accordance with the Earnest Money paragraph above. All agreed-upon repairs and replacements shall be completed in a good and workmanlike manner prior to closing.

Buyer(s)

Initials

OR

B. Property Sold "As Is." All parties agree that the Property is being sold "as is," with all faults including but not limited to lead-based paint and lead-based paint hazards and damage from termites and other wood destroying organisms. The Seller shall have no obligation to make repairs to the Property.

9. <u>Other Provisions.</u>
    A. Binding Effect, Entire Agreement, Modification, Assignment: This Agreement shall be for the benefit of, and be binding upon, Buyer and Seller, their heirs, successors, legal representatives and permitted assigns. This Agreement constitutes the sole and entire agreement between the parties hereto and no modification or assignment of this Agreement shall be binding unless signed by all parties to this Agreement. No representation, promise, or inducement not included in this Agreement shall be binding upon any party hereto. Any assignee shall fulfill all the terms and conditions of this Agreement.

B. **Survival of Agreement:** All conditions or stipulations not fulfilled at time of closing shall survive the closing until such time as the conditions or stipulations are fulfilled.

C. **Governing Law:** This Agreement may be signed in multiple counterparts, is intended as a contract for the purchase and sale of real property and shall be interpreted in accordance with the laws of the State of Georgia.

D. **Time of Essence:** Time is of the essence of this Agreement.

E. **Terminology:** As the context may require in this Agreement: (1) the singular shall mean the plural and vice versa; and (2) all pronouns shall mean and include the person, entity, firm, or corporation to which they relate.

F. **Responsibility to Cooperate:** All parties agree to timely take such actions and produce, execute, and/or deliver such information and documentation as is reasonably necessary to carry out the responsibilities and obligations of this Agreement.

G. **Notices.** Except as otherwise provided herein, all notices, including offers, counteroffers, acceptances, amendments and demands, required or permitted hereunder shall be in writing, signed by the party giving the notice and delivered either: (1) in person, (2) by an overnight delivery service, prepaid, (3) by facsimile transmission (FAX) (provided that an original of the notice shall be promptly sent thereafter if so requested by the party receiving the same) or (4) by the United States Postal Service, postage prepaid, registered or certified return receipt requested. The parties agree that a faxed signature of a party constitutes an original signature binding upon that party. Notice shall be deemed to have been given as of the date and time it is actually received. Notwithstanding the above, notice by FAX shall be deemed to have been given as of the date and time it is transmitted if the sending FAX produces a written confirmation with the date, time and telephone number to which the notice was sent. Receipt of notice by the Broker representing a party as a client shall be deemed to be notice to that party for all purposes herein, except in transactions where the Broker is practicing designated agency, in which case, receipt of notice by the designated agent representing a party as a client shall be required to constitute notice. All notice requirements referenced herein shall be strictly construed.

10. **Disclaimer.** Buyer and Seller acknowledge that they have not relied upon any advice, representations or statements of Brokers and waive and shall not assert any claims against Brokers involving the same. Buyer and Seller agree that Brokers shall not be responsible to advise Buyer and Seller on any matter including but not limited to the following: any matter which could have been revealed through a survey, title search or inspection of the Property; the condition of the Property, any portion thereof, or any item therein; building products and construction techniques; the necessity or cost of any repairs to the Property; hazardous or toxic materials or substances; termites and other wood destroying organisms; the tax or legal consequences of this transaction; the availability and cost of utilities or community amenities; the appraised or future value of the Property; any condition(s) existing off the Property which may affect the Property; the terms, conditions and availability of financing; and the uses and zoning of the Property whether permitted or proposed. Buyer and Seller acknowledge that Brokers are not experts with respect to the above matters and that, if any of these matters or any other matters are of concern to them, they should seek independent expert advice relative thereto. Buyer further acknowledges that in every neighborhood there are conditions which different buyers may find objectionable. Buyer shall therefore be responsible to become fully acquainted with neighborhood and other off site conditions which could affect the Property.

11. **Agency and Brokerage.**
    A. **Agency.**
    (1) In this Agreement, the term ABroker@ shall mean a licensed Georgia real estate broker or brokerage firm and where the context would indicate the broker's affiliated licensees. No Broker in this transaction shall owe any duty to Buyer or Seller greater than what is set forth in their brokerage engagements and the Brokerage Relationships in Real Estate Transactions Act, O.C.G.A. § 10-6A-1 et .seq.;

    (2) Seller and Buyer acknowledge that if they are not represented by a Broker they are each solely responsible for protecting their own interests, and that Broker's role is limited to performing ministerial acts for that party.

    (3) The Broker, if any, working with the Seller is identified on the signature page as the "Listing Broker"; and said Broker is ☐ **OR**, is **NOT** ☐ representing the Seller;

    (4) The Broker, if any, working with the Buyer is identified on the signature page as the ASelling Broker@, and said Broker is ☐ **OR**, is **NOT** ☐ representing the Buyer; and

    (5) If Buyer and Seller are both being represented by the same Broker, a relationship of either designated agency ☐ **OR,** dual agency ☐ shall exist.
        (a) **Dual Agency Disclosure.** [*Applicable only if dual agency has been selected above*] Seller and Buyer are aware that Broker is acting as a dual agent in this transaction and consent to the same. Seller and Buyer have been advised that:
            1 - In serving as a dual agent the Broker is representing two clients whose interests are or at times could be different or even adverse;
            2 - The Broker will disclose all adverse, material facts relevant to the transaction and actually known to the dual agent to all parties in the transaction except for information made confidential by request or instructions from another client which is not otherwise required to be disclosed by law;
            3 - The Buyer and Seller do not have to consent to dual agency; and
            4 - The consent of the Buyer and Seller to dual agency has been given voluntarily and the parties have read and understood their brokerage engagement agreements.
            5 - Notwithstanding any provision to the contrary contained herein, Seller and Buyer each hereby direct Broker, while acting as a dual agent, to keep confidential and not reveal to the other party any information which could materially and adversely affect their negotiating position.
        (b) **Designated Agency Assignment.** [*Applicable only if the designated agency has been selected above*] The Broker has assigned _____ to work exclusively with Buyer as Buyer's designated agent and _____ to work exclusively with Seller as Seller's designated agent. Each designated agent shall exclusively represent the party to whom each has been assigned as a client and shall not represent in this transaction the client assigned to the other designated agent.

(c) **Material Relationship Disclosure.** The Broker and/or affiliated licensees have no material relationship with either client except as follows:_____.
(A material relationship means one actually known of a personal, familial or business nature between the Broker and affiliated licensees and a client which would impair their ability to exercise fair judgment relative to another client.)

B. **Brokerage.** The Broker(s) identified herein have performed valuable brokerage services and are to be paid a commission pursuant to a separate agreement or agreements. Unless otherwise provided for herein, the Listing Broker will be paid a commission by the Seller, and the Selling Broker will receive a portion of the Listing Broker's commission pursuant to a cooperative brokerage agreement. The closing attorney is directed to pay the commission of the Broker(s) at closing out of the proceeds of the sale. If the sale proceeds are insufficient to pay the full commission, the party owing the commission will pay any shortfall at closing. If more than one Broker is involved in the transaction, the closing attorney is directed to pay each Broker their respective portion of said commission. In the event the sale is not closed because of Buyer's and/or Seller's failure or refusal to perform any of their obligations herein, the non-performing party shall immediately pay the Broker(s) the full commission the Broker(s) would have received had the sale closed, and the Selling Broker and Listing Broker may jointly or independently pursue the non-performing party for their portion of the commission.

12. <u>Time Limit of Offer</u>. This instrument shall be open for acceptance until_____ o'clock _____M. on the _____ day of
_____, 20_____.

13. <u>Exhibits and Addenda</u>. All exhibits and/or addenda attached hereto, listed below, or referenced herein are made a part of this Agreement. If any such exhibit or addendum conflicts with any preceding paragraph, said exhibit or addendum shall control:

SPECIAL STIPULATIONS: The following Special Stipulations, if conflicting with any exhibit, addendum, or preceding paragraph, shall control.

☐ **(Mark box if additional pages are attached.)**

_____   (_____)
Selling Broker   MLS Office Code

By: _____
    Broker or Broker's Affiliated Licensee

Print or Type Name:_____

Bus. Phone:_____ FAX #_____

Multiple Listing #_____

_____   (_____)
Listing Broker   MLS Office Code

By: _____
    Broker or Broker's Affiliated Licensee

Print or Type Name: _____

Bus. Phone: _____ FAX#_____

_____
Buyer's Signature: SS/FEI#

Print or Type Name:_____

_____
Buyer's Signature: SS/FEI#

Print or Type Name:_____

_____
Seller's Signature: SS/FEI#

Print or Type Name:_____

_____
Seller's Signature: SS/FEI#

Print or Type Name:_____

Acceptance Date
The above proposition is hereby accepted, _____ o'clock_____ m. on the_____ day of _____, 20_____.

Binding Agreement Date
This instrument shall become a binding agreement on the date ("Binding Agreement Date") when notice of the acceptance of this Agreement has been received by offeror. The offeror shall promptly notify offeree when acceptance has been received.

Reprinted with permission from the Georgia Association of REALTORS®

COUNTEROFFER #_____

_____ o'clock _____ m. on the _____ day of _____, 20_____ .

2002 Printing

This is a Counteroffer from: *[Select A or B below. The one not selected is not a part of this Agreement.]*

☐ **A. Seller to Buyer**   OR   ☐ **B. Buyer to Seller**

The following is a counteroffer to that certain offer to purchase or sell set forth in the Purchase and Sale Agreement dated _____, 20_____ ("Agreement") for the purchase and sale of real property located at:

_____, _____ , Georgia _____ .

All terms and conditions of the Agreement are agreed to and accepted by the undersigned with the express exception of the following:

Continued on next page

Reprinted with permission from the Georgia Association of REALTORS®

☐ **(Mark box if additional pages are attached.)**

The provisions set forth in this counteroffer shall control over any conflicting or inconsistent provisions set forth in the Agreement or any prior counteroffer. By signing below, all parties agree and acknowledge that they are accepting the Agreement subject to the terms and conditions set forth herein. While Buyer and Seller need to sign only this counteroffer for there to be an offer and acceptance of the Agreement (subject to the terms and conditions set forth herein), each party agrees if so requested by the other party, to promptly sign a conformed copy of the Agreement incorporating therein the terms and conditions set forth in this counteroffer.

Time Limit of Offer.
This instrument shall be regarded as an offer by the Buyer or Seller who first signs to the other and is open for acceptance until:
_____ o'clock _____M. on the _____ day of _____, 20_____.

_____ (_____)
Selling Broker   MLS Office Code

By: _____
     Broker or Broker's Affiliated Licensee

Print or Type Name:_____

Bus. Phone:_____ FAX #_____

Multiple Listing #_____

_____ (_____)
Listing Broker   MLS Office Code

By: _____
     Broker or Broker's Affiliated Licensee

Print or Type Name: _____

Bus. Phone:_____FAX#_____

_____
Buyer's Signature: SS/FEI#

Print or Type Name:_____

_____
Buyer's Signature: SS/FEI#

Print or Type Name:_____

_____
Seller's Signature: SS/FEI#

Print or Type Name:_____

_____
Seller's Signature: SS/FEI#

Print or Type Name:_____

Acceptance Date
The above proposition is hereby accepted, _____ o'clock _____M. on the day of _____, 20_____

Binding Agreement Date
This instrument shall become a binding agreement on the date ("Binding Agreement Date") when notice of the acceptance of this Agreement has been received by offeror. The offeror shall promptly notify offeree when acceptance has been received.

         F22, Counteroffer, Page 2 of 2 01/01/02

EXCLUSIVE LEASING/MANAGEMENT
AGREEMENT

2002 Printing

State law prohibits Broker from representing Owner as a client without first entering into a written agreement with Owner under O.C.G.A. § 10-6A-1 et. seq.

This Agreement, made and entered into this _____ day of _____, 20_____, by and between _____ (hereinafter referred to as "Owner") and_____ (hereinafter referred to as "Broker");

WHEREAS, Owner owns that certain real estate property described as follows:
All that tract of land lying and being in Land Lot _____ of the _____ District, _____ Section of _____ County, Georgia, and being known as Address _____ _____, City _____, Zip Code _____, according to the present system of numbering in and around this area, being more particularly described as Lot _____, Block _____, Unit _____, Phase/Section _____ of _____ subdivision, as recorded in Plat Book _____, Page _____, _____ County, Georgia, records together with all fixtures, landscaping, improvements, and appurtenances, all being hereinafter collectively referred to as the "Property." The full legal description of the Property is the same as is recorded with the Clerk of the Superior Court of the county in which the Property is located and is made a part of this Agreement by reference.

WHEREAS, Owner desires to retain Broker as Owner's agent to exclusively rent, lease, operate, and manage the property for and in behalf of the Owner;

NOW THEREFORE, In consideration of the premises and mutual covenants herein set forth, the parties agree as follows:

1. **Term.** Broker shall have the exclusive right to lease and manage the Property for the period of _____ beginning on the _____ day of _____, _____. If Owner terminates this Agreement, Owner shall pay Broker all fees which would be due both from the present and future months by virtue of any unexpired rental agreement in effect at the time of termination. Broker may deduct the full amount of such fees from any monies coming to Broker which would be due Owner.

2. **Leases.** Broker is authorized to enter into a lease of the Property on Owner's behalf if it is for a term of no more than _____ months or less than _____ months at a monthly rental of at least $_____. The Property may be occupied by a tenant obtained by Broker as of _____, 20 _____. Any such lease will be in writing on Broker's standard lease form then in use.

3. **Broker's Authority.** The Owner hereby gives the Broker the following authority and powers and agrees to assume the expenses in connection with:
   A. To exclusively advertise the Property for rental and to display "for rent" signs thereon; to sign, renew, and cancel leases for the Property; to collect rents due or to become due and give receipts therefor; to terminate tenancies and to sign and serve in the name of the Owner such notices as are appropriate; to institute and prosecute actions; to evict tenants and to recover possession of the Property; to sue in the name of the Owner and recover rents and other sums due; and when expedient, to settle, compromise, and release such actions or lawsuits or reinstate such tenancies.
   B. To make or cause to be made and supervise repairs and alterations, and to do decorating on the Property; to purchase supplies and pay bills therefor; the Broker agrees to secure the prior approval of the Owner on all expenditures in excess of $_____ for any one item, except monthly or recurring operating charges and/or emergency repairs in excess of the maximum, if in the opinion of the Broker such repairs are necessary to protect the Property from damage or to maintain services to the tenants as called for in their leases.
   C. To hire, discharge and supervise all contractors and/or employees required for the operation and maintenance of the Property; it being agreed that any employees hired shall be deemed employees of the Owner and not the Broker, and that the Broker may perform any of its duties through Owner's attorneys, agents, or employees and shall not be responsible for their acts, defaults, or negligence if reasonable care has been exercised in their appointment and retention.
   D. To make contracts for electricity, gas, fuel, water, telephone, window cleaning, trash or rubbish hauling and other services as the Broker shall deem advisable; the Owner to assume the obligations of any contract so entered into the termination of this Agreement.
   E. To contract with others, including affiliates of broker or companies owned by broker, to perform services including, but not limited to, repairs, maintenance, accounting, data processing, record keeping, legal fees and court costs. Any such arrangement with affiliates or companies owned by Broker will be on terms fair and reasonable to the Owner and no less favorable than could reasonably be realized with unaffiliated persons or companies. The Owner is hereby aware that Broker may deduct these expenses from the monies coming to Broker that are due to the Owner.
   F. To institute and prosecute legal actions and proceedings in Owner's name and behalf to terminate leases for cause, to remove tenants from Property, to recover from damage to the Property, and for such purposes, Broker may employ attorneys and incur

court costs and litigation costs at Owner's expense any and all of these things. Broker in his discretion is also authorized to settle or compromise any such legal actions or proceedings.

4. <u>Compensation.</u> Broker shall be compensated on the following basis:

A. For Leasing: $_____ or _____ % of monthly rent.

B. For Management: $_____ or _____ % of monthly rent.

C. For Refinancing: $_____.

D. For Modernization: $_____ plus _____ % of expenditures

For Restoration: $_____ plus _____ % of expenditures

For Repairs: $_____ plus _____ % of expenditures

E. Other:_____

5. <u>Sale of Property</u>. If Owner sells the Property to a tenant (or spouse or roommate of such tenant) obtained by Broker, either during the term of the lease or thereafter, Owner will pay Broker a commission of _____% of the price for which the Property is sold. This obligation shall survive the expiration or termination of this Agreement.

6. <u>Non-Discrimination.</u> Owner and Broker are subject to state and federal civil rights and discrimination laws, which prohibit discrimination on the basis of race, color, religion, sex, familial status, handicap, or national origin. Neither Owner nor Broker will perform any act which would have the effect of discriminating against any person in violation of law.

7. <u>Emergency Repairs.</u> Broker is authorized to make such emergency repairs to the Property as Broker reasonably believes to be necessary to protect the Property from damage or to maintain services to a tenant for which a lease provides. Owner has paid to and will maintain with Broker the sum of $_____ as a deposit for the cost of such emergency, but expenditures of such repairs are not limited to that amount if for reasons of necessity Broker must spend more. The deposit money shall be deposited in Broker's escrow account with Broker retaining the interest if the account is interest-bearing. In the event any deposit money check is not honored, for any reason, by the bank upon it is drawn, Owner shall deliver good funds to Holder within three days of the bank's notice to Broker. In the event Owner does not timely deliver good funds, the Tenant, in his sole discretion, shall have the right to terminate this Agreement by giving written notice to the Owner. In that event, Owner shall promptly reimburse Broker for the cost of all other emergency repairs which Broker pays for or for which Broker is obligated, but Owner understands that Broker is under no duty to make expenditures in excess of the amount of the deposit.

8. <u>Condition of Property.</u> Owner certifies that unless provided otherwise herein, all systems and furnished appliances are in working condition. Owner certifies that the Property is in good and habitable condition now and Owner, will at all times, be responsible for the maintenance of the Property in a good habitable condition, and in compliance with all applicable laws, ordinances and regulations of all government authorities. Upon the execution of this agreement Owner will provide two sets of keys for the Property and ensure that the Property is clean and the grounds are in good condition.
Owner shall maintain adequate fire and extended insurance coverage on the Property, and Owner will, at all times, maintain landlord's liability insurance for Owner and will cause Broker to be named as additional insured under such liability insurance. Owner will provide Broker with evidence of such insurance coverage prior to date of occupancy of tenant.
Has your property flooded three or more times in the last five years?　☐Yes ☐No

9. <u>Receipt and Payment of Funds.</u> Broker is authorized to deposit all rent received from the Property in a trust account maintained by Broker for that purpose. However, Broker will not be held liable in event of bankruptcy or failure of a depository. Broker shall render Owner, on a monthly basis, a detailed accounting of funds received and disbursed in Owner's behalf and shall remit to Owner the balance of such funds, if any, remaining after Broker deducts any and all commissions, Management fees and other charges due Broker or other parties in Owner's behalf. In the event the disbursements shall be in excess of the rents collected by the Broker, the Owner hereby agrees to pay such excess promptly upon demand of the Broker. Broker to prepare IRS Form 1099 and any other tax related forms or documents as may be required by law. Broker is further authorized to make the following payments for Owner on a monthly basis; however, Broker shall be under no obligation to make such payments if there are insufficient funds on hand in Owner's account with Broker, it being understood that Broker will promptly notify Owner if such funds are not on hand. The Broker is hereby instructed and authorized to pay mortgage indebtedness, property and employees taxes, special assessments, and to place fire, liability, steam boiler, pressure vessel, or any other insurance required, and the Broker is hereby directed to accrue and pay for same from the Owner's funds, with the following exceptions:_____

10. <u>Miscellaneous Charges.</u> Broker is authorized to charge and collect from the tenant for Broker's own account, charges of late payment of rent, bad check processing, credit reports, and such other matters as Broker may deem necessary, and to deposit any security deposits into an interest-bearing account for Broker's own behalf.

11. <u>Indemnity.</u> Owner agrees to save the Broker harmless from all damage suits in connection with the leasing and management of the Property and from liability from injury suffered by an employee or other person whomsoever, and to carry, at his own expense, necessary public liability and worker's compensation insurance adequate to protect the interest of the parties hereto, which policies shall

be so written as to protect the Broker in the same manner and to the same extent they protect the Owner, and will name the Broker as coinsured. The Broker shall not be liable for any error of judgement or for any mistake, fact of law, or for anything which it may do or refrain from doing hereinafter, except in cases of willful misconduct or gross negligence. Notwithstanding any other provisions to the contrary, Broker shall under no circumstances have any liability greater than the compensation actually paid to Broker hereunder including commissions.

12. **Other Provisions.**
    A. **Binding Effect, Entire Agreement, Modification, Assignment:** This Agreement shall be for the benefit of, and be binding upon, the parties hereto, their heirs, successors, legal representatives and permitted assigns. This Agreement constitutes the sole and entire agreement between the parties hereto and no modification or assignment of this Agreement shall be binding unless signed by all parties to this Agreement. No representation, promise, or inducement not included in this Agreement shall be binding upon any party hereto. Any assignee shall fulfill all the terms and conditions of this Agreement.
    B. **Survival of Agreement:** All conditions or stipulations not fulfilled at time of closing shall survive the closing until such time as the conditions or stipulations are fulfilled.
    C. **Governing Law:** This Agreement is intended as a contract for the purchase and sale of real property and shall be interpreted in accordance with the laws of the State of Georgia.
    D. **Time of Essence:** Time is of the essence of this Agreement.
    E. **Terminology:** As the context may require in this Agreement: (1) the singular shall mean the plural and vice versa; and (2) all pronouns shall mean and include the person, entity, firm, or corporation to which they relate.
    F. **Responsibility to Cooperate:** All parties agree to timely take such actions and produce, execute, and/or deliver such information and documentation as is reasonably necessary to carry out the responsibilities and obligations of this Agreement.
    G. **Notices.** Except as otherwise provided herein, all notices, including demands, offers, counteroffers, acceptances, and amendments required or permitted hereunder shall be in writing, signed by the party giving the notice and delivered to the party at the address set forth below (or such other address as the party may provide in writing) either: (1) in person, (2) by an overnight delivery service, prepaid, (3) by facsimile transmission (FAX) (provided that an original of the notice shall be promptly sent thereafter if so requested by the party receiving the same) or (4) by the United States Postal Service, postage prepaid, registered or certified return receipt requested. The parties agree that a faxed signature of a party constitutes an original signature binding upon that party. Notice shall be deemed to have been given as of the date and time it is actually received. Notwithstanding the above, notice by FAX shall be deemed to have been given as of the date and time it is transmitted if the sending FAX produces a written confirmation with the date, time and telephone number to which the notice was sent. Receipt of notice by the Broker representing a party as a client shall be deemed to be notice to that party for all purposes herein, except in transactions where the Broker is practicing designated agency, in which case, receipt of notice by the designated agent representing a party as a client shall be required to constitute notice. All references to any notice required to be given or due dates for rent payments shall be strictly construed.

Owner's address: _____

Broker's Address: _____

_____

_____

_____

_____

_____

_____

Fax #:_____

Fax #:_____

13. **Disclaimer.** Owner acknowledges that Owner has not relied upon any advice, representations or statements of Broker and waives and shall not assert any claims against Broker involving advice, representations or statements not specifically referenced in the Special Stipulations. Owner agrees that Broker shall not be responsible to advise Owner on any matter, including but not limited to the following: insurance, any matter which could have been revealed through a survey, title search or inspection of the Property; the condition of the Property, any portion thereof, or any item therein; the necessity or cost of any repairs to the Property; hazardous or toxic materials or substances; the tax or legal consequences of any lease transaction; the appraised or future value of the Property; any condition(s) existing off the Property which may affect the Property; the creditworthiness of prospective tenants; the uses and zoning of the Property whether permitted or proposed; and any matter relating to crime and security in and around the Property. Owner acknowledges that Broker is not an expert with respect to the above matters and that, if any of these matters or any other matters are of concern to Owner, Owner should seek independent expert advice relative thereto.

14. **Broker's Policy on Agency.** Unless Broker indicates below that Broker is not offering a specific agency relationship, the types of agency relationships offered by Broker are seller agency, buyer agency, designated agency, dual agency, Owner agency, and tenant agency.

The agency relationship(s), if any, **NOT** offered by Broker include the following_____

Dual Agency Disclosure: [*Applicable only if Broker's agency policy is to practice dual agency*] Owner does hereby consent to Broker acting in a dual agency capacity in transactions in which Broker is representing as clients both the Owner and a tenant interested in or leasing the Property, and Broker is not acting in a designated agency capacity. By entering this Agreement, Owner acknowledges that Owner understands that Owner does not have to consent to dual agency, is doing so voluntarily, and that this brokerage engagement has been read and understood. In serving as a dual agent, Broker is representing two parties as clients whose interests are or at times could be different or even adverse. As a dual agent, Broker will disclose to both parties all adverse material facts relevant to the transaction actually known to the dual agent except for information made confidential by request or instructions from client and which is not required to be disclosed by law. Owner hereby directs Broker, while acting as a dual agent to keep confidential and not reveal to the tenant any information which would materially and adversely affect the tenant's negotiating position. Broker or Broker's affiliated licensees will timely disclose to each client the nature of any material relationship the broker and the broker's affiliated licensees have with the other client or clients, other than that incidental to the transaction. A material relationship shall mean any actually known personal, familial, or business relationship between Broker and a client which would impair the ability of Broker to exercise fair and independent judgment relative to another client. The other party whom Broker may represent in the event of dual agency may or may not be identified at the time Owner enters into this Agreement. If any party is identified after the Agreement and has a material relationship with Broker, then Broker shall timely provide to Owner a disclosure of the nature of such relationship.

15. <u>**Limits on Broker's Authority and Responsibility**</u>. Owner acknowledges and agrees that Broker: (a) may show other properties to prospective tenants who are interested in Owner's Property; (b) is not an expert with regard to matters that could be revealed through a survey, title search, or inspection; the condition of property; the necessity, or cost of repairs; hazardous or toxic materials; the availability and cost of utilities or community amenities; conditions existing off the property that may affect the property; uses and zoning of the property; the appraised or future value of the property; termites and wood-destroying organisms; building products and construction techniques; the tax or legal consequences of a contemplated transaction; and matters relating to financing (and if these matters are of concern to Owner, Owner is hereby advised to seek independent expert advice on any of these matters of concern to Owner); (c) shall owe no duties to Owner nor have any authority to act on behalf of Owner other than what is set forth in this Agreement; (d) may make all disclosures required by law; (e) may disclose all information about the Property to others; and (f) shall, under no circumstances, have any liability greater than the amount of the real estate commission paid hereunder to Broker (excluding any commission amount, paid to a cooperating real estate broker, if any).

16. <u>**Required State Law Disclosures**</u>. (a) Broker agrees to keep all information which Owner asks to be kept confidential by express request or instruction unless the Owner permits such disclosure by subsequent work or conduct or such disclosure is required by law; (b) Broker may not knowingly give customers false information; (c) In the event of a conflict between Broker's duty not to give customers false information and the duty to keep the confidences of Owner, the duty not to give customers false information shall prevail; (d) Unless specified below, Broker has no other known agency relationships with other parties which would conflict with any interests of Owner (with the exception that Broker may represent other tenants, and Owners, buyers and sellers in buying, selling or leasing property).

SPECIAL STIPULATIONS: The following Special Stipulations, if conflicting with any preceding paragraph, shall control.

☐ (Mark box if additional pages are attached.)

BY SIGNING THIS AGREEMENT, OWNER ACKNOWLEDGES THAT: (1) OWNER HAS REAL ALL PROVISIONS MADE HEREIN; (2) OWNER UNDERSTANDS ALL SUCH PROVISIONS AND DISCLOSURES AND HAS ENTERED INTO THIS AGREEMENT VOLUNTARILY; AND (3) OWNER IS NOT SUBJECT TO A CURRENT LEASING/MANAGEMENT AGREEMENT WITH ANY OTHER BROKER.

RECEIPT OF A COPY OF THIS AGREEMENT IS HEREBY ACKNOWLEDGED BY OWNER.

The above proposition is hereby accepted, _____ o'clock _____ M., on the _____ day of _____, 20_____.

I certify that I have read and understand the above printed matter. This _____ day of _____, 20_____.

_____ (_____)
Listing Broker   MLS Office Code

By: _____
    Broker or Broker's Affiliated Licensee

Print or Type Name:_____

Bus. Phone:_____ FAX #_____

_____

_____
Owner Signature   SS/FEI #

Print or Type Name:_____

_____
Address

_____

_____
Owner Signature   SS/FEI #

Print or Type Name: _____

Address_____

Reprinted with permission from the Georgia Association of REALTORS®

LEASE FOR
RESIDENTIAL PROPERTY
(NOT TO BE USED FOR LEASE/PURCHASE TRANSACTIONS)

[To be Used When Broker is Managing Property]

Georgia
Association of
REALTORS®

2002 Printing

In consideration of the mutual covenants set forth herein, this Lease is entered into this _____ day of _____, 20_____ between _____, (hereinafter "Landlord") and _____, (hereinafter "Tenant") Landlord leases to Tenant, and Tenant leases from Landlord, the Property described as follows: All that tract of land lying and being in Land Lot _____ of the _____ District, _____ Section of _____ County, Georgia, and being known as Address _____, City, _____, Georgia, Zip Code _____, according to the present system of numbering in and around this area, being more particularly described as Lot _____, Block _____, Unit _____, Building _____, of _____ subdivision, as recorded in Plat Book _____, Page _____, _____ County, Georgia, records together with all fixtures, landscaping, improvements, and appurtenances, all being hereinafter collectively referred to as the "Property." The full legal description of the Property is the same as is recorded with the Clerk of the Superior Court of the county in which the Property is located and is made a part of this Lease by reference.

1. <u>**TERM**</u>. The initial term of this Lease shall be _____ months _____ days beginning on _____, 20_____ ("Commencement Date"), through and including _____, 20_____.

2. <u>**POSSESSION**</u>. If Landlord is unable to deliver possession of the Property on the Commencement Date, rent shall be abated on a daily basis until possession is granted. If possession is not granted within seven days of the Commencement Date, Tenant may terminate this Lease in which event Landlord shall promptly refund all deposits to Tenant. Landlord shall not be liable for delays in the delivery of possession to Tenant.

3. <u>**RENT**</u>. Tenant shall pay rent in advance in the sum of _____Dollars ($_____) per month on the first day of each month during the Lease Term, at the address set forth in the Other Provisions Paragraph (or at such other place as may be designated from time to time by Landlord in writing). If the Commencement Date begins on the 2nd day through the last day of any month, the rent shall be prorated for that portion of the month and shall be paid at the time of leasing the Property.

4. <u>**LATE PAYMENT; SERVICE CHARGE FOR RETURNED CHECKS.**</u> Rent not paid in full by the fifth day of the month shall be late. Landlord has no obligation to accept any rent not received by the fifth of the month. If late payment is made and Landlord accepts the same, the payment must be in the form of cash, cashier's check or money order and must include a late charge of $_____ and, if applicable, a service charge for any returned check of $_____. Landlord reserves the right to refuse to accept personal checks from Tenant after one or more of Tenant's personal checks have been returned by the bank unpaid.

5. <u>**SECURITY DEPOSIT TO BE HELD BY LANDLORD OR BROKER**</u>. *[Select Section A or B below. The Section not marked shall not be part of this Agreement]*

  ☐ **A. <u>Landlord Holding Security Deposit</u>.**

   (1) Tenant agrees to deposit _____ Dollars ($_____) cash, money order and/or check with Landlord before taking possession of the Property as security for Tenant's fulfillment of the conditions of this Lease ("Security Deposit"). The Security Deposit shall be held by Landlord as follows: *[Select Section (a) or (b) below. The section not marked shall not be part of this Agreement.]*

    ☐ (a) <u>Ten or fewer units owned by Landlord or Landlord's spouse or minor children</u>. The Security Deposit is to be deposited in *[check one]* (___) Landlord's escrow/trust bank account or (___) in the general account of Landlord at _____bank, and not in a separate escrow/trust account. If the Security Deposit is to be deposited in the Landlord's general account, Tenant acknowledges and agrees that Landlord shall have the right to use such funds for whatever purpose Landlord sees fit, and such funds will not be segregated or set apart in any manner. Interest earned on such account(s) shall accrue to and be retained by Landlord.

    ☐ (b) <u>More than ten units owned by Landlord or Landlord's spouse or minor children</u>. The Security Deposit shall be deposited in Landlord's escrow/trust account (Account#_____) at _____ bank. Interest earned from such account(s), if any, shall accrue to and be retained by Landlord.

   (2) Tenant recognizes and accepts the risk of depositing the Security Deposit with Landlord. Tenant acknowledges that Tenant

Permission to use forms is given by the Georgia Association of REALTORS®

has not relied upon the advice of Broker or Broker's Affiliated Licensees in deciding to pay such security deposit to Landlord. Landlord and Tenant acknowledge and agree that:

    (a) Broker has no responsibility for, or control over, the Security Deposit deposited with Landlord;

    (b) Broker has no ability or obligation to insure that the Security Deposit is properly applied or deposited;

    (c) The disposition of the Security Deposit is the sole responsibility of Landlord and Tenant as herein provided; and

    (d) Broker has no knowledge of the financial condition or financial stability of Landlord. Landlord and Tenant agree to indemnify and hold harmless Broker and Broker's affiliated licensees against all claims, damages, losses, expenses or liability arising from the handling of the Security Deposit by Landlord.

(3) The Security Deposit will be returned to Tenant within thirty days after Property is vacated if:

    (a) Lease term has expired or Lease has been terminated in writing by the mutual consent of both parties;

    (b) All monies due Landlord by Tenant have been paid;

    (c) Property is not damaged and is left in its original condition, normal wear and tear excepted;

    (d) All keys have been returned; and

    (e) Tenant is not in default under any of the terms of this Lease.

(4) Within one month after termination of this Lease or Tenant's vacating of the property, whichever is later, Landlord shall return Security Deposit to Tenant, after deducting any sum which Tenant owes Landlord hereunder, or any sum which Landlord may expend to repair arising out of or related to Tenant's occupancy hereunder, abandonment of the Property or default in this Lease (provided Landlord attempts to mitigate such actual damages), including but no limited to any repair, replacement, cleaning or painting of the Property reasonably necessary due to the negligence, carelessness, accident, or abuse of Tenant or invitee, guests, or members of Tenant's household. In the event Landlord elects to retain any part of the Security Deposit, Landlord shall provide Tenant with a written statement setting forth the reasons for the retention of any portion of the Security Deposit, including the damages for which any portion of the Security Deposit is retained. The use and application of the Security Deposit by Landlord shall be at the discretion of the Landlord. Appropriation by Landlord of all or part of the Security Deposit shall not be an exclusive remedy for Landlord, but shall be cumulative, and in addition to all remedies of Landlord at law or under this Lease. The Tenant may not apply the Security Deposit to any rent payment.

☐ **B. <u>Broker Holding Security Deposit</u>.**

(1) Tenant has paid $_____ cash, money order, and/or check, as security deposit, to the following Real Estate Broker _____("Holder"), which has been received by Holder. The Security Deposit shall be deposited in Holder's escrow/trust account (with Holder retaining the interest if the account is interest bearing) within five banking days from the Binding Agreement Date. In the event any Security Deposit check is not honored, for any reason, by the bank upon which it is drawn, Holder shall promptly notify Tenant and Landlord. Tenant shall have three banking days after notice to deliver good funds to Holder. In the event Tenant does not timely deliver good funds, the Landlord shall have the right to terminate this Agreement upon written notice to the Tenant.

(2) Holder shall disburse the Security Deposit only as follows: (a) upon the failure of the parties to enter into a binding lease; (b) upon a written agreement signed by all parties having an interest in the funds; (c) upon order of a court or arbitrator having jurisdiction over any dispute involving the security deposit; (d) upon a reasonable interpretation of this Agreement by Holder; or (e) upon the termination of the agency relationship between Landlord and Holder, in which event Holder shall only disburse the Security Deposit, to another licensed Georgia Real Estate Broker selected by Landlord unless otherwise agreed to in writing by Landlord and Tenant after notice to Holder and Tenant. Prior to disbursing the Security Deposit pursuant to a reasonable interpretation of this Agreement; Holder shall give all parties fifteen days notice, stating to whom the disbursement will be made. Any party may object in writing to the disbursement, provided the objection is received by Holder prior to the end of the day notice period. All objections not raised in a timely manner, shall be waived. In the event a timely objection is made, Holder shall consider the objection and shall do any or a combination of the following: (a) hold the Security Deposit for a reasonable period of time to give the parties an opportunity to resolve the dispute; (b) disburse the Security Deposit and so notify all parties; and/or (c) interplead the Security Deposit into a court of competent jurisdiction. Holder shall be reimbursed for and may deduct from any funds interpleaded its costs and expenses, including reasonable attorney's fees. The prevailing party in the interpleader action shall be entitled to collect from the other party the costs and expenses reimbursed to Holder. No party shall seek damages from Holder (nor shall Holder be liable for the same) for any matter arising out of or related to the performance of Holder's duties under this Security Deposit paragraph.

6. **<u>MOVE-IN/MOVE-OUT INSPECTION</u>.** Prior to Tenant tendering a Security Deposit, Landlord shall provide Tenant with a list of any existing damages to the Property using the form entitled "Move-In, Move-Out Inspection Form" which form is attached hereto and incorporated herein by this reference. Prior to taking occupancy, Tenant will be given the right to inspect the Property to ascertain the accuracy of the list. Both Landlord and Tenant shall sign the Move-In, Move-Out Form. Tenant shall be entitled to retain a copy of the Move-In/Move-Out Form. Within three business days after the date of termination of occupancy, Landlord will inspect the Property and compile a comprehensive list of any damage to the Property during Tenant's occupancy using the Move-In/Move-Out Form. Tenant shall have the right to inspect the Property within five business days after termination of Tenant's occupancy at a reasonable time mutually agreeable to Landlord and Tenant. To ascertain the accuracy of the list, Landlord and Tenant shall sign the list. Tenant must sign the list or sign a written statement listing the items of damage which Tenant disputes.

7. **<u>REPAIRS AND MAINTENANCE</u>.** Tenant acknowledges that Tenant has inspected the Property and that it is fit for residential

occupancy. Upon receipt of written notice from Tenant, Landlord shall, within a reasonable time period thereafter, repair the following (a) all defects in the Property which create unsafe living conditions or render the Property uninhabitable, and (b) to the extent required by state law, such other defects which, if not corrected, will leave the Property in a state of disrepair. Except as provided above, the Tenant agrees to maintain the Property in the neat and clean condition presented at the time of rental, reasonable wear and tear excepted.

8. **LEAD-BASED PAINT – DWELLINGS BUILT PRIOR TO 1978.** For any dwelling located on the Property built prior to 1978, Tenant acknowledges that Tenant has received, read, and signed the Lead-Based Paint Exhibit attached hereto and incorporated herein by reference.

9. **NOTICE OF PRIOR FLOODING OF PREMISES.** Landlord hereby notifies Tenant as follows: Some portion or all of the living space on the Property has ☐ or has not ☐ been flooded at least three times within the last five years immediately preceding the execution of this Lease.

10. **RENEWAL TERM.** Either party may terminate this Lease at the end of the term by giving the other party thirty days written notice prior to the end of the term. If neither party gives notice of termination, the Lease will automatically be extended on a month-to-month basis with all terms remaining the same. Thereafter, Tenant may terminate this Lease upon thirty days written notice to Landlord and Landlord may terminate this Lease upon sixty days written notice to Tenant, except that Landlord reserves the right to increase the amount of rent upon delivery of written notice to Tenant sixty days prior to the effective date of any increase.

11. **SUBLET AND ASSIGNMENT.** Tenant may not sublet the Property in whole or in part or assign this Lease without the prior written consent of Landlord. This Lease shall create the relationship of Landlord and Tenant between the parties hereto; no estate shall pass out of Landlord and this Lease shall create a usufruct only.

12. **RIGHT OF ACCESS, SIGNAGE.** Landlord and Landlord's agents shall have the right of access to the Property for inspection, repairs and maintenance during reasonable hours. In the case of emergency, Landlord may enter the Property at any time to protect life and prevent damage to the Property. Landlord and/or Landlord's agents may place a "for rent" or "for sale" sign in the yard or on the exterior of any dwelling on the property in whole or in part, may install a lockbox and may show the Property to prospective tenants or purchasers during reasonable hours. Tenant agrees to cooperate with Landlord, Landlord's agent and Brokers (as defined in Agency and Brokerage herein) who may show the Property to prospective Tenants. In the event a lockbox is installed, Tenant shall secure jewelry and other valuables and agrees to hold Landlord and/or Landlord's Agent harmless for any loss thereof. For each occasion where the access rights described above are denied. Tenant shall pay Landlord the sum of $_____ as liquidated damages; it being acknowledged that Landlord shall be damaged by the denial of access, that Landlord's actual damages are hard to estimate, and that the above amount represents a reasonable pre-estimate of Landlord's damages rather than a penalty.

13. **USE.** The Property shall be used for residential purposes only and shall be occupied only by the _____ (#) persons listed as follows_____.
The Property shall be used so as to comply with all federal, state, county, and municipal laws and ordinances and any applicable declaration of condominium; declaration of covenants, conditions, and restrictions ;all rules and regulations pursuant thereto; and any community association bylaws; and rules and regulations. Tenant shall not use or permit the Property to be used for any disorderly or unlawful purpose; nor shall Tenant engage in any activity on the Property which would endanger the health and safety of other Tenants or which otherwise creates a nuisance.

14. **PROPERTY LOSS.** Storage of personal property by Tenant shall be at Tenant's risk and Landlord shall not be responsible for any loss or damage. Tenant shall be responsible to insure Tenant's personal property against loss or damage. Landlord shall not be responsible for any damage to Tenant's property, unless such damage is caused by Landlord's gross negligence.

15. **DEFAULT.**
    A. If Tenant defaults under any term, condition or provision of this Lease, including, but not limited to, failure to pay rent or failure to reimburse Landlord for any damages, repairs or costs when due, Landlord shall have the right to terminate this Lease by giving written notice to Tenant and to pursue all available legal and equitable remedies to remedy the default. Such termination shall not release Tenant from any liability for any amount due under this Lease.
    B. If Tenant abandons the Property or violates any of the Rules and Regulations set forth herein, or otherwise fails to abide by and perform any of the obligations, terms, conditions or provisions of this Lease, each and any such breach shall constitute a default under this Lease. If any such default continues for three calendar days after Landlord delivers written notice of said default to Tenant, Landlord may, at his option, terminate this Lease by delivering written notice thereof to Tenant.
    C. All rights and remedies available to Landlord by law or in this Lease shall be cumulative and concurrent.

16. **RULES AND REGULATIONS.**
    A. Tenant is prohibited from adding, changing or in any way altering locks installed on the doors of Property without prior written permission of Landlord. If all keys to the Property are not returned when Tenant vacates the Property, Landlord may charge a re-key charge in the amount of $_____.
    B. Non-operative vehicles are not permitted on the Property. Any such non-operative vehicle may be removed by Landlord at the expense of Tenant, for storage or, for public or private sale, at Landlord's option, and Tenant shall have no right or recourse against Landlord thereafter.
    C. Other than for normal household use, no goods or materials of any kind or description which are combustible or would increase fire risk shall be kept in or placed on the Property.

D. No nails, screws or adhesive hangers except standard picture hooks, shade brackets and curtain rod brackets maybe placed in walls, woodwork or any part of the Property.

E. No pets are allowed unless the exhibit entitled "Pet Exhibit" is attached to this Lease.

F. Lawn and Exterior Maintenance: *[Select one. The section not marked shall not be a part of this Agreement].*
- ☐ (1) Tenant shall keep the lawn mowed, shrubs trimmed, gutters cleaned out, trash and grass clippings picked up on a regular basis (minimum of once every two weeks in growing season and fall leaf season) and shall keep the Property, including yard, lot, grounds, house, walkways and driveway clean and free of rubbish.
- ☐ (2) Partial maintenance by tenant - Tenant shall maintain the following: _____
- ☐ (3) Landlord or Landlord's designated agent shall provide all yard/exterior maintenance.

17. <u>UTILITIES.</u> Applicable utilities and/or service to be paid by Tenant:

UTILITY	INITIALS	UTILITY	INITIALS
( ) Water	_____	( ) Sewer	_____
( ) Electricity	_____	( ) Natural Gas	_____
( ) Garbage	_____	( ) Cable Television	_____
( ) Telephone	_____	( ) Other _____	_____

Tenant must provide proof of payment of final bills for all utilities or service termination (cutoff) slips. Landlord may, at landlord's option, pay utilities and be reimbursed by Tenant along with next month's rent.

18. <u>ABANDONMENT.</u> If Tenant removes or attempts to remove personal property from the Property other than in the usual course of continuing occupancy, without having first paid Landlord all monies due, the Property may be considered abandoned, and Landlord shall have the right, without notice, to store or dispose of any personal property left on the Property by Tenant. Landlord shall also have the right to store or dispose of any of Tenant's personal property remaining on the Property after the termination of this Lease. Any such personal property shall become Landlord's personal property.

19. <u>DISCLAIMER.</u> Tenant and Landlord acknowledge that they have not relied upon any advice, representations or statements of Brokers and waive and shall not assert any claims against Brokers involving the same. Tenant and Landlord agree that Brokers shall not be responsible to advise Tenant and Landlord on any matter, including but not limited to the following: any matter which could have been revealed through a survey, title search or inspection of the Property; the condition of the Property, any portion thereof, or any item therein; building products and construction techniques; the necessity or cost of any repairs to the Property; hazardous or toxic materials or substances; termites and other wood destroying organisms; the tax or legal consequences of this transaction; the availability and cost of utilities or community amenities; the appraised or future value of the Property; any condition(s) existing off the Property which may affect the Property; the terms, conditions and availability of financing; and the uses and zoning of the Property whether permitted or proposed. Tenant and Landlord acknowledge that Brokers are not experts with respect to the above matters and that, if any of these matters or any other matters are of concern to them, they should seek independent expert advice relative thereto. Tenant further acknowledges that in every neighborhood there are conditions which different tenants may find objectionable. Tenant shall therefore be responsible to become fully acquainted with neighborhood and other off site conditions which could affect the Property.

20. <u>OTHER PROVISIONS.</u>
A. **Time of Essence:** Time is of the essence of this Lease.
B. **No Waiver:** Any failure of Landlord to insist upon the strict and prompt performance of any covenants or conditions of this Lease or any of the rules and regulations set forth herein shall not operate as a waiver of any such violation or of Landlord's right to insist on prompt compliance in the future of such covenant or condition, and shall not prevent a subsequent action by Landlord for any such violation. No provision, covenant or condition of this Lease may be waived by Landlord unless such waiver is in writing and signed by Landlord.
C. **Definitions:** "Landlord" as used in this Lease shall include its representatives, heirs, agents, assigns, and successors in title to Property. For the purposes herein, Broker shall be the authorized agent of Landlord and shall have the full and complete authority to act on behalf of Landlord under this Lease including without limitation the right to execute this Lease in a representative capacity on behalf of Landlord. "Tenant" shall include Tenant's heirs and representatives. The terms "Landlord" and "Tenant" shall include singular and plural, and corporations, partnerships, companies or individuals, as may fit the particular circumstances.
D. **Entire Agreement:** This Lease and any attached addenda constitute the entire Agreement between the parties and no oral statement or amendment not reduced to writing and signed by both parties shall be binding.
E. **Attorney's Fees and Costs of Collection:** Whenever any sums due hereunder are collected by law, or by attorney at law to prosecute such an action, then both parties agree that the prevailing party will be entitled to reasonable attorney's fees, plus all costs of collection.
F. **Indemnification:** Tenant releases Landlord and Broker from liability for and agrees to indemnify Landlord and Broker against all losses incurred by Landlord or Broker as a result of: (a) Tenant's failure to fulfill any condition of this Lease; (b) any damage or injury happening in or about the Property to Tenant or Tenant's invitee or licensees or such persons' property, except where such damage or injury is due to gross negligence or willful misconduct of Landlord or Broker; (c) Tenant's failure to comply with any requirements imposed by any governmental authority; and (d) any judgment, lien or other encumbrance filed against the Property as a result of Tenant's actions.
G. **Notices:** Except as otherwise provided herein, all notices, including demands, required or permitted hereunder shall be in writing and delivered either: (1) in person; (2) by an overnight delivery service, prepaid; (3) by facsimile transmission (FAX); or (4) by the United States Postal Service, postage prepaid, registered or certified return receipt requested. Notwithstanding the above, notice

by FAX shall be deemed to have been given as of the date and time it is if the sending FAX produces a written confirmation with the date, time and telephone number to which the notice was sent. Receipt of notice by the Broker representing a party as a client shall be deemed to be notice to that party for all purposes herein except in transactions where the Broker is practicing designated agency, receipt of notice by the designated agent representing a party as a client shall be required to constitute notice to that party. Notices shall be sent to Landlord at:_____

_____.

All references to any notice required to be given or due dates for rental payments shall be strictly construed.

H. Waiver of Homestead Exemption: Tenant for himself and his family waives all exemptions or benefits under the homestead laws of Georgia.

I. Governing Law: This Agreement may be signed in multiple counterparts and shall be governed by and interpreted pursuant to the laws of the State of Georgia.

21. **AGENCY AND BROKERAGE.**

   A. Agency.

     (1) In this Agreement, the term "Broker" shall mean a licensed Georgia real estate broker or brokerage firm and where the context would indicate the broker's affiliated licensees. No Broker in this transaction shall owe any duty to Tenant or Landlord greater than what is set forth in their brokerage engagement and the Brokerage Relationships in Real Estate Transactions Act, O.C.G.A. § 10-6A-1 et. seq.

     (2) Landlord and Tenant acknowledge that if they are not represented by a Broker they are each solely responsible for protecting their own interests, and that Broker's role is limited to performing ministerial acts for either party.

     (3) The Broker, if any, working with the Landlord is identified on the signature page as the "Listing Broker"; and said Broker is ☐ **OR**, is **NOT** ☐ representing the Landlord;

     (4) The Broker, if any, working with the Tenant is identified on the signature page as the "Leasing Broker", and said Broker is ☐ **OR**, is **NOT** ☐ representing the Tenant; and

     (5) If Tenant and Landlord are both being represented by the same Broker, a relationship of either designated agency ☐ , **OR**, dual agency ☐ shall exist.

       (a) Dual Agency Disclosure. [*Applicable only if dual agency has been selected above*] Landlord and Tenant are aware that Broker is acting as a dual agent in this transaction and consent to the same. Landlord and Tenant have been advised that:

         1 - In serving as a dual agent the Broker is representing two clients whose interests are or at times could be different or even adverse;

         2 - The Broker will disclose all adverse, material facts relevant to the transaction and actually known to the dual agent to all parties in the transaction except for information made confidential by request or instructions from another client which is not otherwise required to be disclosed by law;

         3 - The Tenant and Landlord do not have to consent to dual agency; and

         4 - The consent of the Tenant and Landlord to dual agency has been given voluntarily and the parties have read and understood their brokerage engagement agreements.

         5 - Notwithstanding any provision to the contrary contained herein Landlord and Tenant each hereby direct Broker, while acting as a dual agent, to keep confidential and not reveal to the other party all information which could materially and adversely affect the negotiating position of the party.

       (b) Designated Agency Assignment. [*Applicable only if the designated agency has been selected above*] The Broker has assigned _____ to work exclusively with Tenant as Tenant 's designated agent and _____ to work exclusively with Landlord as Landlord's designated agent. Each designated agent shall exclusively represent the party to whom each has been assigned as a client and shall not represent in this transaction the client assigned to the other designated agent.

       (c) Material Relationship Disclosure. The Broker and/or affiliated licensees have no material relationship with either client except as follows: _____. (A material relationship means one actually known of a personal, familial or business nature between the Broker and affiliated licensees and a client which would impair their ability to exercise fair judgment relative to another client.)

   B. Brokerage. The Brokers listed below have performed a valuable service in this transaction and are made parties hereunder to enforce their commission rights. Payment of commission to a Broker shall not create an agency or subagency relationship between Leasing Broker and either Landlord or Landlord's Broker. Landlord agrees to pay the Broker listed below and representing Landlord to lease and/or manage the Property ("Listing Broker") a commission (which commission has already been negotiated in a separate agreement) of $_____ or _____% of the Lease amount, which shall be due and payable upon occupancy. In the event the Lease is made in cooperation with another Broker listed below as the Leasing Broker, the Listing Broker shall receive _____% of the total real estate commission paid hereunder and the Leasing Broker shall receive _____% of the total real estate commission paid hereunder. In the event Tenant and/or Landlord fail or refuse to perform any of their obligations herein, the non-performing party shall immediately pay the Listing Broker and the Leasing Broker their full commissions. The Listing Broker and Leasing Broker may jointly or independently pursue the non-performing party for that portion of the commission which they would have otherwise received under the Lease.

22. **MILITARY ACTIVATION.** If Tenant is called to active duty during the term of this Lease, Tenant shall present to Landlord official orders activating Tenant; then and in that event, this Lease shall be controlled by the Soldiers' and Sailors' Civil Relief Act of 1940 as amended in 50 U.S.C.A. §§ 50-590 and O.C.G.A. §§ 44-7-37 as amended.

23. **EXHIBITS.** All exhibits attached hereto, listed below or referenced herein are made a part of this Lease. If any such exhibit conflicts with any preceding paragraph, said exhibit shall control:

24.   <u>**SPECIAL STIPULATIONS.**</u> The following Special Stipulations, if conflicting with any exhibit or preceding paragraph, shall control:

☐ **(Mark box if additional pages are attached.)**

IN WITNESS WHEREOF, the parties hereto have set their hand and seal the day and year first written above.

_____ (_____)		_____
Leasing Broker MLS Office Code		Tenant's Signature SS/FEI #
		Print or Type Name:_____
By: _____		
Broker or Broker's Affiliated Licensee		_____
		Tenant's Signature SS/FEI #
Print or Type Name:_____		Print or Type Name:_____
Bus. Phone:_____ FAX #_____		
		_____
		Landlord's Signature (or Authorized Agent for Landlord)
_____ (_____)		
Listing Broker MLS Office Code		Print or Type Name:_____
Multiple Listing # _____		_____
		Landlord's Signature (or Authorized Agent for Landlord)
By: _____		
Broker or Broker's Affiliated Licensee		Print or Type Name:_____
Print or Type Name: _____		_____
Bus. Phone:_____ FAX #_____		TELEPHONE # for Emergency Repairs
		Landlord's address for notices and mailing of rent:
		_____
		_____, _____

Reprinted with permission from the Georgia Association of REALTORS®

Appendix B: Complaint Procedure

The ten possible steps in handling complaints against a licensee are as follows:

1. When the Georgia Real Estate Commission (GREC) receives a complaint, the GREC staff reviews it. If the complaint is deficient in form, i.e., unsigned or not notarized, it is returned to complainant as rejected with an explanation for the rejection.
2. If the complaint is adjudged by the GREC staff to be in good form and contains facts that suggest that a violation of the license law or rules of the commission has taken place the Director of Investigations assigns the complaint to an investigator.
3. The investigator gathers evidence, using subpoenas if necessary.
4. The investigator reports findings to supervisors.
5. The commission reviews report and findings of investigation.
   A. If no evidence of violations has been found, the case is closed.
   B. If evidence has been found of a minor violation, a citation might be issued and a fine imposed. See Rule 520–1–.43.

 WWWeb.Link
To see rule 520–1–.43, go to the Web Site of the Georgia Real Estate Commission, http://www.grec.state.ga.us/, click on the button for the Georgia Real Estate Commission, and then click on the button for Rules.

   C. If evidence has been found of a more serious violation, the commission will offer to settle the matter through a consent agreement with the licensee.
6. If no agreement is reached, the commission refers the case to the attorney general for a hearing.
7. The Office of State Administrative Hearings assigns an Administrative Law Judge who schedules a due process hearing. The licensee is notified and can choose to be represented by an attorney.
8. If the administrative law judge finds no violation, the matter is dismissed.
9. If the administrative law judge finds a violation, the administrative law judge imposes a sanction on the licensee.
10. If a sanction is imposed on the licensee, the licensee may appeal to the commission. If the commission affirms the sanction, the licensee may appeal to the courts.

Appendix C: Useful Real Estate Web Sites

GEORGIA WEB SITES

http://www.state.ga.us/
Georgia State Government
Use this site for all Georgia Government Information, including
- all Georgia laws,
- all Georgia rules, and
- sex offenders.
An easy way to navigate is to click on Index and find topic.

http://www.grec.state.ga.us/
Georgia Real Estate Commission
This is a short cut to information related to real estate.

http://www.garealtor.com/
Georgia Association of REALTORS®
Members can access all contracts and forms at this site.
You can also use this site to locate REALTORS® around the state.

http://www.usbooksinc.com/
Greg Dunn's Homepage
Use this site to contact the consulting editor of *Georgia Real Estate: Practice and Law.*

http://goamp.com
AMP (Georgia's testing service)
Use this site to schedule the state exam and for information about the test.

NATIONAL WEB SITES

https://entp.hud.gov/idapp/html/hicostlook.cfm
Federal Housing Administration Mortgage Limits

http://www.va.gov/
Veterans Administration

http://www.usdoj.gov/crt/housing/title8.htm
Federal Fair Housing Act

http://www.federalreserveeducation.org/
Federal Reserve Education

Appendix D: Suggested Documents To Use in a Georgia Residential Real Estate Transaction

1. At Listing
   A. Exclusive Seller Listing Agreement
   B. Seller Property Disclosure
   C. Termite Letter
2. At Time of Showing Buyer
   A. Exclusive Buyer Brokerage Agreement
   B. Or Customer Election
3. At Time of Contract
   A. Purchase and Sale Agreement (one of four types) must contain: legal description, method of payment, agency disclosure, special stipulations.
      i. Purchase and Sale
      ii. New Construction
      iii. Land or Lot
      iv. Lease Purchase
   B. Exhibits
      i. Legal Description
      ii. Finance
      iii. Occupancy
      iv. Seller Property Disclosure
      v. Termite Letter
   C. Amendments
      i. To Change Closing Date
      ii. To Remove Inspection Contingency

Note: Federal Lead-Based Paint Disclosure is part of seller's property disclosure form and is required for all property where any part of the main dwelling was built prior to 1978.

4. At Time of Closing
   A. HUD-1 Closing Statement
   B. Commission Check

Answer Key

Chapter Quizzes

Chapter 1
License Law

1. d(8)
2. a(11)
3. d(14)
4. b(12)
5. d(8)
6. c(13)
7. c(4)
8. a(3)
9. a(14)
10. a(12)
11. b(3)
12. a(8)
13. b(6)
14. d(14)
15. d(8)
16. c(16)
17. b(14)
18. b(13)
19. d(13)
20. c(10)
21. d(1)
22. d(7)
23. a(9)
24. b(10)
25. d(11)

Chapter 2
Rules

1. c(20)
2. b(20)
3. c(26)
4. c(26)
5. a(27)
6. c(22)
7. a(23)

8. a(28)
9. b(27)
10. c(27)
11. d(25)
12. c(28)
13. d(26)
14. c(26)
15. a(21)
16. c(20)
17. d(23)
18. c(25)
19. b(27)
20. c(27)

Chapter 3
BRRETA

1. d(34)
2. a(32)
3. d(33)
4. a(35)
5. c(32)
6. d(34)
7. c(32)
8. a(32)

Chapter 4
Anti-Trust

1. a(37)
2. b(37)
3. c(39)
4. c(38)
5. d(38)

Chapter 5
Legal Descriptions

1. c(41)
2. d(42)
3. a(41)
4. b(42)
5. b(43)

6. c(43)
7. b(44)
8. b(41)
9. c(44)
10. b(44)

Chapter 6
Listing the Seller

1. a(47)
2. c(49)
3. d(52)
4. b(52)
5. b(53)
6. c(49)
7. a(48)
8. d(48)
9. c(53)
10. a(48)

Chapter 7
Pricing Property

1. d(58)
2. b(59)
3. b(59)
4. a(59)
5. c(59)
6. c(59)
7. b(59)

Chapter 8
Seller's Cost

1. a(67)
2. c(67)
3. b(67)
4. a(69)
5. d(68)
6. b(67)
7. a(68)
8. c(68)
9. c(71)

10. a(66)
11. b(69)
12. a(66)
13. c(68)
14. c(68)
15. d(68)
16. c(65)
17. a(67)
18. b(68)
19. d(68)
20. c(68)
21. d(70)

Chapter 9
Listing the Buyer

1. a(77)
2. b(75)
3. a(76)
4. b(76)
5. a(77)
6. c(78)
7. b(80)

Chapter 10
Buyer's Cost

1. a(84)
2. d(86)
3. c(86)
4. c(86)
5. d(90)
6. c(90)
7. a(84)
8. a(85)
9. a(89)
10. a(89)
11. d(87)
12. d(85)
13. c(83)
14. d(83)
15. a(84)

16. b(85)
17. d(87)
18. c(86)
19. c(84)
20. c(85)
21. c(88)
22. a(87)
23. a(90)
24. b(89)

Chapter 11
Writing Contracts

1. b(97)
2. d(105)
3. d(101)
4. b(94)
5. d(96)
6. a(101)
7. b(96)
8. d(105)
9. d(102)
10. a(97)
11. b(93)
12. a(102)
13. d(93)
14. b(104)
15. a(105)

Chapter 12
Property
Management

1. a(114)
2. d(117)
3. c(112)
4. b(113)

Chapter 13
Writing Leases

1. b(124)
2. a(127)
3. b(124)
4. d(123)
5. b(127)
6. b(127)
7. c(126)

8. d(124)
9. b(123)
10. d(125)
11. d(123)
12. c(125)
13. b(124)

Chapter 14
Community
Association
Management

1. c(137)
2. c(140)
3. a(140)

Index